Performing Statecraft

Methuen Drama Agitations: Text, Politics and Performances

Theatre has always offered immediate responses to political, social, economic, and cultural crisis events that are local, national, and global in dimension, establishing itself as a prime medium of engagement. Methuen Drama Agitations interrogates these manifold intersections between theatre and the contemporary: What is the relationship between theatre and reality? Which functions does the theatre perform in public life? Where does the radical potential of the theatre reside and how is it untapped?

Methuen Drama Agitations addresses issues from across a number of spectrums, including contemporary politics, environmental concerns, issues of gender and race, and the challenges of globalization. The series focuses on text as much as performance, on theory as much as practice. It investigates the lively dialogues between theatre and contemporary lived experience.

Series Editors
William C. Boles (Rollins College, USA)
Anja Hartl (University of Innsbruck, Austria)

Advisory Board
Lynnette Goddard (Royal Holloway, University of London, UK)
Anton Krueger (Rhodes University, South Africa)
Marcus Tan (Nanyang Technological University, Singapore)
Sarah J. Townsend (Penn State University, USA)
Denise Varney (University of Melbourne, Australia)

Theater of Lockdown: Digital and Distanced Performance in a Time of Pandemic
Barbara Fuchs

Theater in a Post-Truth World: Texts, Politics, and Performance
Edited by William C. Boles

Forthcoming Titles

Contemporary Black Theatre and Performance: Acts of Rebellion, Activism, and Solidarity
Edited by Martine Kei Green-Rogers, Khalid Y. Long, and DeRon S. Williams

Performing Left Populism: Performance, Politics and the People
Edited by Théo Aiolfi and Goran Petrović-Lotina

Performing the Queer Past: Bodies Possessed
Fintan Walsh

Theatre and its Audiences: Reimagining the Relationship in Times of Crisis
Kate Craddock and Helen Freshwater

Performing Statecraft

The Postdiplomatic Theatre of Sovereigns, Citizens, and States

Edited by
James R. Ball III

methuen | drama
LONDON · NEW YORK · OXFORD · NEW DELHI · SYDNEY

METHUEN DRAMA
Bloomsbury Publishing Plc
50 Bedford Square, London, WC1B 3DP, UK
1385 Broadway, New York, NY 10018, USA
29 Earlsfort Terrace, Dublin 2, Ireland

BLOOMSBURY, METHUEN DRAMA and the Methuen Drama logo are trademarks of
Bloomsbury Publishing Plc

First published in Great Britain 2023
This paperback edition published 2024

Copyright © James R. Ball III and contributors, 2023

James R. Ball III has asserted his right under the Copyright, Designs and
Patents Act, 1988, to be identified as Editor of this work.

For legal purposes the Acknowledgments on p. x constitute an
extension of this copyright page.

Series design by Ben Anslow
Cover image: World leaders, La Moneda Presidential Palace during the
APEC Summit, 21 November, 2004, Santiago, Chile.
(© TIM SLOAN/AFP via Getty Images)

All rights reserved. No part of this publication may be reproduced or transmitted
in any form or by any means, electronic or mechanical, including photocopying,
recording, or any information storage or retrieval system, without prior
permission in writing from the publishers.

Bloomsbury Publishing Plc does not have any control over, or responsibility for,
any third-party websites referred to or in this book. All internet addresses given
in this book were correct at the time of going to press. The author and publisher
regret any inconvenience caused if addresses have changed or sites have ceased
to exist, but can accept no responsibility for any such changes.

A catalogue record for this book is available from the British Library.

Library of Congress Cataloging-in-Publication Data
Names: Ball, James R., III, editor.
Title: Performing statecraft : the postdiplomatic theatre of sovereigns,
citizens, and states / edited by James R. Ball III.
Description: London ; New York : Bloomsbury Academic, 2022. |
Series: Methuen drama agitations : text, politics and performances |
Includes bibliographical references and index.
Identifiers: LCCN 2022014175 (print) | LCCN 2022014176 (ebook) |
ISBN 9781350285170 (hardback) | ISBN 9781350285200 (paperback) |
ISBN 9781350285187 (epub) | ISBN 9781350285194 (ebook)
Subjects: LCSH: International relations and culture. | Arts and diplomacy.
Classification: LCC JZ1251 .P467 2022 (print) | LCC JZ1251 (ebook) |
DDC 327.101–dc23/eng/20220729
LC record available at https://lccn.loc.gov/2022014175
LC ebook record available at https://lccn.loc.gov/2022014176

ISBN: HB: 978-1-3502-8517-0
PB: 978-1-3502-8520-0
ePDF: 978-1-3502-8519-4
eBook: 978-1-3502-8518-7

Series: Methuen Drama Agitations: Text, Politics and Performances

Typeset by Newgen KnowledgeWorks Pvt. Ltd., Chennai, India

To find out more about our authors and books visit www.bloomsbury.com
and sign up for our newsletters.

Contents

List of Figures ix
Acknowledgments x

Introduction: Postdiplomatic Theatre 1
James R. Ball III

1 (En)Acting the Republic: The 1916 Rising as a Spectacle of Self-Sacrifice for Ireland 29
 Áine Josephine Tyrrell
2 An "Indian Princess," a King and a Queen, and a President: Diplomatic Performance and Indigenous Sovereignties at the 1939 Royal Visit 47
 Christiana Molldrem Harkulich
3 The President's Yellow Batakari: Performance and the Sartorial in Ghanaian Politics 63
 David Afriyie Donkor
4 Windrush Strikes Back: "Rivers of Blood," Performance, and Guerrilla Diplomacy 91
 Mary Karen Dahl
5 Organ Failure: Medicalized Torture During the Iraq War 119
 Warren Kluber
6 Viral Diplomacy: Music, Masks, and Maritime Borders Between China and the Philippines 139
 Adam Kielman
7 The President Makes a Play: Putin and Erdoğan's Sporting Statecraft 165
 Sean Bartley and Jared Strange
8 Statecraft and Revolution: Remaking Bolívar for an Anti-Imperialist Transnational Alliance 189
 Angela Marino

Afterword: The Future of Dissensus: Performance Postdiplomatic Postdemocracy   207
Tony Perucci

Selected Bibliography   211
List of Contributors   225
Index   229

Figures

0.1	Actors Benjamin Goldman and Dean Malissa perform for French President Nicolas Sarkozy and President Bush during the entertainment portion of a social dinner at the White House on Tuesday, November 6, 2007, in Washington, DC	2
3.1	President Jerry Rawlings gestures to a crowd of 60,000 people at the Accra Stadium as he campaigns for reelection to the presidency of Ghana, July 26, 1996	76
5.1	US Ambassador to Iraq, L. Paul Bremer, watches video of Saddam Hussein going through his medical examination shortly after his capture. The video presented at a briefing to the media gathered at the Iraqi Forum (formerly known as the Baghdad Convention Center) in Baghdad during Operation IRAQI FREEDOM	120
8.1	Pavel Égüez, *La Patria naciendo de la ternura* (Patriotism Is Born from Tenderness). Mural on the Avenida Baralt in downtown Caracas, 2010	200

Acknowledgments

This book emerged from a meeting of the Theatres of Public Diplomacy Working Session at the annual conference of the American Society for Theatre Research in November, 2019, in Arlington, VA. The Working Session was convened by James R. Ball III, David Donkor, and Derek Goldman, and included the participation of Sean Bartley, Dr. Natka Bianchini, Mary Karen Dahl, Gad Guterman, Olivia Eljaiek-Hendricks, Christiana Molldrem Harkulich, Marcus Johnson, Warren Kluber, Kelli Coleman Moore, Dr. des. Rashna Darius Nicholson, Tony Perucci, Jared Strange, and Áine Josephine Tyrrell. The chapters that follow all owe much to the Working Session's conversations in 2019.

Excerpts from the play *Lidless* appear courtesy of Frances Ya-Chu Cowhig. Excerpts from "Bill's Big Lie," by Byron York, appear courtesy of *The American Spectator*. Portions of Chapter 8 were previously published in *Populism and Performance in the Bolivarian Revolution of Venezuela* (Evanston: Northwestern University Press, 2018), by Angela Marino. All the contributors to *Performing Statecraft* are deeply thankful to Mark Dudgeon and Ella Wilson at Bloomsbury Publishing, and the editors of the Methuen Drama Agitations series, Anja Hartl and William C. Boles, for their enthusiasm and support for this project.

Introduction: Postdiplomatic Theatre

James R. Ball III

Consider the state visit: its itineraries, its meals, its set pieces, and its performances. On November 6, 2007, the president of the French Republic, Nicolas Sarkozy, arrived in Washington for a twenty-six-hour visit that would include a social dinner, an address to Congress, and a visit to the historical site and museum, Mount Vernon. There would not be a *state* dinner, officials stressed, as the trip was billed as a working visit, but few news outlets or historical records joined them in splitting hairs.[1] Indeed, Sarkozy arrived to the White House at 7:00 p.m. in black tie, and by 7:35, he and President George W. Bush were exchanging toasts in the *State* Dining Room, in front of 130 guests.

The American president practiced his French—"Bienvenue à la Maison Blanche"—before returning to English to name the visit's theme:

> In 1777, another George W. welcomed to America another Frenchman. His name was Lafayette. The two leaders built a strong friendship, based on common values and common virtues. They both recognized the power of human freedom. They both served with courage in freedom's cause. And they both anticipated that freedom would advance in other lands following its victory here in America.[2]

Recalling history and marking its repetitions, Bush activated the theatricality of the diplomatic moment: he and Sarkozy were re-performing a bit of diplomatic theatre more than two centuries old, setting the stage for a visit that would performatively locate each nation's identity in its capacity to spread democracy around the globe. His toast cited diplomatic precedents, recirculating them to charge their

Figure 0.1 Actors Benjamin Goldman, second from left, and Dean Malissa, left, perform for French President Nicolas Sarkozy and President Bush during the entertainment portion of a social dinner at the White House on Tuesday, November 6, 2007, in Washington, DC. AP Photo/Evan Vucci.

effects, pulling the past into the present to do the work of statecraft.[3] In the space of a social ritual, the time of diplomacy cycles through centuries to rearticulate the nation on a global stage, a performance that reinforces and advances policy goals.

Sarkozy reiterated the theme, redeploying it and other diplomatic discourses to reaffirm the allies' commitments to each other. It was a new phase in relations, but also a return to shared principles and a shared past:

> I've come to Washington to bear a very simple, straightforward message, and I bear it on behalf of all French men and women: I wish to reconquer the heart of America ... So here I am in Washington on a first Tuesday in November ... a very special day because it's the day on which Americans elect their President.[4]

Reconquering hearts (and presumably minds) and reaffirming American democracy, Sarkozy walked in Lafayette's footsteps. Pains were taken to make sure the connection would not be missed: the guest list included Joey Durel, city-parish president of Lafayette, Louisiana, and Arthur J. Rothkopf, president emeritus of Lafayette College, and a cake was served featuring a chocolate cameo of the Marquis, to honor his 250th birthday. Writing for the *Washington Post* the next day, Dana Milbank noted, "the theme [of transatlantic friendships renewed] could not have been any more over the top if the two men wore powdered wigs and false teeth."[5] As it repeats historical precedents to new ends, statecraft generates theatrical excesses.

At the entertainment following dinner, two men wore powdered wigs, if not false teeth. Guests retired to the East Room where a small platform stage had been set with two red upholstered chairs. There, General George Washington and General Marie Joseph Paul Yves Roch Gilbert du Motier, the Marquis de La Fayette (played by actors Dean Malissa and Benjamin Goldman, respectively), staged the 1777 encounter yet again (Figure 0.1). The short play, "On Fire for Liberty" by William Sommerfield, was a White House commission of the American Historical Theatre. In a brief excerpt of the performance uploaded to YouTube years following the event, Washington raised his glass in toast to Lafayette, proclaiming, "Liberty." Lafayette returned the toast, "Égalité." They both turned to acknowledge their audience, especially the heads of state seated in the front row, offering with one voice in each character's native tongue, "Fraternité"/"Fraternity." Turning back to each other, the fourth wall reestablished, Washington continued, "My dear Marquis, it is my hope that someday we shall make wine of this ilk here in America." The audience laughed politely.[6] The theatre acknowledged the statesmen, and the politicos indulged the actors; boundaries between them all proving permeable. From reiterating past precedents, the evening's participants began to rewrite the incidental details of history to serve the goals of twenty-first-century diplomacy.

The 22-member US Army Chorus followed, a rather more conventional choice of state dinner entertainment than the historical playlet. The performers at US state dinners have served multiple functions, but always and especially to manifest particular configurations of national community: the self-image of America preferred by a given regime. Since the Cold War, high culture and American forms like jazz and Broadway most often graced White House stages. More recently, popular music has also gotten its foot in the door; among others, Gloria Estefan sang for the visit of Brazilian President Fernando Collor de Mello in 1991, Lou Reed rocked for President of the Czech Republic Václav Havel in 1998, and Mary J. Blige performed for Sarkozy's successor, François Hollande, in 2014. The United States performs itself: as a cultural equal to old Europe, as economically entwined with its hemisphere and the globe, as a multicultural and plural society. In the 2007 entertainments, diplomacy and war blended into each other: as politicians watched actors play generals and soldiers sang after supper, the United States of America appeared as guarantor of democracy around the globe through alliance and force.

At the end of the night, the *Washington Post* reported, the president told his guests, "they could stay and dance 'if you wish.'"[7] It is not clear from newspaper reports whether any did. Indeed, the *Post*'s Style section largely went through the motions in recounting the visit: "We can tell you what was served, and what the first lady wore, because that's what we do at these things."[8] Via the mediatizations that make diplomacy public, state and citizen encounter one another and size each other up. *Washington Post* staff writer Hank Stuever snarked at "one of the most uninspired guest lists in White House dinner-party reporting history," and offered little imagery to describe Laura Bush's "midnight blue Oscar de la Renta gown."[9] It was not quite "The Death of Fashion Diplomacy" that the *New York Times* would declare following Donald Trump's state visit to the UK in 2019, but it remained faint praise.[10] As the public minutiae of statecraft accumulate before the scrutinizing eyes of journalists and their readers, opportunities for dissent multiply. Public political performance establishes a theatrical interface where citizens and sovereigns (and various intermediaries) converge.

The next day, Sarkozy addressed a joint session of Congress, extolling American soft power and finding little disagreement among his audience. He invoked a legion of US performers, interpellating them as diplomats: "My generation ... shared all the American dreams. Our imaginations were fueled by the winning of the West and Hollywood. By Elvis Presley ... By Duke Ellington, Hemingway. By John Wayne, Charlton Heston, Marilyn Monroe, Rita Hayworth."[11] He declared his love for America, and Congress reciprocated. The *New York Times* reported, "President Nicolas Sarkozy of France was greeted with cheers and standing ovations ... a sign that France was forgiven for opposing the American-led war in Iraq."[12] Sarkozy performed Redress and ratified Reintegration, in the explicit terms of a Social Drama, as theorized by Victor Turner and championed by Richard Schechner.[13] The schism dividing the allies was forgiven, freedom fries were forgotten.

And the visit continued to Mount Vernon, the one-time home of George Washington, now a museum—a third stage set on which to perform American democracy and transatlantic alliance. There, Bush and Sarkozy held a closed-session meeting on security and democracy in the Middle East. Though they followed closely in the footsteps of Washington and Lafayette, adherence to the centuries-old script provided opportunities for new choreographies. Diplomatic performance reveals the ways in which time and space flow into one another in statecraft. Performance proves handy for modulating the time of statecraft, whether folding together centuries or enlarging a space for alliance to be reaffirmed.

A luncheon followed, and then a brief press appearance. "I can't thank the president enough for his willingness to stand with young democracies," Bush exclaimed, reminding all of the policy agenda the performances had been designed to reinforce. Meanwhile, Sarkozy returned to the reenactments reenacted, "I especially enjoyed the skit of the dialogue between Washington and Lafayette that we witnessed." And a bit of candor emerged as the Presidents bantered with each other and their press corps. "You want to call on somebody?" Bush asked Sarkozy, who chuckled, "You know in France I don't pick the journalists." As Sarkozy laughed, Bush continued, "I choose? Who would you like me to choose?" Both men gestured to the corps, and Bush corrected himself, "Oh he chose. Wait a minute, it didn't last very long, did it?" Sarkozy concluded the bit, "I didn't choose, I indicated a general direction."[14] As the visit wound down to its close, we watched a blustery American and a nonchalant Frenchman on the world stage, separated from them by distance and decades, their power remaining legible though hardly invulnerable. Performance is also useful for shifting scales and viewing positions to assess the power of those who perform on the world stage anew.

Consider the state visit, even an unexceptional visit like Sarkozy's, and the complex ways it performs two states, two nations, in conjunction. Consider the spaces invested with history—the White House, the Capitol, Mount Vernon—animated anew, theatrically. Consider the oratory—the toasts, the speeches, the negotiations, the press appearances—the precedents cited, discourses deployed, and speech acts felicitous and infelicitous. Consider the entertainments, the costuming, the star power of the guests, the food. Consider the dramaturgy, the scripted moments, the planned instances of candor, the authentically unexpected, the arrangement of on stage and off. Consider the audience, reading the Politics page at NYTimes.com or the Style section of the *Washington Post*, applauding from the floor of congress, seated in the East Room, snorting at a computer screen. To what end this mass of theatrical material, such profusive trappings of performance?

Statecraft, the art of conducting or managing the public affairs of a state, requires theatre—the overt, performative presentation of a particular arrangement of global and domestic affairs. The alliance between the US and France could not simply be made, it needed to be enacted, and better still reenacted in choreography and oratory, just as the actors re-performed Lafayette and Washington, and just as Sarkozy and Bush followed in their footsteps. This theatre is neither without substance, nor divorced from the exercise of power. The use of force requires intensely theatrical diplomatic performances. Beyond the two actors in powdered wigs were the ongoing wars in Iraq and Afghanistan, conflicts that required the discourse of democracy promotion that Bush and Sarkozy performed, and a discourse that could only be staged, advanced, and maintained in performance. Performance is neither an alternative to nor screen for the military power of states on the world stage, it is a concomitant part of any foreign policy.

Statecraft is spectacular, theatrical, and performative, qualities that reach their apotheosis in events like Sarkozy's Lafayette-inspired tour of Washington and environs. This book investigates the performances of states, their leaders, and their people on an expanded field of the global arts of statecraft—arts that include, inter alia, diplomacy, law and jurisprudence, public administration, public finance, ceremony and protocol, and the use of force. What is the role of performance in governance? How do nations use performance to advance their interests? How can artists, scholars, and activists intervene in politics and policy? What new fissures in the monolithic presentations of states appear when statecraft is performed? Treating theatre as both an art form and as a practice of political actors, this book draws together scholars who take up and analyze the performances of heads of state, governments, legislators, diplomats, soldiers, activists, artists, and citizens.

To turn our attention to the performance of statecraft, to the acts of states and their agents performed for audiences at home and abroad, is to return to fundamental questions that animate any project in the field of performance studies: *who* is performing? *How* are they performing? And *what* is performed? One might imagine statecraft requires a set of actors in near lockstep performing a national self-image to global and domestic audiences. Yet, on the world stage, performance is a tool wielded by amateurs and professionals alike to articulate national identities, aspirations, and imaginaries. Attending to such performances reveals a nuanced set of activities and contestations, as citizens and state actors converge and enter into conflict. Tracing these conflicts, new histories appear in which a performing body reasserts itself as an essential component of a global politics that would erase it. New times and spaces of politics emerge and new powers are exercised. Returning to these fundamental questions, *Performing Statecraft* puts pressure on our usual answers, as audience and actor merge, as power proves vulnerable, and as old certainties evaporate. In their wake, a postdiplomatic theatre may appear.

Performing Statecraft

Who or what performs the state? In some ways, such performance appears most explicitly in scenes of public diplomacy, and diplomacy figures as a primary arena for performing statecraft throughout this book. Yet, when seeking who or what performs diplomacy, one finds roles proliferating and the boundaries between them blurring. Certainly, there are individual players, ranging from interns, to low-level technocrats, to first secretaries, to ambassadors, to cabinet ministers, to heads of state, but there are also other, more nebulous actors. Constituencies, populations, and the nations they make up. Republics, kingdoms, and confederations. Intergovernmental institutions and regional alliances drawing states and nations together. Each performs and their performances are tightly interrelated. An individual can perform an institution or state, and a nation may call an individual to perform in a particular way.

Political science literature tends to treat the question of who performs the state far more narrowly. For example, the authors of "Who is Acting in International Relations?" reduce the question to a binary opposition between an imagined unitary state and (following Bruno Latour) a distributed network of entities that compose the state.[15] The more varied and nuanced answers to the same question that appear in this volume speak to the richness of continuing performance studies interventions in political science. The framework of performance expands the repertoires of states, their leaders, and citizens, as much as it enhances the toolkits of scholars.

In theatre and performance studies and their cognate fields, nations and states performed have long been a privileged subject of study. This interest may have its origins in anthropology. In *Negara: The Theatre State in Nineteenth-Century Bali*, anthropologist Clifford Geertz provides one image of a state performed, "in which the kings and princes were the impresarios, the priests the directors, and the peasants the supporting cast, stage crew, and audience." Importantly, theatre in this case was no metaphor; in nineteenth-century Bali, "power served pomp, not pomp power."[16] Similarly, Benedict Anderson's *Imagined Communities: Reflections on the Origin and Spread of Nationalism*, provides an account of the emergence of nations in shared acts and the embodied choreographies of those who performed them: as the printed word spread it created networks "of fellow-readers ... connected through print [who] formed ... the embryo of the nationally imagined community,"[17] an embryo that grew into a nation-state via (among other things) "the established skein of journeys through which each state was experienced by its functionaries."[18] From nineteenth-century Bali, a state quite literally performed, to the twentieth-century nation-state, constituted in the acts and choreographies of its people and administrators.

In each case we get some sense of what Michael Taussig more directly names "the magic of the state." In his book of the same title, Taussig details the circulating imagery, mobilized by the representatives of governments, independent citizens, and others, that constitutes the power of a state. From *who* performs we may now ask *how* they are performing. Insofar as the magic of the state is a power available to both authorities and subjects, it indicates the degree to which performance may serve as the ground on which competing notions of a nation or state come into conflict.[19] Performance studies has also been profoundly interested in the performing arts as a site in which such contests emerge. One exemplar of this literature is Karen Shimakawa's *National Abjection: The Asian-American Body on Stage*, in which the framework of abjection reveals where and how national myths of "Americanness" incorporate or exclude Asian Americans.[20] Performance on stage and off provides the terms by which a state may fashion its image for itself and for others, an image with peculiar and substantial powers.

What, then, *is* performed when individuals or groups perform a state? Beyond the actors, what is enacted? National identities and national myths figure as the most prominent answers to be found in works in and beyond performance studies that examine cases in Africa, Europe, Asia, and elsewhere.[21] Authority, unity, and the power they project often also prove performative, in the strictly Austinian sense that these traits are only manifested where they are explicitly performed.[22] Adam Kielman's recent article, "Sites and Sounds of National Memory: Performing the Nation in China's Decennial National Day Celebrations," argues for the role of "mediatized emplaced sounds" in the "performative manifestation of national community," in the context of China's broad ethnic diversity; in this case officially sanctioned performances commemorating a civic holiday make the state whole by prompting its population to perform on stage and off.[23] Similarly, Diana Taylor's *Disappearing Acts: Spectacles of Gender and Nationalism in Argentina's "Dirty War"* details the ways the military junta ruling Argentina "engender[ed] and control[ed] a viewing public through the performance of national identity, traditions, and goals."[24] And in "Playing King," Maria Berlova highlights the ways that by theatrically performing his power, the Swedish King Gustav III was able to raise militia forces and levy special war taxes at the end of the eighteenth century.[25]

Thus, a state may also perform or be performed to affect policies and discourses. Roxanne Doty highlights how power and performance are entwined on the world stage in *Imperial Encounters*, which details aesthetic representations of the Third World by the Global North that produced the diplomatic reality faced in the Global South. In this case, to perform a state is also to stabilize it discursively, as a representation "constituting particular interpretive dispositions that create certain possibilities and preclude others … a kind of power that produces meanings, subject identities, their interrelationships and a range of imaginable conduct."[26] Elsewhere in political science, performance is not often a primary rubric through which politics is understood, but there are exceptions that look closely at the role it can play. Julia C. Strauss notes that in the cases of the People's Republic of China and Taiwan, "how policy was communicated and performed was as important as what policies were decided and implemented," performances that quite literally made those states.[27] Similarly, political geographer Alex Jeffery notes that "states are improvised. Their legitimacy and ability to lay claim to rule rely on a capacity to perform their power."[28] And *Staging Politics: Power and Performance in Asia and Africa* (coedited by Strauss and Donal B. Cruise O'Brien) draws together essays by political science scholars who turn to "the whys and hows of effective public performance" in order to understand "the 'softer' ... categories of affect, emotional engagement, and imagination" and their role in "the evolution of state and society in Asia and Africa."[29]

What comes to the fore across these literatures is the fact that performing statecraft is something more than expressive action or ornament: it is a substantive political act, an exercise of power. As Geertz noted in Bali, "The dramas of the theatre state, mimetic of themselves, were, in the end, neither illusions nor lies, neither sleight of hand nor make-believe. They were what there was."[30] Even those performances with discursive ends make action possible or impossible on the world stage; following Geertz, often performance is all there is. Performing statecraft, then, is something other than a question of representation; it is more than a matter of image or identity. As many of the chapters in this book reveal, such performances make spaces and undermine sovereigns, they serve as acts of liberation or they legitimate acts of war, and they establish authority or lay bare its vulnerability.

The chapters that follow provide a broad survey of performances by state and non-state actors that afford opportunities to reexamine key questions that emerge from the conjunction of performance and politics in the twenty-first century. Our authors track performances of national legitimacy and authority that show fissures or invite contestation, and performances of everyday citizens that lay claim to power on the world stage. As I have written elsewhere on diplomatic performance, "the necessity of performance is power's Achilles heel."[31] Focused on recent events and the early twenty-first century, the chapters in this book also turn regularly to the past, tracing statecraft's logic of reiteration to reactivate concerns that have long preoccupied scholars. Our authors take up anew the question of the role of the nation-state in international relations, adding to debates on the subject by understanding that figure as an actor made and remade in performance. Performance also provides insights into the relationship between citizens and the broader assemblages (community, state, international organization) in which they perform. We embrace the central role played by arts and artists on the world stage, as embassies in their own right who exceed the pigeonholes of cultural diplomacy or soft power. In what follows, the boundaries between art and politics dissolve to reveal that governance is always an artful practice, and that aesthetic performance can always have effects on the world stage.

Postdiplomatic Theatre

This book takes stock of what it means to perform statecraft two decades into the twenty-first century. Performing statecraft is not just about discourse and policy, it also refers to a set of specific gestures, a professional habitus, a particular sort of handicraft (as Costas Constantinou reminds us in *On the Way to Diplomacy*).[32] Statecraft is carried out at the highest levels by a professional class that has been well trained in etiquette and protocol, that dresses and behaves in particular ways. Raymond Cohen's *Theatre of Power* is representative of a common understanding that diplomatic negotiation, and perhaps politics more broadly, consists not just in explicit verbal sparring but in a complex and unique sign system of body language, attitudes, and cues that is relatively stable and can be deciphered by the initiated.

Theatre of Power also tracks the degree to which the mediatization of politics in the twentieth century, and the concomitant expansion of the mass audience it reaches, has transformed political performance. As new platforms and norms emerge on which and by which diplomacy is practiced, old ways are often remediated to meet changed conditions, since, Cohen asserts, the need of diplomacy to clearly communicate a set of intentions and meanings remains the same. "The professional diplomat lives and breathes the carefully-drafted text and the exegesis of slight shades of emphasis that are his stock-in-trade. But mass publics and politicians alike are less impressed by such nuances. It is the human touch, the direct visual message, the appeal to the senses, which they notice and remember."[33] Cohen's work thus highlights two trends in tension in statecraft, and especially in its performance—one an art of subtle shades of meaning following well-worn practices and conventions, another an art of grand gestures that disrupt the old ways to strike at the bodies of new audiences directly.

These trends have broken into open conflict at the start of the 2020s. Indeed, the notion that either politics or international relations is made up of a legible and readable system of signs, stable and predictable in its current and future course, though more urgently desired than ever, feels a bit dubious as I write at the end of the Trump presidency and start of the Biden presidency. As Fiona McConnell puts it, throughout the history of international relations, adherence to codes of diplomatic decorum "has varied considerably, not least in the present geopolitical environment, as illustrated by the rise of social media's less scripted modes of communication and President Trump's flagrant disregard for the conventions of diplomatic protocol."[34] From 2017 to 2021, a boorish and theatrical American regime undid ties with traditional allies,[35] played a whiplash diplomacy with dictators,[36] and stirred controversy and made peace in equal measure in the Middle East,[37] at all points defying the conventional wisdom on which any stable lexicon of diplomatic performance may be built. Disruption—and the disruption of established scripts and scenarios in particular—has become the name of the game, and will likely continue as a salient figure in global politics despite President Biden's stated interest in cultivating "stable and predictable" international relationships in Trump's wake.[38]

In the present moment, it seems a bit crazy to think that diplomacy could proceed in a straightforward manner as a set of signs encoded and decoded either between accredited diplomats or between publics. More importantly, to do so would be an impoverished way of thinking about what the performance of statecraft might entail or why it might be a useful object of study. One needs to account for words, bodies, gestures, affects, and their meanings as much as the spectacular events that intervene in those meanings, but any analysis of the performance of politics should never be reducible to either a guide to body language or to spectacle. Instead, to study the performance of statecraft is to study global politics in its most explicit guise—to refuse the notion that we might denude global affairs of their theatricality.

To Jacques Rancière,

> Trump's people is … a people produced by a specific institution in which many stubbornly see the supreme expression of democracy: that which establishes an immediate and reciprocal relationship between an individual deemed to embody the power of all and a collective of individuals deemed to recognize themselves in him.[39]

Trumpism makes a political bloc via Cohen's techniques of visceral address on the world stage; medium is not merely message but the articulation of a relationship that constitutes the political lives of citizens and sovereigns. The performance is attractive to its adherents precisely because it enacts an ideal political configuration for them—one in which a political leader brooks no censor in regurgitating the xenophobic desires of his followers on the world stage. To study performance on the world stage, then, is to get to the root of how politics operates in the twenty-first century. Politics plays out as theatre—as a set of performances that express and manifest the relations by which they proceed. To understand this milieu, I offer the figure of postdiplomatic theatre.

The notion that we might be in a time and space of the postdiplomatic arose in conversations among this volume's contributors as we sought to parse the relevance of our distinct research agendas—spanning the twentieth and twenty-first centuries, multiple continents, and heterogenous performance practices—in a world that increasingly seemed to lack the fixed coordinates by which orderly relations had proceeded. Well versed in the excesses performance generates, we were nevertheless overwhelmed by the global situation we had set out to study. In the Theatres of Public Diplomacy working group at the annual conference of the American Society for Theatre Research we lamented the surface clarity of Trump's performance on the world stage (what need have we to point out to the world we are watching performance?) and our inability to change hearts and minds in an era of polarized disbelief (what difference can a critical reading make to those unwilling to think otherwise?). Of course, this was not just a matter of accounting for Trumpism, but for a period in which traditional categories are shifting and new actors and relationships appear, from rivers granted personhood,[40] to teams of multinational refugees competing at the Olympics under a shared flag,[41] to Denmark's appointment of the first ambassador to Silicon Valley and the technology industry.[42] What is public diplomacy for the person without a human body, for the human body without a state, for the state dwarfed by a transnational corporation? This is also an era in which, as many have pointed out, "information manipulation has become a global phenomenon, a prominent instrument in the strategic foreign policy toolkit of a great deal of governments, at bilateral, regional, and global levels."[43] What future might there be for global cooperation or multilateral solutions to the world's problems when agreement on the same facts or reality proves so elusive?

Postdiplomatic theatre is a performance studies intervention into political science that names a genre of political performance. It is a critical frame for the study of the performances of sovereigns, citizens, and states that brings the insights of theatre and performance studies to bear on the analysis of statecraft. Each performance detailed in this book is an instance of postdiplomatic theatre.[44]

Postdiplomatic theatre is firstly a way of thinking about political performance on the world stage that decenters the textuality of diplomacy (e.g., the words and instruments it uses, on which negotiations so often center), much as Hans-Thies Lehmann's *Postdramatic Theatre* names theatrical trends that break with an emphasis on the dramatic text, to recenter on relations between performers and spectators and to foreground their bodies. To Lehmann, "theatre is the site not only of 'heavy' bodies but also of a real gathering, a place where a unique intersection of aesthetically organized and everyday real life takes place ... The theatre performance turns the behavior onstage and in the auditorium into a joint text," that supplants any dramatic text, and postdramatic theatre, in turn, "has made use of this basic given of theatre, has specifically reflected on it and directly turned it into the content and theme of its presentation."[45] Postdiplomatic theatres, then, recognize that the work of international relations happens wherever performing bodies encounter one another on the world stage, regardless of the credentials they carry or the textual instruments they execute. To return to the question of who performs the state, we find an expanded field where those played-to perform in turn and where forms of address move in multiple directions. Postdiplomatic theatres locate statecraft's power precisely in its theatrical interfaces and the excesses they give rise to.

Of course, this postdiplomatic is hardly the break with the diplomatic past it implies. Here too the term follows in the footsteps of the postdramatic, for which "post-" "is to be understood neither as an epochal category, nor simply as a chronological 'after' drama, a 'forgetting' of the dramatic 'past', but rather as a rupture and a beyond that continue to entertain relationships with drama."[46] The postdiplomatic does not imply the obsolescence of diplomacy, or the inadequacy of its structures, or its inability to communicate. Rather, postdiplomatic theatre is a way to renew the promise and potential of performance studies to intervene in the fields of international relations and political science, and in the practice of global politics. Postdiplomatic theatre recenters diplomacy on the moments in which it is performed, recognizing that the content it putatively transmits is inseparable from the times and spaces in which it operates, the forces it deploys, the affects and atmospheres it generates, and the ways it is embodied.

Postdiplomatic theatre modulates the time of diplomacy, bringing the past into the present and placing the future in question. I have previously argued that theatre's power vis-à-vis diplomacy is in part that it "remembers performance; it is a structure that refuses to allow performance to forget or be forgotten."[47] The instances of postdiplomatic theatre collected in this volume make clear the ways in which performance opens spaces in which timeframes collapse together, recur, and expand. As individuals perform cultural memory and states perform hegemonic histories, postdiplomatic theatre becomes an arena in which the irreversibility of historical time may be arrested, opened to new scrutiny, or diverted.

In such blurred and cycling temporal frames, certain political categories lose their stability and reveal their contingency. The state and its alternatives are each enacted and compete for legitimacy within a postdiplomatic theatre. Postdiplomatic theatres are centered on dissent and dissensus. Postdiplomatic theatres are sites of struggle, as states perform to distinguish themselves from one another, articulating visions that invite opposition from within and without. In postdiplomatic theatres, diplomacy and its one-time goal of agreement become decoupled, recentering attention from ends once more on means, for example the moments of performance that compose it. Citizens and sovereigns, artists and activists vie, each finding tools, audiences, and stages. Postdiplomatic theatre *is* a theatre of power, a theatre in which images of authority are undermined by the citizen rejoinders that meet them.

In such encounters, postdiplomatic theatres also feature postdiplomatic biopolitics. Being irreducible to the transmitted content of diplomatic speech or signaling, this is a diplomacy that is necessarily embodied. Diplomacy has always been embodied and has always been about the body; as war by other means it has always been about bodies oppressed, in pain, and facing death. But the body often disappears from view in scholarship on global politics. A recent volume notes, "in [the discipline of international relations] the human appears in manifold terminological shapes and forms: as actor, subject, individual, person, body/being, self, mind, psyche and so forth," giving the body fifth billing, and forcing it to share its stage, awkwardly, with being.[48] The study of diplomacy has not exactly been fleshy; our images of diplomacy eschew the body (think of the antiseptic conference rooms of embassies and institutions) though they often become punctuated by viscera (think of George H. W. Bush vomiting at a state dinner).[49] Ethnicity, race, imperialism, colonialism, and white supremacy each imagine and mold the body, and so too have they configured the performance of statecraft; their forces reach far into the twenty-first century. The body becomes tantamount, foregrounded in a postdiplomatic theatre as medium and message, that which performs and that which is at stake. Asking *how* we perform the state invites us to rethink where and why the body disappears from politics. It asks us to attend to our bodies in shared space, and to attend to the bodies of others on the world stage. As David Donkor remarked in the conference proceedings at this book's origins, "diplomacy cannot begin until we have performed who the other is; performance inaugurates this time of encounter." Postdiplomatic theatres reveal the predicates on which global politics are built.

Sovereigns, Citizens, and States

In organizing this book to follow a sensible arc of topics and arguments, the chapters fell into roughly chronological order, taking up events and phenomena stretching from the early twentieth century to the present day. Even so, this book is addressed to our contemporary moment, a moment for which the past always figures as a resource to be put to new ends by statecraft in the present. Here, then, is another way to think about the postdiplomatic—it names at once a set of practices and approaches that have been the stuff of diplomacy for at least a century, and it points to a question of what may or may not have unraveled in the practice of statecraft in the years since. Indeed, as we travel from revolution to disruption, we may find ourselves asking what has, in fact, changed.

This volume is not divided into sections, but its organization reveals exciting affinities. Our first three chapters, which look back to the early and middle decades of the twentieth century, provide views of nations performed, and the complexities and fissures that emerge as a national formation is asserted on the world stage. The first four chapters also consider the unique role of performance in settler colonial states, anticolonial struggles, and independence movements. Chapters 4 and 5, in turn, share an interest in the discursive fields produced by the performances of states, institutions, and individual politicians. Chapter 5 also shares with Chapter 1 an interest in the use of performance as an adjunct to armed conflict. And Chapter 6 locates aesthetic performance as a ground on which territorial disputes play out. The second half of the book (Chapters 5–8) is set squarely in the twenty-first century. These chapters see a small parade of dictators and others with totalitarian tendencies: Saddam Hussein (Chapter 5), Vladimir Putin, and Recep Tayyip Erdoğan (Chapter 7). In Chapters 6–8, too, the capacity of citizens to press back against or provide alternatives to the statecraft performed by sovereigns becomes increasingly salient.

The chapters of *Performing Statecraft* investigate a broad field of practices under the umbrella of statecraft. Some consider the performative dimensions of law and policy, including The British Nationality Act (Chapter 4), the memos providing the legal justification for the use of torture by the United States (Chapter 5), and Venezuela's Law Against Racial Discrimination (Chapter 8). Ceremony and protocol prove important in such varied contexts as the propriety of photographing a monarch eating a hot dog (Chapter 2), the implicit and explicit meanings associated with traditional ethnic dress (Chapter 3), and as part and parcel with the production of a music video (Chapter 6). Economic policy and the economic dimensions of diplomacy and war are also rarely far from view, as insurrectionists target factories (Chapter 1), as civil society members disrupt trade negotiations (Chapter 4), as foreign aid wins diplomatic dividends (Chapter 6), or as the sports-industrial complex exercises its own political powers (Chapter 7). And the use of force appears in diverse forms with diverse effects, from the continuing trauma of the US invasion of Iraq (Chapter 5) to the celebrated history of Simón Bolívar's wars of revolution and liberation (Chapter 8).

Reading these chapters alongside one another reveals sets of related concerns that speak to the necessity of ongoing performance studies engagement with political science. As our chapters trace dramas of recognition and misrecognition in equal measure, they offer new avenues for considering the politics of visibility and invisibility. As they find performance mobilized to transform discursive fields, our chapters continue the important work of dismantling the false opposition between speech and action on the world stage. And as each chapter navigates between the efforts of citizens and sovereigns to perform the state, they offer new insights into modes of dissent that can change the world.

In Chapter 1, "(En)Acting the Republic: The 1916 Rising as a Spectacle of Self-Sacrifice for Ireland," Áine Josephine Tyrrell examines the aesthetic choices made by the leaders of the Irish Easter Rising, a six-day insurrection against the British Empire in Dublin in 1916. Considering the spatial politics at play in the sites chosen for the insurrection, Tyrrell highlights the insurrection as a performance of national spirit that ultimately manifested a counter public to British imperial rule. Via their conscientious dramaturgy, the insurrection's planners effectively established the oppressiveness of British rule and their own self-sacrificing heroism, providing the essential foundation for revolutionary acts to come. The book thus begins not at the negotiating table, but on the battlefield, amid revolution, at the symbolic start of a far longer struggle for recognition.

Christiana Molldrem Harkulich is also interested in colonized nations performed and legitimated against an international backdrop, but traces a drama of misrecognition. In Chapter 2, "An 'Indian Princess', a King and a Queen, and a President: Diplomatic Performance and Indigenous Sovereignties at the 1939 Royal Visit," she turns to the first state visit of the king and queen of England to the United States, and the performance of Te Ata Fisher, a member of the Chickasaw nation, at Franklin Delano Roosevelt's so-called Hot Dog Summit. Performing indigeneity to contribute to a particular image of the United States and its policy goals, Te Ata's performance, and its misrecognition by the assembled sovereigns, also troubles a stable interpretation of the idea of nation and state, pointing to the imaginative and diplomatic power of disruption inherent in an Indigenous body within a colonial framework, and the limits of that power.

Chapter 3 turns to further colonial struggles and independence movements. In "The President's Yellow Batakari: Performance and the Sartorial in Ghanaian Politics," David Afriyie Donkor provides a social history of the batakari, a type of tunic smock woven from narrow, hand-spun strips of cotton, worn in northern Ghana. He follows the batakari from its origins in Islam's arrival in Africa in the seventh century, through Kwame Nkrumah's use of the garment during his involvement in the anti-colonial struggle and Ghana's independence. Donkor argues that Nkrumah engaged a "sartorial politics" that exploited symbolic opportunities to legitimate his leadership over newly sovereign Ghana. Closing with a striking image of the Batakari's continued political use by current President of Ghana, Nana Akufo-Addo, Donkor reveals fashion to be a crucial site of postdiplomatic interface between citizens and heads of state.

Chapter 4 returns to Britain for another view of performance and the postcolonial. In "Windrush Strikes Back: 'Rivers of Blood', Performance, and Guerrilla Diplomacy," Mary Karen Dahl examines British Member of Parliament Enoch Powell's 1968 "Rivers of Blood" speech, "a deliberately performative articulation of ethnonationalism," that targeted black British subjects recruited from Caribbean colonies to work in postwar Britain. Dahl takes up the legacy of the speech in the decades since, the way it provided the terms for its own repudiation and contestation by a coalition of Caribbean diplomats, British parliamentarians, journalists, and civil society groups in the 2018 Windrush scandal. Chapter 4 makes explicit the ways in which postdiplomatic theatres expand the category of statecraft, transform discursive fields, and open times and places for citizen intervention into the making of policy.

Warren Kluber's "Organ Failure: Medicalized Torture During the Iraq War" (Chapter 5) details a similarly contested discursive field.

Kluber's analysis of the 2004 televised medical examination of Saddam Hussein by US Army doctors finds war, diplomacy, and domestic politics bleeding into one another yet again. Kluber argues that this "military-media performance" substantiates the metaphor of war-as-medicine, a node in a network of state performances designed to produce "spectatorial amnesia: a numbing of the pain of witness." Contrasting the state performance with Frances Ya-Chu Cowhig's 2009 play *Lidless*, Kluber considers an alternative relationship of care that could emerge from medical metaphors. In this chapter, aesthetic drama emerges as a tool used by artists and citizens to heal from state violence.

Chapter 6, "Viral Diplomacy: Music, Masks, and Maritime Borders Between China and the Philippines," provides a view of public diplomacy that misfired—a music video produced by the Chinese Embassy in the Philippines, featuring diplomats and pop stars, and extolling China's "mask diplomacy" (*kouzhao waijiao*) amid the global Covid-19 pandemic. Philippine audiences were quick to decry the thinly veiled territorial encroachment implied by the song, which laid claim to the "One Sea" stretching between the nations. To Adam Kielman, the case provides an opportunity to move beyond narrow Western-centric accounts of "musical diplomacy" common in musicological literature. Instead, Kielman builds his analysis from the Confucian *Yue Ji* ("Record of Music") to recognize that ritual, music, policy, and force are tightly braided together in any statecraft.

Chapter 7, "The President Makes a Play: Putin and Erdoğan's Sporting Statecraft," by Sean Bartley and Jared Strange takes us to new arenas of state performance: football fields and ice hockey rinks. The authors take up the performances of authority staged by Russia's Vladimir Putin and Turkey's Recep Tayyip Erdoğan, looking closely at the ways those carefully cultivated performances prove prone to misfire. Bartley and Strange invite us to consider the conjoining of politics and sports power as "sport-as-politics," efforts that use sports to exercise, expand, or contest the power of governments and heads of state. Located between institutions and actors, sport-as-politics offers a rich site in which to recognize the competing agencies of politicians, athletes, sports governing bodies (like FIFA), and fans. As such, our authors remind us, sport remains a scenario in which dissent and conflict are constitutive and inescapable.

Conflicts between citizens and states continue in Chapter 8, as artists, historians, and national leaders each lay claim to and deploy icons and symbols overloaded with meanings. In "Statecraft and Revolution: Remaking Bolívar for an Anti-Imperialist Transnational Alliance," Angela Marino reveals "the instability of states and the staying power of performance" via popular performances that take advantage of the image of the nineteenth-century revolutionary Simón Bolívar. Marino focuses on efforts by Afro-descendant historians to make visible an Afro-Venezuelan history that had been suppressed. Doing so, she traces phenomena that can "open… the very parameters of state power" in exciting ways.

Finally, Tony Perucci's Afterword, "The Future of Dissensus: Performance Postdiplomatic Postdemocracy," closes the volume by returning to the figure of postdiplomatic theatre, highlighting the terrain in which new forms of dissensus may emerge as practices of radical antagonism against antidemocratic rule.

The case studies that follow lay out an agenda for continued work by theatre and performance studies scholars in the fields of politics and international relations. Our authors model new and exciting approaches to global political performance, asserting the importance of always assessing politics through a performance lens. Performance is the medium and message of statecraft, a substantive location of global politics. These chapters map a postdiplomatic theatre in which the practice of statecraft emerges as a multiform performance in which state officials and private individuals are both interpellated. On the world stage we perform to make the world, its stratifications, its oppressions, and its opportunities for liberation. Doing so we encounter the bodies that global politics might otherwise eschew, and return to the most basic terms by which international relations proceed. As the chapters that follow attend rigorously to the performance of statecraft, they open new avenues for dissent, and new strategies for world-making.

Notes

1. Courtney Thompson, "White House Dinner Serves U.S.A.-Loving Sarkozy American Wine," *BizBash,* November 8, 2007, https://www.bizbash.com/style-decor/social-events/article/13226440/white-house-dinner-serves-usaloving-sarkozy-american-wine (accessed April 18, 2022).
2. White House Office of the Press Secretary, "President Bush and President Sarkozy of France Exchange Toasts," *News Release*, November 6, 2007, https://georgewbush-whitehouse.archives.gov/news/releases/2007/11/text/20071106-14.html (accessed April 18, 2022).
3. In my book, James R. Ball III, *Theater of State: A Dramaturgy of the United Nations* (Evanston: Northwestern University Press, 2020), 73–4, I detail the performative structure of such acts of citation.
4. White House Office of the Press Secretary, "President Bush and President Sarkozy."
5. Dana Milbank, "Sarkozy's Lafayette Tour," *Los Angeles Times—Washington Post News Service*, November 7, 2007, *NewsBank: America's Newspapers.* https://infoweb.newsbank.com/apps/news/document-view?p=NewsBank&docref=news/11CCC22793F51D98 (accessed April 18, 2022).
6. AP Archive, "Banquet, Post Dinner Entertainment with Bush," *YouTube Video*, 2:30, July 21, 2015, https://www.youtube.com/watch?v=utsuvfmN9cI (accessed April 18, 2022).
7. Hank Stuever, "All Fraternité for Sarkozy at a Cozy White House Fete," *The Washington Post*, November 7, 2007, https://www.washingtonpost.com/wp-dyn/content/article/2007/11/06/AR2007110602756_2.html (accessed April 18, 2022).
8. Stuever, "All Fraternité."
9. Stuever, "All Fraternité."
10. Vanessa Friedman, "Critic's Notebook: The Death of Fashion Diplomacy," *The New York Times*, June 7, 2019, https://www.nytimes.com/2019/06/07/fashion/the-death-of-fashion-diplomacy.html (accessed April 18, 2022).
11. 153 Cong. Rec. H13211 (daily ed. November 7, 2007) (Address by His Excellency Nicolas Sarkozy, president of the French Republic).
12. Elaine Sciolino, "Sarkozy Is Greeted Warmly By Congress," *The New York Times,* November 7, 2007, https://www.nytimes.com/2007/11/07/washington/07cnd-sarkozy.html (accessed April 18, 2022).

13 In Victor Turner, *Dramas, Fields, and Metaphors: Symbolic Action in Human Society* (Ithaca: Cornell University Press, 1974), Turner outlines a four phase process of Social Drama: (1) a *Breach* of regular social relations is followed by, (2) mounting *Crisis*, which precipitates, (3) *Redressive Actions*, which leads to either, (4) *Reintegration* or *Schism* (37–41). See also, Richard Schechner, *Performance Theory*, Revised and Expanded Edition (London: Routledge Classics, 2003). Social Drama provides one conceptual framework with which to make sense of Sarkozy's performance, but it does not exhaust the analytical potential of his state visit.

14 ProfGP, "George W. Bush: The American Presidency Project," *YouTube Video*, 18:42, January 24, 2013, https://youtu.be/Z6TjnQcUoFU (accessed April 18, 2022).

15 Jan-Hendrik Passoth and Nicholas J. Rowland, "Who Is Acting in International Relations?" in *Human Beings in International Relations*, ed. Daniel Jacobi and Annette Freyberg-Inan (Cambridge: Cambridge University Press, 2015), 302.

16 Clifford Geertz, *Negara: The Theatre State in Nineteenth-Century Bali* (Princeton: Princeton University Press, 1980), 13.

17 Benedict Anderson, *Imagined Communities: Reflections on the Origin and Spread of Nationalism*, Revised Edition (London: Verso Books, [1983] 2006), 44.

18 Anderson, *Imagined Communities*, 115.

19 Michael Taussig, *The Magic of the State* (New York and London: Routledge, 1997).

20 Karen Shimakawa, *National Abjection: The Asian American Body on Stage* (Durham: Duke University Press, 2003).

21 In Africa, see, for example, Kelly Askew, *Performing the Nation: Swahili Music and Cultural Politics in Tanzania* (Chicago: University of Chicago Press, 2002), which highlights the role music played in official efforts to define national culture and Laura Edmondson, *Performance and Politics in Tanzania: The Nation on Stage* (Bloomington and Indianapolis: Indiana University Press, 2007). Edmondson finds artists "performing, transforming, and reforming the nation in a continuous cycle of collaboration, complicity, and conviviality" (7). In Europe, see Nadine Rossol, *Performing the Nation in Interwar Germany: Sport, Spectacle*

and Political Symbolism, 1926–36 (New York: Palgrave Macmillan, 2010), and Mona Ozouf, *Festivals and the French Revolution*, trans. Alan Sheridan (Cambridge, MA: Harvard University Press, 1988), each of which examines the role mass spectacles and public festivities played in fostering community and "connecting the population with the republic" (Rossol, 160). In Asia, see Hyunjung Lee, *Performing the Nation in Global Korea: Transnational Theatre* (Basingstoke: Palgrave Macmillan, 2015), for an account of Korean theatres as a site in which national self-identity and global preconceptions meet and compete.

22 See J. L. Austin, *How to Do Things With Words*, ed. J. O. Urmson and Marina Sbisà (Cambridge, MA: Harvard University Press, 1955).

23 Adam Kielman, "Sites and Sounds of National Memory: Performing the Nation in China's Decennial National Day Celebrations," *International Communication of Chinese Culture* 7, no. 2 (2020): 155.

24 Diana Taylor, *Disappearing Acts: Spectacles of Gender and Nationalism in Argentina's "Dirty War"* (Durham: Duke University Press, 1997), ix.

25 Maria Berlova, "Playing King," *Nordic Theatre Studies* 26, no. 1 (2014): 81.

26 Roxanne Lynn Doty, *Imperial Encounters: The Politics of Representation in North–South Relations* (Minneapolis: University of Minnesota Press, 1996), 4.

27 Julia C. Strauss, *State Formation in China and Taiwan: Bureaucracy, Campaign, and Performance* (Cambridge: Cambridge University Press, 2020), 27.

28 Alex Jeffrey, *The Improvised State: Sovereignty, Performance and Agency in Dayton Bosnia* (Chichester: John Wiley & Sons, 2013), 2. In the discipline of political geography, see also Fiona McConnell, *Rehearsing the State: The Political Practices of the Tibetan Government-in-Exile* (Chichester: John Wiley & Sons, 2016).

29 Julia C. Strauss and Donal B. Cruise O'Brien, eds., *Staging Politics: Power and Performance in Asia and Africa* (London: I.B. Tauris, 2007), 2.

30 Geertz, *Theatre State,* 136.

31 Ball, *Theater of State*, 19.

32 Costas Constantinou, *On the Way to Diplomacy* (Minneapolis: University of Minnesota Press, 1996), 69–95.

33 Raymond Cohen, *Theatre of Power: The Art of Diplomatic Signalling* (London: Longman, 1987), 212–13.

34 Fiona McConnell, "Performing Diplomatic Decorum: Repertoires of 'Appropriate' Behavior in the Margins of International Diplomacy," *International Political Sociology* 12 (2018): 364.
35 See Michael Crowley, "Allies and Former U.S. Officials Fear Trump Could Seek NATO Exit in a Second Term," *The New York Times*, September 3, 2020, https://www.nytimes.com/2020/09/03/us/politics/trump-nato-withdraw.html (accessed April 18, 2022).
36 See Chris Cillizza and Brenna Williams, "15 Times Donald Trump Praised Authoritarian Rulers," *CNN.com*, July 2, 2019, https://www.cnn.com/2019/07/02/politics/donald-trump-dictators-kim-jong-un-vladimir-putin (accessed April 18, 2022).
37 See Alexia Underwood, "The Controversial US Jerusalem Embassy Opening, Explained," *Vox*, May 16, 2018, https://www.vox.com/2018/5/14/17340798/jerusalem-embassy-israel-palestinians-us-trump (accessed April 18, 2022). See also, Rich Lowry, "How Jared Kushner Proved His Critics Wrong," *Politico.com*, September 16, 2020, https://www.politico.com/news/magazine/2020/09/16/how-jared-kushner-proved-his-critics-wrong-416527 (accessed April 18, 2022).
38 White House Briefing Room, "Readout of President Joseph R. Biden, Jr. Call with President Vladimir Putin of Russia," April 13, 2021, https://www.whitehouse.gov/briefing-room/statements-releases/2021/04/13/readout-of-president-joseph-r-biden-jr-call-with-president-vladimir-putin-of-russia-4-13/ (accessed April 18, 2022).
39 Jacques Rancière, "The Fools and The Wise," trans. David Fernbach, January 22, 2021, https://www.versobooks.com/blogs/4980-the-fools-and-the-wise (accessed April 18, 2022).
40 See Ashley Westerman. "Should Rivers Have the Same Legal Rights as Humans? A Growing Number of Voices Say Yes," *National Public Radio*, August 3, 2019, https://www.npr.org/2019/08/03/740604142/should-rivers-have-same-legal-rights-as-humans-a-growing-number-of-voices-say-ye (accessed April 18, 2022).
41 See, Baidruel Hairiel, Abd Rahim, Nurazzura Mohamad Diah, and Mohd Salleh Aman, "From Immigrants to Sports Figures: The Case Study of the IOC Refugee Team in Rio Olympics 2016," *Al-Shajarah: Journal of the International Institute of Islamic Thought & Civilization*, Special Issue: Migration and Refugee Studies (2018): 137–54.

42 See Adam Satariano, "The World's First Ambassador to the Tech Industry," *The New York Times*, September 3, 2019, https://www.nytimes.com/2019/09/03/technology/denmark-tech-ambassador.html (accessed April 18, 2022).

43 André W. M. Gerrits, "Disinformation in International Relations: How Important Is It?" *Security and Human Rights* 29 (2018): 4.

44 In political science literature, the terms postdiplomacy and postdiplomatic appear only occasionally. In some instances, they identify shifting phases in the relations between states (see, for example, Shaun Breslin, "Beyond Diplomacy? UK Relations with China Since 1997," *The British Journal of Politics and International Relations* 6 (2004): 409–25), in others, the terms indicate a "disconnection between foreign policy formulators … and traditional implementers (mostly diplomats)." Dawisson Belém Lopes, "De-westernization, Democratization, Disconnection: The Emergence of Brazil's Post-Diplomatic Foreign Policy," *Global Affairs* 6, no. 2 (2020): 169.

45 Hans-Thies Lehmann, *Postdramatic Theatre*, trans. Karen Jürs-Munby (New York: Routledge, 2006), 17.

46 Karen Jürs-Munby, "Introduction," *Postdramatic Theatre* (New York: Routledge, 2006), 2.

47 Ball, *Theater of State*, 27.

48 Daniel Jacobi, and Annette Freyberg-Inan, "Introduction: Human Being(s) in International Relations," in *Human Beings in International Relations*, ed. Daniel Jacobi and Annette Freyberg-Inan (Cambridge: Cambridge University Press, 2015), 8. For literature in international relations that does do justice to the body, see Laura Wilcox, *Bodies of Violence: Theorizing Embodied Subjects in International Relations* (New York: Oxford University Press, 2015).

49 ABC News, "Jan. 11, 1992: President Bush Gets Sick in Japan," Filmed 1992 at the Japanese Prime Minister's Residence, Tokyo, Japan, 1:58, https://abcnews.go.com/Archives/video/jan-11-1992-president-bush-sick-japan-9357727 (accessed July 18, 2021).

1

(En)Acting the Republic: The 1916 Rising as a Spectacle of Self-Sacrifice for Ireland

Áine Josephine Tyrrell

On a Sunday in 1916, James Connolly, Pádraig Pearse, and five other Irish men led the newly formed IRA (Irish Republican Army) in the first major revolt against British colonial rule since the United Irishmen Rebellion of 1798. Today, this uprising is generally framed as the founding act of the Irish democratic state. At the time, however, it was perceived to be an unwarranted, bloody act of treason that was unrepresentative of the Irish public's preference for Home Rule. The uprising itself, as a battle for independence, was far from successful: the rebels ultimately surrendered and sixteen of their more prominent fighters were executed by firing squad by British soldiers. However, it was as a direct result of the Irish soldiers' sacrifice and the violence of British retaliation, that public opinion in Ireland was quickly swayed in favor of the rebels' cause. In short, the effects the Rising had on the Irish collective consciousness cannot be overstated. The Rising quickly became—and still is today—a symbol of the triumph of failure *to* and *for* Ireland.

The Rising was fought across a number of locations in Dublin's city center; each locale was selected for its aesthetic and ideological power, its capacity to steer the insurrection in *favor* of Irish Republicanism.

The leaders' attention to the symbolism that imbued each space indicates that these men understood the political value of theatre and the intrinsic theatricality of politics.[1] This is not surprising when we consider that, of the seven-man military council that choreographed the events, three were playwrights (Thomas MacDonagh, James Connolly, and Pádraig Pearse) and one was a theatre founder (Joseph Mary Plunkett).[2] The locations where the Rising took place were, I argue, chosen for the same reasons that a director tends to choose their set: for their aesthetic and for their ability to shape *how* the action takes place and is subsequently interpreted by its intended audience. These parallels between the Rising and theatre are no coincidence as theatre was at the heart of Irish political life at the time. Indeed, Douglas Hyde, Lady Gregory, W. B. Yeats, and other literati were in the midst of the Irish Literary Revival and their Abbey Theatre was at the height of its political significance. Joseph Holloway—the Abbey Theatre's most frequent and prominent patron—even admits in his private journals that he mistook the Irish Proclamation for a playbill, due in large part to the fact that two of the signatories were also founders of the Irish National Theatre Society.[3]

The sites chosen for the Rising were: the Northumberland Hotel (today, known as Liberty Hall), the General Post Office (GPO), the Four Courts, St. Stephen's Green Square/Park, Jacob's Biscuit Factory, the South Dublin Union, and Boland's Mill.[4] Here, I shall restrict myself to an analysis of the spatial politics at play at the GPO and Kilmainham Gaol. As the rebels' headquarters and the site of their executions respectively, I argue that these two edifices were the most vital for the ontological reconfiguration of Ireland. By using these sites as case studies, I hope to broadly convey my larger thesis: that the Rising's events successfully created a counter-public[5] to British imperialism by framing self-sacrifice as a performance of national spirit. The rhetoric and staging of Sacrifice provided the Irish rebels with a rationale for framing their deaths, as *not* deaths. Instead, death was reconfigured: it became a techne for the rebirth and regeneration that eventually gave rise to the Irish Republic.

The Rise of the Fenian Leaders: Socio-Cultural Context of the Rising

In the 1880s, Douglas Hyde published a revolutionary essay titled "The Necessity for De-Anglicising Ireland" in which he called for a renaissance of the Irish culture, language, and Gaelic sports lost under Britain's colonial control, as well as the establishment of a new national literature and theatre. Through the lens of Pheng Cheah's scholarship, this cultural-pedagogical project constituted a search for an "original culture," an effort to win back a "self-supporting" national identity by solidifying a collective cultural subjectivity.[6] Language is central as it is not merely the product of a people's shared life experience or, to quote Cheah, "metaphorical expressions of the supersensible world," but is formative to the constitution of a nation's spiritual unity.[7] By this logic, the act of speaking a native tongue becomes both a revival and a propagation of one's traditions; the use of idioms, cultural references, language and so on unifies nationalist thought and action, knowledge and practice.

When one considers Dublin at the turn of the century, it is of little wonder that Hyde quickly banded together with figures such as W. B. Yeats and Lady Augusta Gregory to begin mining and recuperating Ireland's past. This new movement of cultural nationalism quickly led to the establishment of a variety of organizations, the most prominent of which were: Conradh na Gaeilge (the Gaelic League) that initiated an Irish language revival movement; the more general Irish Literary Revival, which sought to create and propagate a uniquely Irish national literature; and the Irish national theatre.[8] Most of those involved in the Easter rebellion were of the newly urbanized Catholic middle and lower classes of Irish society, the increasingly militant labor movement, and a minority were also of the Protestant Ascendancy (aristocracy).[9] Dublin's compactness relative to other European capital cities meant that the various strands of Irish nationalism quickly began to "cross-fertilize"; the leaders of the Rising increasingly moved in the same social and political circles as Ireland's new prolific and renowned literary figures. For example, Pádraig Pearse, Thomas MacDonagh, James Connolly,

Arthur Griffith and their fellow Gaelic Leaguers began their political careers by dedicating themselves to Hyde's cultural activism.

This being said, the rebel leaders were quickly drawn away from the creation of art and toward political and military action: they embraced the ideas of republicanism and separatism preached by generations of Fenian politicians and fighters. By the end of May 1915, three influential Republicans (or Fenians), namely Pádraig Pearse, Joseph Plunkett, and Éamonn Ceannt, were secretly[10] appointed by the Irish Republican Brotherhood (IRB) to oversee preparations for an insurrection against the British in Ireland.[11] This military committee was later expanded to include Tom Clarke and Séan McDermott.[12] Together, these men plotted for the remainder of 1915 and into 1916. The end of 1915 also saw the head of the Irish Citizens' Army,[13] James Connolly, join the council; he was approached by the IRB because they feared his increasing vociferousness for revolutionary insurrection would jeopardize the conspirators' burgeoning plans.[14] Connolly quickly agreed to join their efforts and the secret council went about finalizing their plan of action. On April 23, Easter Sunday, the leaders of the Rising met at the Northumberland Hotel (today, Liberty Hall) to finalize preparations. Meanwhile, downstairs, copies of the Proclamation of the Irish Republic were hurriedly being printed in the basement; later that night these were signed[15] by the council for distribution about the city the following morning.[16]

The Easter Rising as Theatre

Much can be gained from reading the Rising, not only as a political event but as a performance with a distinctly political agenda of creating a new form of Irish nationalism. Indeed, if one considers the Rising through the lens of performance studies,[17] one sees that there was an attention to the aesthetic and the symbolic that suggests the leaders had an understanding of the political value of theatre and the intrinsic theatricality of politics.[18] Such a reading is bolstered by the fact that, of the seven-man military council that choreographed the Rising, three were playwrights (MacDonagh, Connolly, and Pearse) and one was a theatre founder (Plunkett).[19] The use of spectacle as a means of transforming Irish society into a (nationalist) public[20] is discernable from the outset of the Rising but particularly from the rebels' arrival at the GPO. At 10:00 a.m. on Easter Monday, April 24, 1916, the leaders took to the steps of Liberty Hall to rally and unify the various rebel militia and to inaugurate the Irish Republican Army (IRA). Pearse, Plunkett, and Connolly then marched their troops up Sackville Street to the GPO. Once arrived, they began establishing their headquarters: all customers were ushered from the premises and the windows were sandbagged. Upon the completion of these military operations, Pearse—dressed smartly in his volunteers' uniform and flanked on either side by his councilmen—emerged to address the small crowd of very confused civilians that had assembled outside the edifice. With as much ceremony as could be mustered, Pearse proceeded to read aloud from the Proclamation of the Irish Republic.

While some have written about the theatricality of Pearse's reading of the Proclamation, others have noted that the public reading can be understood as an Austinian performative, one that spoke the Irish State into being. However, little attention has been paid to the stage upon which the reading occurred. The GPO building boasts a stern and grandiose façade adorned with a portico in the style of an ancient Greek temple: it has a triangular roof, ionic columns, a frieze, a pediment, and ornate moldings. Upon first glance, it is, therefore, easily comparable to a *skene* in the tradition of Greek theatre, a building that served as a backdrop and that was typically decorated as a palace, temple, or another civic building depending upon the needs of the play being staged. Analysis of the leaders' letters suggests this parallel with ancient Greek theatre was intentional. The GPO was selected as a backdrop to imbue the Proclamation, Pearse, and his fellow leaders, with all the solemnity, authority and potential for catharsis of a Greek tragic play. Perhaps the most persuasive evidence for this connection can be found in the papers of Michael Collins. Collins was one of

Ireland's most famous revolutionaries and—most importantly—one of the soldiers who fought alongside Pearse in the GPO. He expressed considerable skepticism toward the aesthetic and symbolic dimensions of the rebellion in his writings from the Welsh prison camp (Frongoch) where he was imprisoned for participating in the Rising. The following is a passage from one such letter:

> I do not think the Rising week was an appropriate time for the issue of memoranda couched in poetic phrases, nor of actions worked out in a similar fashion ... Looking [back] at [the events in the GPO] from inside it had the air of a Greek tragedy about it.[21]

Admittedly, as a practical man of action, Collins likely had a better understanding of military strategy than the romantic (possibly naive?) poets and scholars who planned and led the 1916 insurrection. However, what Collins fails to acknowledge in this passage is the ideological power of the aesthetics of the Rising and the myths it appropriated. As teachers, artists, and playwrights, Pearse and his fellow rebels were conscious of the fact that the GPO's architecture simultaneously gestured toward the ancient (idealized) time of the Athenian *demos* while also symbolizing the harmony (stereo)typically associated with a social context in which there is a prevalence of authority and order. They consciously set about reappropriating these classical associations by adorning the roof of the GPO's portico with flags. These banners served as visual signifiers, to Dublin and to the British forces, of their reclamation of the authority of this site in the name of the Republic. Indeed, the flags that they flew were a green, white, and orange tricolor—which is, even today, the flag of the Irish Republic—and a green flag adorned with an Irish harp, above which were the words "The Irish Republic" in gold lettering.[22]

Aside from drawing upon visual signifiers of classical Greek culture, the rebels also sought to appropriate and redefine the GPO's associations with Empire and institutional power. The cornerstone for the GPO building was laid by Lord Whitworth on August 12, 1814 and, upon its completion, quickly became integral to the lives of all Irish citizens as the hub for all mail, financial services, telegraphs, and telephone communication on the island.²³ More importantly, as the center for communications, the GPO became increasingly intertwined with discourses of British influence and domination. The rebels' decision to occupy the structure, therefore, spoke to their desire to reappropriate this dominant symbol of colonial oppression in the collective consciousness.

Overall, then, the use of the GPO as the rebel Headquarters (HQ) was carefully calculated to emphasize the authority and legitimacy of the Provisional Government; the weight of their demand for the allegiance of the Irish people; their power/ability to strike at the heart of the British Empire in Ireland; and, as I hope to demonstrate shortly, the nobility of their call for all Irish to self-sacrifice for the emergence of a Republican Nation.

The British Performance of Colonial Power

This reclaiming of a quintessential colonial space in the name of the Irish popular national movement inevitably provoked a British response. The Empire's desire for revenge on the political resistors was such that it could only be satisfied with endlessly reproduced "spectacles of suffering."²⁴ These spectacular practices of violence were calculatedly enacted upon Irish streets and Irish bodies to legitimize the colonial power via bombings, shellings, and the deployment of British troops across the capital. Patrick Anderson and Jisha Menon explain this phenomenon in that they posit that the precondition for the forging of violence by resistors as "resistance" and "liberation" is, precisely, state-sanctioned violence.²⁵ The inevitable conclusion of their view is that the distinction between "righteous brutality" and "insurgent aggression" is a false one: both forms are simply manifestations of the same violence that underpins social representations in the same social fabric. The performance of British imperial power in the aftermath of the Rising was as spectacular as those staged against the rebels during the insurrection itself. Indeed, General John Grenfell Maxwell²⁶ was merciless in his prosecution of the rebel leaders. Upon their surrender, Maxwell immediately sentenced the Fenian men to court-martial and execution by firing squad.[27] In so doing, he sought to frame the insurrection as an aberration, an act of terrorism against the British King's legitimate rule.

The very evening of their sentencing, the rebel leaders were transferred to Kilmainham Gaol,[28] placed in separate cells, and informed they were to be shot at dawn.[29] If the GPO was *skene* for the Fenians' performative acts, Kilmainham was a dead-end: a hellhole built for British retribution that was utterly impenetrable, inescapable, and engineered for death. This contrast is immediately discernible in the architecture of the gaol. The entrance to Kilmainham is found at the convergence of the two wings of the prison, in a shallow square featuring a single, heavy door. With three large, rounded windows standing sentinel on second level above it, the impressive doorway stands center-stage, drawing the eye. Its design invokes the opening passages of Dante's *Divine Comedy* ("Abandon all hope, ye who enter here") or Auguste Rodin's *Gates of Hell*. The door is thick, black, and iron reinforced; it sits below an ornately carved portico featuring a carving of a hydra whose multiple heads struggle against their bondage, their teeth furiously gnashing at their chains. It is said that the hydra represents the five worst crimes, each of which led to the prison and its gallows: murder, piracy, rape, theft, and treason.[30] Surrounding the door and carved over-panel is a rusticated and vermiculated doorcase. Before the door rest two ornate black iron gates boasting sharpened points along their top edges. Above are two granite inserts where the gallows used for public hangings were once attached. Together with the carving of the chained hydra, the façade's design makes clear that this prison will contain and/or obliterate all those who oppose or otherwise threaten society and the (British) rule of law.

It is unsurprising, then, that the prisoners' detainment here was crucial to the power play intended to reinforce British supremacy over Ireland. The building had long been associated with Irish rebellion; it had been used to detain (and sometimes also execute) political prisoners—mainly the leaders of Irish insurrections—since1789.[31] The gaol, therefore, literally physically subsumed the leaders into a long lineage of *failed* acts of resistance. In his text *A History of Kilmainham Gaol,* Pat Cooke describes this relationship between the gaol and the Anglo-Irish political scene as follows:

> Thus the opening ... of the Gaol more or less coincided with the making ... of the Union between Great Britain and Ireland ... the Gaol functioned like a political seismograph, recording most of the significant tremors in the often turbulent relations between the two countries. At the epicentre of these relations lay the Irish aspiration to political independence, setting off shockwaves of varying force throughout the nineteenth century and reaching a climax in the years 1916–22. There can be few places, therefore, that more intensely crystallize the forces that shaped modern Irish nationalism than Kilmainham Gaol.[32]

Their imprisonment within this edifice built upon the oppressive theatricality of the trials in that it reenforced the magnitude of the British Empire and its power to reestablish order in its colonies in the past, the present, and far into their futures.

Creating an Irish Nationalist Counter-Public via Self-Sacrifice

The British performance of power, however, backfired. Whereas the British sought to strengthen their control by instilling a fear of death, they ended up providing the rebels with the discursive and institutional frameworks of violence they needed to position themselves as morally superior combatants for the freedom of Ireland. Though they may have solidified their colonial position as the agents of death, this positionality was precisely what led the British to be perceived by the Irish people as the oppressive force responsible for the stultification of the vitality and idealism—literally and metaphorically—of the rebel forces.[33] Indeed, the public came to sympathize with the chained (Fenian) hydra.

This sense of the leaders' moral superiority over their colonizers first entered general circulation by virtue of newspaper headlines of the time. In the weeks that followed the Rising, the *Irish Times* slowly began to print articles that suggested that the erasure of the rebel leaders from the public sphere was, in fact, a crime against humanity. This framing gradually led to public outrage: the leaders' executions came to be seen as violations of the basic human rights of these men who, by publicly surrendering, had—for all intents and purposes—become prisoners of war under international law.

Interestingly, if we return to examine the aesthetics and symbols that were employed in the GPO over the course of the insurrection, then we can see that the seeds for such a reframing were planted by the leaders themselves. Over the course of the six days of battle, Pearse and his fellows were very careful to publicly cast their violence as being imbued with a *moral* integrity. By continually drawing upon Catholic imagery in their speeches and letters, Pearse and his fellows ensured that the Rising retrospectively became—both in the collective consciousness of Ireland (then and now) and in the eyes of the *world*—a symbol of the *triumph* of failure.

This careful framing of rebel (and, implicitly also British) violence is readily apparent in the last bulletin Pearse wrote and delivered to his forces in the GPO on the eve of their surrender. In this text he establishes that the measure for success, at least as far as *his* forces are concerned, was not military victory but an ideological and moral one: "If they do not win this fight, they will, at least, have deserved to win it. But win it they will, although they may win it in death."[34] With the words "they will ... have deserved to win," he attributes the rebel cause with a higher degree of morality than the British counterattack. This emphasis upon the rebels' righteousness is set up to frame his conclusion "they may win it in death" in a specific manner; it allows Pearse to open up a space for reimagining the dead rebels as the ultimate victors.

This last project came to the fore on Saturday April 29 when Pearse bowed to the unbearable pressure of the circumstances and surrendered unconditionally to the British.[35] Joe Sweeney, a soldier stationed at the GPO garrison, recalls that Sean McDermott addressed the men directly after the surrender: "This is only the beginning of the fight. All the leaders would be executed but it's up to you men to carry it on."[36] By framing execution as "only the beginning," McDermott was reinforcing that institutionally realized self-sacrifice was to be the means by which the Irish nation, as imagined by him and his fellow intellectuals, could/would become a concrete reality. McDermott's declaration that, "it's up to you men to carry it on," emphasizes that self-sacrifice was not just an inherited ideal but also a living tradition or destiny that was to be transmitted from one revolutionary generation of Irish to the next. The imagined tradition in question was, in the words of the Proclamation, a readiness within the Irish people to "sacrifice themselves for the common good," to "pledge [their] lives and the lives of [their] comrades-in-arms to the cause of [Ireland's] freedom, of its welfare, and of its exaltation among the nations."[37]

Pheng Cheah explains that the intended result of such a deliberate summons of an inherited tradition is to "implant the seeds of change" in a public.[38] While meditating upon the process by which revolutionaries come to reincarnate "original culture" and "national spirit," Cheah reflects upon the spectrality of nationalism. He notes that the victims of a colonial state's cruelty literally haunt the nation for "they leave contaminating marks on the colonial archive's pristine sheets."[39] The unjust, invisible deaths of the Irish rebels,[40] by this logic, haunted the Irish people by impressing them with the cruelty and oppressiveness of the British Empire. They also haunted the British, as colonizers, by revealing the power they derived from the obstruction and degradation of native Irish bodies and ideals. However, the rebels' Fenian nationalism can also be read as "spectral" or "phantasmagorical" in that, for the Fenians, Irish national regeneration could only occur if the living were haunted into action by Ireland's ghosts. The term "ghosts" in this context refers to, in Cheah's words, "the indelible marks of the absence of what is destroyed but cannot be exorcised" that "herald" the inevitable return and reincarnation of what was lost.[41] In short, the ghosts necessary for the successful interpellation of the Irish people to self-sacrifice for Ireland were: that which "cannot be exorcised," namely the nation's precolonial history; and that which must be "heralded," namely the future possibility of national freedom.[42]

Conclusion: The Spectrality of Irish Nationalism

In conclusion, cultures adjust to ensure self-preservation and this process of collective perpetuation is built upon the following paradox: in the words of Joseph Roach "memory is a process that depends crucially on forgetting."[43] The Rising, as a process of nation-making, was designed to erase the public's memory of the civilian casualties, the devastation to the city's infrastructure, and the distinct lack of popularity of the rebels among Dubliners. It was orchestrated to perpetuate a sense of uncanniness among the people of Dublin such that, within days of the news of the leaders' executions, they could forget their animosity toward the Fenians and embrace the revolutionaries as national heroes. This phenomenon was captured by Pádraic Colum—poet, founder of the *Irish Review,* and member of Irish Revival Movement, the Abbey Theatre, and the National Theatre Society—when, upon being asked to reflect upon the Rising, he merely quoted the following passage from Yeats's *Cathleen Ni Houlihan:*

> An Irish-man knows well how those who met their deaths will be regarded.
> They shall be remembered for ever; they shall be speaking for ever; the people shall hear them for ever.[44]

In 1916, the Fenians' actions were viewed extremely unfavorably and many of the names of the participants of the Rising were forgotten or remained obscure. Many of these individuals (particularly the civilians and children) have remained unnamed, details about the events of the Rising have been lost, and the city has been rebuilt where the fighting destroyed it. Yet, as Colum predicted, in the weeks, months, and years since, the men and women who fought during Easter 1916 have entered into Irish history as role models, as sources of inspiration, and as foundational figures for the national identity of the Irish Republic.

Notes

1 Fearghal McGarry, *The Abbey Rebels of 1916: A Lost Revolution* (Dublin: Gill and Macmillan, 2015), 8.
2 McGarry, *The Abbey Rebels*, 8.
3 McGarry, *The Abbey Rebels*, 9.
4 Though the focus of this particular chapter however, shall be on the symbolism and occupation of the GPO, it is important to recognize the political and social significances of these other locations. The Four Courts occupied an extremely strategic location in the heart of Dublin city center. It was (and still is today) located on Inn's Quay on the banks of the Liffey, between Sackville Street (today, O'Connell Street) and Kingsbridge Station (today, Heuston Station), the terminus for the Southern and Western Railways. The building function(ed) as the central pillar of the colonial judicial system and, as such, was an integral institution for the propagation of British rule (and the implementation of their punitive powers) on Irish soil. Whereas the occupation of the Four Courts and the GPO presented a challenge to the political apparati of imperial Britain, the occupation of St. Stephen's Green was a "strike" against the British socio-cultural colonization of Ireland. Though the Green was—since its reopening in 1887—open to the general public, its location at the heart of one of the most fashionable districts of Dublin city meant that it remained firmly associated with the elegant and refined Protestant Anglo-Irish aristocracy. The usurpation of this land by (for the most part) lower-to-middle-class Catholic Irishmen thus presented the British authorities and the ruling class with a vivid visual challenge to their occupancy and social dominion over Irish land. Of the last three remaining sites of the Rising, Jacob's Factory was one of the largest employers of the lower classes in the nation and the South Dublin Union was home to the most deprived and destitute members of Irish society. Boland's Mill, meanwhile, was located in one of the few socially diverse neighborhoods in which slum tenements stood alongside upper-middle-class housing. By virtue of their Fenian

occupation and politicization, these three sites embodied the Provisional Government's (and the Proclamation's) insistence on social equality and the protection of all Irish people, regardless of religious, social, or political backgrounds. These also emphasized their drive to eradicate the sociopolitical evils/divides that arose under British rule.

5 Michael Warner's views on "publics" are expressed in his book *Publics and Counterpublics*. The notion of public being employed here is borrowed from Michael Warner who frames publics as things that exist "only by virtue of their imagining." He positions them as "a kind of fiction that has taken on life." In order for a public to work, the participants must pertain to the same background and/or self-understanding: they must think of themselves as a "certain kind of person" within a "certain kind of social world" with certain media and genres at their disposal, be motivated by "a certain normative horizon" and speak with a "certain language ideology." Thus, the idea of a public enables a degree of reflexivity to emerge in the circulation of texts among a group of strangers; it is by virtue of this reflexive circulation of discourse that a heterogeneous mass is reconfigured into a singular social entity. See Michael Warner, *Publics and Counterpublics* (New York: Zone Books, 2005), 8–12.

6 Pheng Cheah, *Spectral Nationality: Passages of Freedom from Kant to Postcolonial Literatures of Liberation* (New York: Columbia University Press, 2003), 121.

7 Pheng Cheah, *Spectral Nationality*, 122.

8 Bríona Nic Dhiarmada, *The 1916 Irish Rebellion*, Forward by Mary McAleese (Notre Dame, Indiana: University of Notre Dame Press, 2016), 18.

9 Nic Dhiarmada, *The 1916 Irish Rebellion*, 18.

10 Theirs was a conspiracy within a conspiracy; Eoin MacNeill, though still the nominal head of the Irish Volunteers, was not made privy to the existence of this council or to their plans for an uprising. The year 1912 saw the formation of The Irish Volunteers in response to the formation of a Unionist militia in Northern Ireland. Thousands of nationalists in (Southern) Ireland gathered at the Rotunda hospital in Dublin on November 25, 1912 to form this counter-militia under the direction of Eoin MacNeill. In their manifesto, the volunteers identified the British Conservative Party as their principal enemy as, to their minds, the party

had conspired to: "[M]ake the display of military force and the menace of armed violence the determining factor in the future relations between Britain and Ireland" (Manifesto of the Irish Volunteers). Among the 4,000 men that enrolled that evening were Pearse, MacDonnagh, Tom Clarke, Plunkett, and Éamon de Valera. See Bríona Nic Dhiarmada, *The 1916 Irish Rebellion*, Forward by Mary McAleese (Notre Dame, Indiana: University of Notre Dame Press, 2016), 54.

11 Bríona Nic Dhiarmada, *The 1916 Irish Rebellion*, Forward by Mary McAleese (Notre Dame, Indiana: University of Notre Dame Press, 2016), 70.

12 Nic Dhiarmada, *The 1916 Irish Rebellion*, 70.

13 The Irish Citizen Army (ICA) was subsequently formed during the Dublin Lock-out, a labor dispute between factory owners and working-class manual laborers, in 1913. The force was created to enable the locked-out factory hands to defend themselves in their armed clashes with the Dublin Metropolitan Police. The ICA was formed under the direction of James Connolly and James Larkin, two of the most prominent figures in the Irish Socialist Movement at the time. See *BBC History*, http://www.bbc.co.uk/history/british/easterrising/profiles/po14.shtml (accessed November 2, 2017).

14 Nic Dhiarmada, *The 1916 Irish Rebellion*, 70.

15 Tom Clarke was bestowed with the honor of being the first leader to sign the Proclamation; the other six signatures were Pearse, MacDonagh, Plunkett, Ceannt, Mac Diarmada, and Connolly. See Bríona Nic Dhiarmada, *The 1916 Irish Rebellion*, 76.

16 Nic Dhiarmada, 75–6.

17 I am thinking here, particularly, of Martin Esslin's view of theatre as the site where a state or nation "thinks in public in front of itself" and his insistence that there is a very close link between the general beliefs of a society, its notions of "proper" behavior, and the political climate of the nation. For more, see Martin Esslin, *An Anatomy of Drama* (New York: Hill and Wang, 1976), 101. Esslin's view speaks to William I. Thompson's writings on the Easter Rising; Thompson argues that the conventional binary of art versus reality implodes in a moment of revolution: "When the revolutionary fails as artist, he turns from art to history and attempts to make of the state a work of art." For more

information see William Irwin Thompson, *The Imagination of an Insurrection: Dublin, Easter 1916* (Manchester, UK: The Lindisfarne Press, 1982), 115.
18 Fearghal McGarry, *The Abbey Rebels of 1916: A Lost Revolution* (Dublin, Ireland: Gill and Macmillan, 2015), 8.
19 McGarry, *The Abbey Rebels of 1916*, 8.
20 According to Michael Warner, the idea of a public is as much a motivating factor as it is an instrument for the *constitution* of a social imaginary: "the making of publics is the meta-pragmatic work newly taken up by every text in every reading" (12). The act of attempting to answer the questions, "What kind of public is this?" and "How is it being addressed?" has concrete and determining consequences upon the social world that the public belongs to and for the delineation of what actions and subjectivities are possible within it (Warner 12). Thus, in addressing the Irish public the rebels were also, automatically, struggling with the conditions that bring people together as a public.
21 Michael Collins quoted by Dermot McEvoy, "Michael Collins: From the GPO to Béal Na MBláth," *Irish America* (February–March 2016), 52.
22 Nic Dhiarmada, *The 1916 Irish Rebellion*, 92.
23 Irish Architectural Archive, Cartlann Ailtireachta Na HÉireann, http://www.iarc.ie/exhibitions/previous-exhibitions/the-gpo-two-hundred-years/ (accessed November 3, 2016).
24 Patrick Anderson and Jisha Menon, *Violence Performed: Local Roots and Global Routes of Conflict* (London: Palgrave Macmillan, 2009), 1.
25 Anderson and Menon, *Violence Performed*, 3.
26 Sir John Grenfell Maxwell was appointed the Commander-in-Chief of all British troops in Ireland; by virtue of martial law, his appointment to this position also resulted in him assuming legal, juridical, and political power over Ireland at this time.
27 Nic Dhiarmada, *The 1916 Irish Rebellion*, 144.
28 Kilmainham Gaol was opened in 1796 by the British to serve as the County Dublin jail. Today, the building symbolizes the tradition of militant and constitutional nationalism of Ireland that began with the rebellion of 1798 and ended with the Irish Civil War of 1922 and 1923. The leaders of the rebellions from 1798 to 1916 were detained (and most also executed) in this building. As a county gaol, the edifice also housed

ordinary prisoners (men, women, and children) whose crimes ranged from petty offences—stealing food—to murder and rape. See "Prison Life." Kilmainham Gaol Museum | The Office of Public Works, http://kilmainhamgaolmuseum.ie/ (accessed November 4, 2016).

29 There were twenty-two guilty verdicts in total and all twenty-two prisoners received death sentences though, after Pearse, Clarke, and MacDonagh, only four more executions actually took place: those of Ned Daly, Willie Pearse (Pádraig Pearse's younger brother), Michael O'Hanrahan (second-in-command to MacDonagh at Jacob's Biscuit Factory), and Joseph Mary Plunkett. Most of the other sentences were converted to penal servitude as Maxwell came under serious pressure, both from the Irish public and the British government, to not overreact and still punish the parties guilty of high treason. Most of these individuals were, therefore, deported to internment camps and prisons in England and Wales. By Monday May 8, eight men had been executed, over 3,500 people had been arrested (double the number of those who had actually fought in the Rising), and Ireland was under martial law. See Bríona Nic Dhiarmada, *The 1916 Irish Rebellion*, 151–6.

30 "Kilmainham Gaol, Inchicore Road, Kilmainham, Dublin 8," *National Inventory of Architectural Heritage*, May 2016, https://www.buildingsofireland.ie/building-of-the-month/kilmainham-gaol-inchicore-road-kilmainham-dublin-8/ (accessed March 4, 2022).

31 "Prison Life." Kilmainham Gaol Museum | The Office of Public Works, http://kilmainhamgaolmuseum.ie/ (accessed November 4, 2016).

32 Quoted by The Office of Public Works | Kilmainham Gaol Museum, http://kilmainhamgaolmuseum.ie/ (accessed November 2, 2017).

33 Pheng Cheah, *Spectral Nationality: Passages of Freedom from Kant to Postcolonial Literatures of Liberation* (New York: Columbia University Press, 2003), 308.

34 Pádraig Pearse quoted by Padraic Colum, Maurice Joy, James Reidy, Sidney Gifford, Rev. T. Gavan Duffy, Mary M. Colum, Mary J. Ryan, and Seumas O'Brien, *The Irish Rebellion of 1916 and Its Martyrs: Erin's Tragic Easter*, ed. Maurice Joy (New York: The Devin-Adair Company, 1916), 120.

35 On Sunday April 30, Pearse's letter of surrender was delivered to the other garrisons about the city. There was sporadic resistance but by Monday

May 1, all the garrisons had surrendered. By the end of the Rising the death toll was as follows: 64 Irish volunteers, 107 British soldiers, 16 Dublin-based police officers, and 254 civilians of which 40 were still only children. Meanwhile 357 British soldiers, 29 police officers, and 2,217 civilians were injured while 9 British soldiers went missing and their bodies were never recovered. There are insufficient records to determine how many of the IRA soldiers were injured during the insurrection. The majority of the non-combatant casualties during the Rising were the direct result of British artillery shelling of Dublin city center from the safety of Trinity College Dublin, located on College Green. See Bríona Nic Dhiarmada, *The 1916 Irish Rebellion*, 138 and Marion R. Casey, "1916: The Easter Rising," *Irish America* (February/March 2016), 30–1.
36 Quoted by Bríona Nic Dhiarmada, *The 1916 Irish Rebellion*, 131.
37 The Provisional Government of the Republic of Ireland, "Proclamation of the Irish Republic," *CAIN*, http://cain.ulst.ac.uk/issues/politics/docs/pir24 416.htm (accessed November 1, 2016).
38 Pheng Cheah, *Spectral Nationality*, 253–4.
39 Pheng Cheah, *Spectral Nationality*, 310.
40 Many felt that the executions of the rebel leaders were, in fact, crimes against humanity/violations of basic human rights in view of the fact that the men had surrendered and were, under international law, prisoners of war.
41 Pheng Cheah, *Spectral Nationality*, 317.
42 Pheng Cheah, *Spectral Nationality*, 264.
43 Joseph Roach, *Cities of the Dead: Circum-Atlantic Performance* (New York: Columbia University Press, 1996), 2.
44 James Moran, *Staging the Easter Rising: 1916 as Theatre* (Cork: Cork University Press, 2005), 4.

2

An "Indian Princess," a King and a Queen, and a President: Diplomatic Performance and Indigenous Sovereignties at the 1939 Royal Visit

Christiana Molldrem Harkulich

On June 11, 1939, an unprecedented meeting occurred: the reigning king and queen of the UK visited the sitting US president at his personal home at Hyde Park, New York, and had hot dogs. This is the major narrative of the Hot Dog Diplomacy of Franklin Delano Roosevelt to King George VI and his wife Queen Elizabeth.[1] It was the first time that a sitting ruler of England had ever visited the rebellious former colony, and it was also the first time the king and queen had eaten a hot dog.[2] This informal setting for a formal encounter between two world powers at the beginning of the Second World War was both novel and important in cementing goodwill and good feeling between the two sovereign nations. While the UK and the United States were the two recognized foreign powers engaging in diplomacy at this event, they weren't the only sovereign representatives present. Engaged to perform for the day, Te Ata, billed as Princess Te Ata of the Chickasaw and Choctaw tribal nations, represented the Indigenous nations who were previously displaced from the land by colonialism.

The consumption of hot dogs, while a performance unto itself and the more written about (although undocumented since it was thought unseemly to photograph a king or queen stuffing a hot dog in their face), was not the formal performance engaged for the day. First Lady Eleanor Roosevelt organized a whole afternoon of outdoor entertainment for the visiting royals and their entourage. The Roosevelts had carefully crafted a narrative of the day that was about the American-ness of the encounter. From hot dog to country picnic (at the "cottage" that was really a mansion), this event was designed as a performance of diplomacy, a soft power demonstration of folksy camaraderie to cement cooperation with the UK on the eve of the Second World War. The UK would not declare war against Germany until September of that year, so this was truly a visit of goodwill and diplomacy before conditions became extreme. Diplomacy is a dance between nations, sometimes quite literally, and the full implications of this visit are beyond the scope of this chapter. Rather, I'm interested in the political implications of including Te Ata Fisher's program of Indigenous storytelling as the outdoor post-meal performance.

Billed as "Princess Te Ata" on the program provided by the Roosevelt White House for the day's events, her presence was on purpose—chosen by Eleanor Roosevelt specifically for what it means for the United States to encompass Indigenous identity. Te Ata was not selected by benevolent decision-making, rather she heavily advocated to Mrs. Roosevelt to be the performer for this part of the event. This agency on her part, and the choices she made within her theatrical program, complicates the simple narrative of US culture presented on the outdoor green in Hyde Park, New York, while digesting hot dogs. The white settler culture of the United States has constantly tried to differentiate itself from its imperial British roots. What makes white Americans different from the Brits? The specifics of that answer have changed over time, but at nearly every moment Indigenous cultures have been used or appropriated to delineate that difference. Settler-colonial Americans required the appropriation of Indigenous identity to differentiate themselves from the British.[3]

Diplomatic performance is often symbolic and also often (as the introduction to the collection points toward) reenacts previous state engagements. This was true at Hyde Park as well. This was not just a meeting between two nation-states, but a reenactment of colonial powers, of breaches between colonies and imperial powers, and of the colonized Indigenous people. This was a meal meant to perform friendship, and to reify and recognize US identity as separate from imperial rule. Where did this leave the recognition of Indigenous peoples? The Roosevelts' strategy throughout the royal visit was to showcase the diversity of the United States through entertainment. Prior to arriving at Hyde Park, Mrs. Roosevelt put together a variety entertainment for the king and queen in Washington, DC, that included singer Marian Anderson, opera star Lawrence Tibbett, cowboy Alan Lomax, radio star Kate Smith, the WPA sponsored North Carolinian Negro Chorus, and the Soco Gap dancers (from the Appalachian Mountains).[4] This wide range of entertainments was meant to showcase the diversity and plurality of identity within the United States to a royal visitor.

Eleanor Roosevelt's entertainments mark a recognition of the many social groups within the United States. Recognition in a political setting, as Glen Sean Coulthard writes, supports a multicultural identity that often denies power to groups in exchange for admitting that they exist. While many activist groups fight for recognition, in doing so they allow the state to control their ultimate definition through the act of recognition. This creates an imbalance of power, and tends to reify colonial value patterns, for example the United States does not need the Chickasaw nation to recognize them, but the Chickasaw need the United States to recognize their rights to land and sovereignty. As Coulthard writes "in these contexts, the 'master'—that is, the colonial state and state society—does not require recognition from the previously self-determining communities upon which its territorial, economic and social infrastructure is constituted. What it needs is land, labor, and resources."[5] Certainly the pattern of government involvement in US policy, as I write about later, points toward this pattern in Oklahoma and the Chickasaw nation. Mis-recognition or non-recognition of a group can cause self-alienation and be damaging. The desire to be recognized is also where those who have the implicit power of the state behind them can make demands that minority groups perform authenticity to the state's standards in order to be recognized in the first place. Authenticity in this context becomes meaningless and a colonial tool.

While she was not the daughter of the chief, nor in anyway a princess, the newspapers and the White House were fond of titling her Princess Te Ata in their accounts of her performances. This is a misrecognition that benefited the United States by making Te Ata more "authentic" in the eyes of the white popular media. In the lead-up to the Royal Visit, The *New York Times* described Te Ata's contribution thus: "The king and queen will hear Indian folktales, which antedate the coming of the first white men to this country, told by Princess Te Ata, a Choctaw-Chickasaw, of five-eights Indian blood, from Oklahoma."[6] The language the *New York Times* uses presents this not only as a meeting of a president and the king, but also an additional foreign dignitary, an "Indian Princess," who will represent Indigenous culture for the foreign sovereign as the world approaches the brink of war.

Te Ata did not refer to herself as a princess in her materials, although the press and White House did. She was born Mary Thompson in 1895 in the Chickasaw nation in Indian territory right before Oklahoma became a state. Her father was the last tribally elected treasurer of the Chickasaw nation before it was absorbed into the state of Oklahoma, and her uncle was the last governor of the Chickasaw nation. She changed her name to Te Ata specifically for the stage. Her name is not Chickasaw word, but rather a Maori word for "Bearer of the Morning," a name that a family friend called her in her youth.[7] Te Ata was a formally trained actress—with training from both the Oklahoma College for Women and the Carnegie Institute (later known as Carnegie Mellon University). During her time at Oklahoma College for Women she made an income in the summers performing on the Chautauqua circuit. On the circuit she developed a program of stories, song, and dance composed of Indigenous stories from a wide range of tribal nations as well as some materials on native themes from white writers (e.g., she performed parts of Longfellow's *Hiawatha* early in her career). During the 1930s, Te Ata was based out of New York, where she performed in plays as well as performing her storytelling programs.

The *New York Times* did not mention her background or training, rather they qualify her Indigenous status by conflating race and citizenship through the use of a blood-quantum designation of five-eighths "Indian blood." Blood-quantum, as Kim Tallbear has explained, is a colonial concept of status enforced and codified by the US government in order to delineate who could and could not have treaty resources.[8] It was also a method to delineate how Indigenous cultures could be bred away through interracial marriages over time. The eventual goal of this policy is to erase tribal nations' sovereignty.

The *New York Herald Tribune* made the leap to interracial marriage by making a comparison between Te Ata and Pocahontas. Their column on June 5, 1939 ran with the headline "Modern Pocahontas to Recite for Royal Couple at Hyde Park: Princess Te Ata, Like Her 17th Century Predecessor, Is Wed to White Man."[9] Within the article they further clarified that Te Ata "married a white man, Dr. Clyde Fisher, curator of astronomy at the American Museum of Natural History."[10] The column goes on to make comparison that "thus Te Ata will be repeating in more than one respect the story of Pocahontas, first Indian princess to have a name in history. Pocahontas married a white man, John Rolfe, and went with him to London in 1616, where she was presented to King James and Queen Anne."[11] This marriage, like the mention of blood-quantum, mirrored the narrative of the Indian princess who loves a white man—a colonial myth made real. The Indian princess was (and remains) a symbol of US national belonging through possession.

While the newspaper does not mention it, theatrical entertainment was also a part of that historic meeting: Pocahontas met the king and queen in January 1617 and a Ben Jonson masque was presented as entertainment. In this reenactment, the stand-in for Pocahontas becomes the theatrical event. To include her in the program, as another newspaper reported, made the performance "an all-American program. In England, of course, tea would have been served. What to do for an American counterpart? … The Tea we served was Te Ata, Chickashaw [*sic*] Indian Princess, more American than baked beans, or hot dogs, or paper napkins."[12] In the eyes of the public, and as a symbolic diplomatic performance, the native-ness of the Indian princess was seen as consumable and uniquely American—something to be served and used. Her performance was a resource to be utilized.

In considering this diplomatic event, and Te Ata's performance within it, I am struck by the proximity of the words Indigenous, foreign, and sovereignty. The definition of Indigenous is to be of a place, of the land. It implies a deep connection with the world and space where a people are from—a storied land. Mishuana Goeman articulates that for Indigenous peoples and epistemologies "the land acts as mnemonic device in many ways, by being the site of stories, which create cohesive understandings of longing and belonging … Land in this moment is living and layered memory."[13] Indigenous place-making is one of the ways in which communities (and by extension tribal nations) are created. Indigenous peoples within the United States have had to remake their identity after the violence of removal policies in the ninteenth century. The Chickasaw people's homelands are located in the southeastern woodlands, in the land that would become Mississippi, Tennessee, and Alabama under settler colonialism. However, by 1839 the US government had removed most of the Chickasaw nation to Indian territory in what would become the state of Oklahoma. Te Ata was born into the Chickasaw nation and the United States in Indian territory—when the Chickasaw nation was sovereign over itself. Her childhood was shaped by the creation of Oklahoma and the loss of that sovereignty in 1907.

Sovereignty, the right to self-govern, is also fraught. In 1939 at Hyde Park, as the sitting US president meets the king of England, many recall the right to sovereignty that the colonists fought for in 1776. This meeting is historic, on the brink of the Second World War, a building of partnerships between sovereign nations months before the sovereign borders of Poland were invaded by Hitler launching declarations of war. In the moment of the Hyde Park picnic, none of that had yet happened. The informal nature of the event, compared to the formal state visit that preceded it, was more relaxed with a goal of friendship between nations and families. The day's entertainment was a continuation of Eleanor

Roosevelt's curation of America as a nation built by diverse voices (and as the program from the June 8 performance in Washington states "an export commodity to all parts of the world").[14] In 1939, the diplomatic performance of nation included framing the United States as diverse and exceptional, and ultimately different culturally from the British and European roots of many of the settlers.[15]

With the addition of Te Ata, princess or not, there are ghosts of the encounters between earlier Indigenous sovereigns, like Powhatan and King Philip and representatives of both colonial and imperial powers, that are called to mind. This is not a moment that is a blank canvas, but rather a performance that exists in the many layers of colonial trauma over the last 400 years. The choice to include Te Ata, and her performance on the day, create a moment of deep history of the space, a moment of the layered past outside on the Hudson Valley, disguised as light entertainment. It is a performance that speaks to the history of the land and the colonial legacy, as well as the possibility of some new way and the radical New Deal politics of the president.

As mentioned previously, Te Ata advocated for her performance as part of the visit. After reading about the royal visit in the newspaper, Te Ata wrote to Mrs. Roosevelt in January 1939 stating "a program of American Indian folk-lore might be quite appropriate to one of your social affairs, while the King and Queen of England are here. Those of other countries always seem greatly interested in *native* [emphasis hers] culture."[16] She received a note of acknowledgment back, and in late April of 1939 the formal invitation to perform at the Roosevelts' home arrived. Her advocacy and inclusion speak to Te Ata's long-term project of making Indigenous voices heard throughout the country and the world (during the 1930s she brought her program to Sweden, and traveled to Peru as well). Still, Te Ata focuses on the word native in her letter, implying a project of first peoples in opposition to both foreignness of the king and queen as foreigners, and the native-born but not native-to position of the Roosevelts themselves. Te Ata's desire to be recognized meant that while she pushed back, she was still consistently mis-recognized in order to be of as much use as possible to the US government.

Citizenry and indigeneity are seemingly implied to be one and the same, but that is a fallacy of settler-colonialism that denies the continued existence and historical presence of Indigenous peoples. Until 1924, with the passage of the Indian Citizenship Act, many Indigenous peoples, despite being native born, were not citizens of the United States. Despite the fourteenth amendment's language that declares that within the borders of the territory of the United States anyone born is automatically a citizen, depending on the language of the treaty between the United States and the particular tribal nation, members of that nation might not be citizens and may in fact be considered wards of the state. With the passage of the act, Indigenous peoples were forced into citizenship whether they wanted it or not, and without concern for their own allegiances to the sovereignty of their first nation. While voting rights are useful, this could be seen as another means of erasing Indigenous nations through citizenship. The founding of Oklahoma superseded the sovereignty of the Chickasaw people and they saw their government absorbed into the state. For a time, the governments of several of the so-called five civilized tribes organized together to create the State of Sequoyah which would have preserved their tribal governments within the bounds of the state. However, the demanding call of the sooners for settlement drowned out any potential state other than Oklahoma. When Te Ata was twelve, Oklahoma was born. Te Ata and all of the Chickasaw were no longer sovereign over their own land, but rather now dual-citizens of land that was held twice over. They were recognized as another nation by the United States, while simultaneously denied the rights of land and self-government.

Te Ata's experience of the duality of living within the United States is not unique. The US government has never protected the sovereignty of Indigenous tribal nations. Te Ata's storytelling performance practice, which gave a voice to a multitude of different Indigenous tribal nations, provided a platform to declare that Indigenous identities have never been absorbed into the US identity. They are not absent, and have not yet been bred out of existence (as the policy of blood-quantum was crafted to do). Her performance in a diplomatic setting offers something more than that "all-American" theme that the Roosevelts crafted for the day.

The Performance

It was a warm and windy day in Hyde Park, New York when Te Ata took the stage. As biographer Richard Green writes in *Te Ata: Chickasaw Storyteller, American Treasure*, Te Ata arrived at the cottage for the performance with a small entourage. She brought her husband Clyde Fisher, her drummer Kuruks, and her friend Margaret Ball on the trip up from New York City.[17] Te Ata split the program with Ish-Ti-Opi, who according to the program was an "American-Indian" baritone. He had argued his way into a joint performance, although Te Ata had initially thought she would be performing alone. Te Ata makes no mention of any other performer but herself in her autobiography, which perhaps is telling of her opinion of Ish-Ti-Opi.[18]

On the shared bill Te Ata and Ish-Ti-Opi each did two sets taking turns between them. The whole performance was scheduled to take about an hour after the meal was served, which left their material at a half hour each. The platform stage was set back from the house, and audience surrounded the platform on all four sides.[19] The king and queen, and the president all watched from the comfort of the porch. Te Ata began the first half of the program with her recitation of H. B. Alexander's "Let It Be Beautiful"; a piece that had been in her repertoire for many years. The program then followed with a romance legend from the Seneca people, another staple of her program, and then a Dakota Lullaby.[20] While it isn't listed on the official program, in her memoir "As I Remember It" she states that she finished this portion of the bill with "The Song of the Maiden Weaving" by Constance Skinner. During the song she incorporated a Salish Basket that was gifted to her by the American Museum for the purpose.[21] This portion of her program demonstrated three distinct Indigenous cultures, the Seneca, the Salish, and the Dakota. It is likely that she sang the Dakota Lullaby in the Dakota language, as she told newspapers prior to the performance that she would be singing at least one song in an Indigenous language.[22]

In the second half of her program, Te Ata performed an "Indian Sign Language" demonstration, the story of "The Blue Duck" by L. Sarett, and finished her program with the Corn Dance Ceremony that she had authored.[23] All three of these pieces were in Te Ata's repertoire for several years before the 1939 performance. They were a set part of her practice of performing a wide range of Indigenous identities that she named explicitly. Her program undermines the colonial idea of "Indian" identity as a monolithic culture or nation, instead she shows that Indigenous people are not one but many nations.

The press leading up to the event, and discussing it afterward focused on the "Indian Sign Language" portion of her program. One article describing her plans for the performance gives this explanation of the sign language:

> Indian sign language, which she will also demonstrate before the King and Queen, developed because a common means of communication was needed, she said. When large tribes of her people migrated to other homes, they met Indians who spoke a different tongue, and herding and camping parties constantly came in contact with tribes that did not speak their language. Thus a sign language slowly grew up to overcome the language barrier. [24]

In describing what she planned to do, the newspaper leaves a record of what this part of the performance might have looked like. The creation of the sign language speaks to the history of settler-colonialism within the United States, a project that began under the colonial project of the English royalty in the 1600s. The sign language performance, while spun in a positive manner, illuminates the history of removal that necessitated its creation. This is a diplomatic means of bringing this narrative to light in front of both the president and the English monarch. A history that is otherwise easily swept aside, through Te Ata's performance is brought gently back into the conversation in a pivotal moment before the Second World War. Te Ata's choice to include this story brings the shared Indigenous story of forced removal by the United States into the conversation of what it meant to be Indigenous in 1939, despite newspapers covering this as a quaint and positive development.

The same article describes exactly what signs she planned to show the king and queen:

> Beginning with the sign of an Indian greeting, Te Ata demonstrated several of the signs she will perform for the entertainment of their majesties on Sunday. Crooking her first finger toward her thumb so that the two formed an almost complete circle, she raised her right hand to a position a few inches above her left shoulder, then brought it in an arc over her head until her right hand was level with her shoulder. "With the finger and thumb held thus, that semi-circular gesture of the right arm represents a day's time," she said. "If you want to indicate a certain time of day you simply raise your hand approximately that distance on the arc. Morning is the extreme left, noon directly overhead, and night the extreme right. You make stars by wiggling the first finger."[25]

Shared language is necessary for diplomacy. While the story of the development of Indian sign language points toward the violence of displacement, it also points toward inter-tribal diplomacy as the many different tribal nations who had many different languages were displaced into the same territory. Finding new language is a diplomatic strategy, an example of performative language. Language also shapes the way we understand the world. The choice to demonstrate and teach sign language as well as sing in an Indigenous language shows that Te Ata was not afraid to alienate her audience when they could not understand her. While English was the shared language amongt the king, queen, president, and "princess," speaking Dakota and teaching sign language in the wilderness setting might evoke the memory of the Indigenous people whose land Hyde Park was built on.

Finally, the newspaper article described the corn dance Te Ata planned to perform that would begin with her storytelling of a legend before beginning the dance (that they claim she created). Te Ata explained:

> "It has been said of the Indian that he didn't talk his religion, he danced it" Te Ata commented. "Most Indian dancing has its origin in the great religious dramas in which all took part. There are really no Indian solo dances. But I will show some of the steps the women do and some that the men do. In the dance, I offer the corn to the north, to the south, to the east, to the west, and to the above and to the below. I ask for the sun and rain to feed it. It is in this dance that I will wear the 100-year-old ceremonial costume of the Dakotas. The dance is entirely authentic, not theatrical." [26]

The newspaper, in trying to recognize Te Ata's authorship and authenticity, in fact demonstrates that Te Ata is sharing authentic-adjacent traditional dances with audiences, and that she is not able to do the true dance or practice the religious aspects by herself. She outlines the possibility of Indigenous religions that are tied to the earth, religions that are not Christianity. Many of these Indigenous religions were outlawed by US policy prior to Roosevelt's Indian New Deal policy, which allowed them again in 1934.[27] Her dance is inclusive and educational, meant to demonstrate steps while also demonstrating a different way of being in relationship to the land. Land that is meant to be honored in each direction and cared for, not colonized. Capitalism and colonialism require us to understand and recognize the land as a resource to be used up. While the dance is a plea for the crop to grow, the dance is not farming labor nor is it magic. It is a movement practice that reminds the dancer where they are in relationship to the earth and sky, to the land around them and to the corn. By wearing the hundred-year-old ceremonial costume of the Dakotas, her costume connects her to older traditions. She is connected to the past and to the present, a chain that is not yet broken.

This performance on the eve of the Second World War, and at the end of the royal visit, went over well with the king and queen. When Te Ata greeted the royal couple and the president she found herself shy in the presence of royalty. She accepted praise from the king and queen, they stated that it was their "pleasure" to hear her stories and program, and expressed concern that these stories were being collected.[28] Even in this moment of appreciation, the response was about perceived loss of a dying culture, rather than appreciation of stories from a wide range of vibrant cultures. Te Ata utilized her body and voice to articulate a complex idea of what it meant to be Indigenous in the United States; and yet the nuances seem to be lost on the king and queen. Her performance is filled with concerns that are far removed from the king and queen and they see her stories as entertainment.

What are the limits of performance—what can it actually do? Te Ata's performance is important, representation in this moment matters. But representation is limited.[29] Te Ata's performance does not radically change the relationship between the Chickasaw nation and the United States or the British Isles. It can't, because ultimately she is only recognized in a way that her authenticity benefits the United States. She is mis-recognized even while she works to be specific and honor the stories of multiple tribes that are not her own. Her narrative centers Indigenous history and peoples, but much like the diplomatic encounter with Pocahontas that this day in 1939 remembers, there is little soft power left for Indigenous people. Her performance was collected and recorded (literally) by the king and queen, and utilized by the president, much like Pocahontas was collected and presented. Te Ata's performance offers an ephemeral moment of story to remind the settler audience that Indigenous people still exist, and have existed in this space prior to the creation of the United States or the landing of British colonies; and to exist in the face of genocidal policies enacted by both of the nations that these powerful men and women represented is itself a radical act.

The mis-recognition that Te Ata encountered in 1939 has not changed drastically in the last century. Indigenous claims to land were debated in the Supreme Court as recently as 2021.[30] In 2018, the Federal Court denied recognition to the Mashpee Wampanoag Tribe in Massachusetts after they were previously granted recognition in 1934 by Roosevelt's administration. That denial of recognition meant that the Wampanoag Tribe were denied their land claim.[31] In 2021, Deb Haaland (Pueblo Laguna) became the first Indigenous American Secretary of the Interior—the position that makes policy changes over reservations across the country as well as the person who dictates policy over land resources. Her appointment is significant and historic. Indigenous representation in the Department of the Interior was long overdue. When Haaland recently visited Cape Cod she failed to make a diplomatic visit to the Mashpee Wampanoag people—who remain unrecognized by the state.[32] As it did in 1939, representation does not always equal recognition.

Notes

1 Not to be confused with the current Queen of England, Queen Elizabeth II, she is commonly referred to now as The Queen Mum.
2 Kat Eschner, "When Franklin Delano Roosevelt Served Hot Dogs to a King," *Smart News*, Smithsonian," https://www.smithsonianmag.com/smart-news/when-franklin-delano-roosevelt-served-hot-dogs-king-180963589/ (accessed November 4, 2019). See also Peter Conradi. *Hot Dogs and Cocktails* (London: Alma Books, 2014).
3 For further exploration of this performative practice see Joseph Philip Deloria, *Playing Indian*, Yale Historical Publications (New Haven: Yale University Press, 1998) and Jill Lepore, *The Name of War: King Philip's War and the Origins of American Identity* (New York: Vintage Books, 1999).
4 "White House Variety to Entertain Royalty," *New York World Telegram*, June 6, 1939. Oversized Box 1 in Te Ata Fisher Collection. WHC M1298. Western History Collection. University of Oklahoma Libraries, Norman, Oklahoma.
5 Glen Sean Coulthard, *Red Skins White Masks: Rejecting the Colonial Politics of Recognition* (Minneapolis: University of Minnesota Press, 2014), 40.
6 "King Will Hear Songs of Our Land," *The New York Times*, May 23, 1939.
7 See Te Ata Fisher. *As I Remember It*. Te Ata Fisher Collection. WHC M1298. Western History Collections, University of Oklahoma Libraries, Norman, Oklahoma.

8 Kimberly Tallbear, *Native American DNA: Tribal Belonging and the False Promise of Genetic Science* (Minneapolis: University of Minnesota Press, 2013), 55–61.

9 Emma Bugbee, "Modern Pocahontas to Recite for Royal Couple at Hyde Park," June 5, 1939, *New York Herald-Tribune* clipping in oversized Box 1. Te Ata Fisher Collection. WHC M1298. Western History Collections, University of Oklahoma Libraries, Norman, Oklahoma.

10 Bugbee, "Modern Pocahontas."

11 Bugbee, "Modern Pocahontas."

12 "Hot Dogs and Te Ata," Newspaper Clipping, unattributed in oversized Box 1. Te Ata Fisher Collection. WHC M1298. Western History Collections, University of Oklahoma Libraries, Norman, Oklahoma.

13 Mishuana Goeman, "From Place to Territories and Back Again: Centering Storied Land in the Discussion of Indigenous Nation-Building," *International Journal of Critical Indigenous Studies* 1, no. 1 (2008): 24–5.

14 "A Program of American Music" for the White House State Dinner on June 8, 1939. Eleanor Roosevelt Papers. Accessed online through FDRlibrary.org.

15 The June 8 performance concluded with a performance by Marian Anderson, the Black contralto whose exclusion from a DAR concert venue in Washington, DC, earlier that year caused Eleanor Roosevelt to resign from the DAR and invite her to perform during the royal visit. See also, "Eleanor Roosevelt and Marian Anderson—FDR Presidential Library & Museum," https://www.fdrlibrary.org/anderson (accessed March 8, 2022).

16 Te Ata Fisher, quoted in Richard Green, *Te Ata: Chickasaw Storyteller, American Treasure* (Norman: University of Oklahoma Press, 2006), 201.

17 Green, *Te Ata: Chickasaw Storyteller*, 207–8.

18 Fisher, *As I Remember It*.

19 There is a short film of clips taken by the king with a hand-held camera. The footage is film only, with no sound. FDR Archives. FDR Library Film ID MP 83–5.

20 Official Program for the June 11, 1939, performance. Oversized Box 1. Te Ata Fisher Collection. WHC M1298. Western History Collections, University of Oklahoma Libraries, Norman, Oklahoma.

21 Fisher, *As I Remember It*, 172.

22 Ernesto Paine, "Royal Indian Greeting to Come from the Heart," *Canto Press*, 1939. Oversized Box 1. Te Ata Fisher Collection. WHC M1298. Western History Collections, University of Oklahoma Libraries, Norman, Oklahoma.
23 Official Program for the June 11, 1939, performance. Oversized Box 1. Te Ata Fisher Collection. WHC M1298. Western History Collections, University of Oklahoma Libraries, Norman, Oklahoma.
24 Paine, "Royal Indian Greeting to Come from the Heart."
25 Paine, "Royal Indian Greeting to Come from the Heart."
26 Paine, "Royal Indian Greeting to Come from the Heart."
27 FDR's New Deal Policy extended explicitly to Indigenous communities under the direction of Bureau of Indian Affairs Commissioner John Collier. This work was made possible in a large part by the Meriam report of 1928 that detailed the terrible conditions on reservations across the United States.
28 Fisher, *As I Remember It*.
29 See also: Coulthard, *Red Skins White Masks*, for further discussion about the limits of representation and recognition for Indigenous peoples in the face of settler-colonial power.
30 Adam Liptak, "Supreme Court May Revisit Ruling on Native American Rights in Oklahoma," *The New York Times*, May 26, 2021, sec. U.S. https://www.nytimes.com/2021/05/26/us/supreme-court-oklahoma-native-american.html (accessed December 17, 2021).
31 "Secretary Of Interior Orders Mashpee Wampanoag Reservation 'Disestablished,' Tribe Says," https://www.wbur.org/news/2020/03/28/mashpee-wampanoag-reservation-secretary-interior-land-trust (accessed December 17, 2021).
32 CAI, "Mashpee Tribe Snubbed by Interior Secretary," November 19, 2021. https://www.capeandislands.org/local-news/2021-11-19/mashpee-tribe-snubbed-by-interior-secretary (accessed December 17, 2021).

3

The President's Yellow Batakari: Performance and the Sartorial in Ghanaian Politics

David Afriyie Donkor

As Montesquieu wrote a Spirit of Laws ... so could I write a Spirit of Clothes ... For neither in tailoring nor in legislating does man proceed by mere Accident, but the hand is ever guided on by mysterious operations of the mind.

Professor Teufelsdrockh in Thomas Carlyle's *Sartor Resartus*[1]

On January 25, 2019, President Nana Akufo-Addo of Ghana arrived in a vehicular convoy on the sandy-brown grounds of Gbewaa Palace at Yendi, in the north of the country. His presidential visit to the seat of the historic Dagbon Kingdom was as a special guest of honor at the enskinment (installation) of the new paramount chief or *Yaa-Naa* of the Kingdom, Abubakari Mahama II, after a protracted (two-decade long) chieftaincy dispute. A small gust, one of those dry and dusty Harmattan winds that come down from the Sahara Desert to the Volta Basin at that time of year, welcomed the president as he stepped out of the convoy toward the forecourt of the palace to greet the *Yaa-Naa*. It was always expected that the president, who had arrived spectacularly with his security detail of uniformed and plainclothes men trotting alongside the convoy of cars, would make a "notable impression" when he stepped off his convoy. He did not disappoint this expectation: as one report of the visit put it, the president "went further to surprise those present with his special outfit for the special occasion."² President Nana Akufo-Addo was dressed in a striking outfit—a distinctively yellow-colored batakari.³

Dress, as Jean Allman notes in *Fashioning Africa*, is embedded in fields of power: it represents, articulates, constitutes, and even contests power.⁴ In this regard the dressed body has a potential for incisive forms of political language and action. As a learned, displayable, revisable, creative-expressive behavior dress is a performance or at least a performance waiting to happen. What was the significance of President Akufo-Addo's sartorial choice that day at Yendi: what did the president seek to perform and how did his yellow outfit serve as the language and/or action for doing so? In this chapter I argue that the president's yellow batakari ensemble was his way of presenting himself to the Dagbon State (and, by extension, to people of Ghana) as a neutral but committed architect-purveyor of the peace and reconciliation that was now possible in the Dagbon State between factions of the protracted chieftaincy feud. Leading to this argument, I situate Akufo-Addo's sartorial choice in a sociopolitical history of the batakari. This history not only shows the polyvalence and the malleability of the meaning of batakari in assorted fields of power—state-political, spiritual, economic—that allowed Akufo-Addo to tell a story with his own dress. It also explains the socioeconomic marginalization of northern Ghana (where Dagbon State is located) compared to the southern parts of the country, a key element of the political motivation for the President Akufo-Addo's performance as the "Peacemaker of/for Dagbon."

It should not be a radical thing to say that the study of dress is "unspeakably important." Yet Angela McRobbie felt obliged to say in 1998 that dress "is a subject worthy of study" despite "its trivialized status," and Emma Tarlo's assertion of similar worth in the title of her 1996 book *Clothing Matters*, both show that we have not been very long past the times when intellectual prejudice placed such study outside the boundaries of academic respectability.⁵ The good news is that studies of dress "have blossomed as new generations of far more open-minded ethnographers ... historians and dress and textile specialists have developed fresh approaches to theory and research" on the subject.[6] Africa is a focus in the blossoming, with several edited volumes and monographs on the subject.[7] Yet it is in merely a few journal articles that we find more than passing attention to dressed bodies of African leaders, despite recognition that dress is embedded in spheres of politics and fields of power.[8] Examination of a *social history* of mobility in the meaning of batakari, is another feature that distinguishes this chapter from scholarship so far on African dress. By exploring the significance of President Akufo-Addo's yellow batakari against that background—a social history of the dress—this chapter adds to the burgeoning area of studies on dress, power, and the performance of presidential politics in Africa.

Islam Meets African Creativity: The Medieval Roots of Batakari

Batakari belongs to a diverse "family" of outfits that are a syncretic result of West Africa's encounter with Islam. In the seventh century, Arab Muslims entered Egypt, headed west across the Sahara and overran Maghreb Berbers to control North Africa. Their expeditions South brought them to gold-rich Sahelian kingdoms. The Arab/Berber Muslim merchants formed trade centers and a commercial diaspora along the Sahel up through the twelfth century.[9] From sometime about then, Mande-speaking Muslim traders of Upper Niger also settled on trade routes from the Niger River to the Volta Basin.[10] In the process, a vast Muslim trade network linked West Africa to the Middle East and Europe. Islam in West Africa was a religion not only of commerce but also of court. The non-Muslim rulers welcomed the literacy and numeracy of Muslims and appointed them to serve as historians, accountants, treasurers, and advisors.[11] Some of the rulers believed that the Muslim clerics had mystical powers and sought supernatural aid from them.[12]

Whether by trade or conquest, the impact of Islam was *syncretic*, not total. Fourteenth-century Arab globetrotter Ibn Battuta saw

Malian Muslims in Mali in public prayer and study of Quran but also (he called them "vile") practices like honoring the king by sprinkling dust and ashes on their heads or singing his praises in red-beaked feather-masked masquerades.[13] Muslim rulers in Mali surrounded themselves with Muslim scholars and holy men *and* paid heed to the priests and philosophers of the ancestral religions. South of the Sahel, in the savanna by the Volta Basin, states like Gonja and Dagbon (where President Akufo-Addo visited) were founded by invader-settlers with Sahelian roots in (or at least routes through) Mali/Songhai. It is thus unsurprising that rulers of these states also appointed imams to their courts and incorporated clerics in the political structure but kept places in the structure for non-Muslim priests/officials of the ancestral religion.[14] Dress was a key arena of West Africa's syncretic encounter with Islam. The Muslim trade networks helped expand the market for cloth and clothing and encouraged import and local manufacture. As garments arrived in West African markets to dress the growing Muslim and Islamized African elite, handy local craftspeople made their own vernacular versions.[15]

Dress was a site of syncretism but also a marker of social-religious distinction, setting apart relatively Islamized urban elite and ruling Africans from the less Islamized rural Africans who held more strongly to ancestral religious practices. Eleventh–thirteenth century Arab and Persian historian-geographers described rural Africans as "naked" or wearing, at the most, skins.[16] On the contrary they describe the urban Africans in contact with Arab traders, and therefore in the orbit of Islam, as emulating "Muslim fashion" (wide, long-sleeved tunics and ankle-length flowing kaftans and capes consistent with Islamic dress code of piety and modesty) draping themselves in cloths and sewn clothes of cotton, wool, brocade, or silk.[17] Similar distinctions pertained in the savannah regions south by the Volta Basin. Less Islamized rural autochthonous people away from urban centers of state power did not weave/make cloth. Rather, they wore small items of dress— leaves, animal skin. Meanwhile the people inhabiting the Islamized kingdoms like Gonja and Dagbon, Muslims in particular, used cloth on all occasions. Among the former, wearing cloth was variously taboo, "foreign luxury," and a betrayal of local roots. Among the latter, where Islam held more sway, *not* wearing cloth was a sign at once of the pagan and savage (wild, uncivilized "of the bush") who live "without the law of God or man."[18] The social value Islam added to cloth led to the rise of a family of clothes comprising single to multiple-piece ensembles of tunics, kaftans, capes, headgears, and pantaloons whose descendants are found today in the Senegalese *boubou*, Yoruba *agbada*, Hausa *baba riga* (both Nigerian) and the Ghanaian *batakari*.

The batakari itself comprises a smaller family of styles within the larger family of syncretic clothing that West Africa's encounter with Islam produced across the subcontinent. The simplest, commonest style of baṭakari is a sleeveless tunic or *densikyi*. Densikyi is a work garment, street cloth and undergarment in more elaborate ensembles. The short sleeved *Bingmaa bari* is a step higher in prestige. Further up in prestige is *yebili*, which reaches below the knee with sleeves stretching to the wrists, and signals opulence, wealth, and power. Chiefs must fully unfold and swing out both sleeves. Princes without titles must fold the right sleeve. Commoners who happen to be able to afford it must fold both sleeves over the shoulders. Batakari can bestow an air of dignity, flair, confidence, and lofty pride on wearers due to numerous gussets around the waist that lets the dress to flow or flare outward in circles when one wheels around, or drape around the body in various ways depending on one's posture or activity. Batakari may be worn over pouched, drawstring pantaloons. These "hernia trousers," as nicknamed, have long gathers before and between the legs and tight-fitting leg-ends for trucking into leather boots. If a person wearing batakari choses to wear a cap, it must be adjusted appropriately. A stiff tall posture of the cap is traditionally the preserve of "self-actualized" people. Pointing the cap backward says "let us put the past behind us" and forward is a provocative, offensive claim of superiority. People usually avoid the latter except rascals looking for trouble. The safest gesture is to bend the cap sideways in the manner of saying, "I come in peace."[19]

The Call of an Asante Ritual Market: Batakari Travels "South"

From the seventeenth century onward the two powerful Islamized states of the northern Volta Basin, Gonja and Dagbon were, subordinated to a southern political force, the Asante empire, as the latter rose in strength from the forest belt below the savannah. The Asante perceptions of the inhabitants of the northern savannah region varied to the degree of civilization Asante attributed to them. True, Asante regarded Gonja and Dagomba (people of Dagbon) as aliens. However, to the Asante, who had a highly hierarchical imperial state, Gonja and Dagbon were recognizable: polities whose hierarchies Asante could see tied to its empire by formal treaty arrangements. On the other hand, Asante saw northern people outside the hierarchical centers of power, who had more or less "acephalous," "stateless" polities and tended to be clothless, as barbarians fit to be exploited as "*ndonko*" (connoting outsiders … non-Asante, bought). Thus, for Asante, not just the absence of a stark political hierarchy but *also* the abhorrence of wearing cloths rendered the less Islamized communities uncivilized. Most of the 1000–2000 or so slaves that the Islamized states delivered per year as tribute to the Asante overlords between the eighteenth and nineteenth centuries, came from small stateless unclothed societies that both Islamized states and Asante regarded as uncivilized. *Asantehene* (Asante King) Nana Kwaku Duah may have been an extreme voice in Asante when he called the people of the stateless communities "stupid," just a "little better than beasts," and of "no use for anything but slaves." However, even the more toned-down opinion of his descendant Nana Osei Bonsu, that the people of those communities are "little civilized" and unable either "to make ornaments of gold," "build comfortable houses," or "weave garments," reflected the derogatory consensus that the Asante apparently held about that part of the North.[20]

In contrast to its derogation of people from the less Islamized stateless communities Asante developed a high regard for Muslim traders, scholars, and diviners of the Volta Basin states and gave them leave to reside in Kumasi, Asante's capital, and to provide crucial services to the royal court as secretaries, accountants, diplomatic attachés, and trade and treaty negotiators. The Asante royalty were especially interested in the Muslims' spiritual skills. As the Asantehene Osei Tutu Kwame put it to a British consul in the 1820s, "Crammo [Muslims] are strong people in *fetische* [objects of magical power]."[21] The Asante interest in the magico-spiritual services of Muslims from the North is rooted in Asante cosmology itself. In the Asante cosmos, beneath the supreme being, *Onyame*, exists a world with spiritual entities of an extraordinary variety but including two categories, *abosom* tutelary deities that possess anthropomorphic personalities and *asuman*, a diverse range of mobile powers manifested in the form of physical talismans/amulets. Asante believed that *asuman*, unlike *abosom*, are potent against witchcraft or other elements of willful maleficence and capable of being *bought or sold*. With this belief Asante established a ritual economy of exotic, imported, commodified, supernatural powers. As an expanding gold-rich empire, especially interested in protection from *asuman* during war, the Asante army had the *nsumankwaahene* (chief of suman-specialists) go before it to spiritually clear any disaster before it. Naturally, the Asante royals were prepared to pay extravagantly to obtain mystic powers from the Muslims of the North, particularly spiritually fortified batakari devised by Muslim clerics.[22]

Already, in Gonja and Dagbon, Muslim clerics prepared and placed scripted Quran verses into pouches sewed on batakari. A hunter or a battle-bound warrior would then wear the fortified tunic for protection against mishap in battle or the hunt. The practice was by itself a syncretic outcome of West Africa's encounter with Islam. Since pre-Islamic times there had been traditions of warrior-hunters in West African societies from the Niger to the Volta rivers who spiritually fortify their apparels and bodies with amulets and talismans. Similarly, in the Islamic world, from Ottoman to Moghul empires, there have been Sufi talismanic traditions of inscribing tunics with verses of the Quran, names of Allah and prophets, special numbers, and astrological images and symbols, as protection from evil and as a spiritual shield in battle. The West

African marabouts replaced (or combined) the traditional talismanic objects with calligraphic scripts of Quranic verses. Various Asantehene purchased war tunics affixed with amulets filled with "letters, cabalistic formulae and quotations from the Qur'an."[23] In 1819, after making a festival sacrifice, *Asantehene* Osei Tutu Kwame stepped in public "in a cloth studded all over in Arabic writings of various inks."[24] In the mid-nineteenth century *Asantehene* Nana Osei Tutu Kwame bought several amulet-fortified batakari for the price of eighty plus slaves from the King of Dagbon.[25] *Asantehene* Nana Osei Bonsu is recorded to have danced before his people in one of such dresses after a battle victory.[26] In 1844, the *Asantehene* Nana Kwaku Dua, instituted the office of *Asantehene Kramo* (the royal Muslim cleric) and appointed Gonja cleric Uthman Kamaate to the office from whom the king received a fortified tunic called *Batakari Kese* (Great Batakari).[27]

The Asante ritual economy thus opened a path for batakari to migrate South where it was associated with a northern Muslim identity. We see the association in the Asante proverb, *nsuo boro kramo ni a, yemmisa ne batakari* (if rain beats a Muslim, don't upset him more by asking if his batakari remained dry). An Englishman noted in the nineteenth century that the term for Muslim cleric up North, "Crambo ... bears the same interpretation as ... *a man clothed.*"[28] If wearing cloth distinguished a northern Muslim from his cloth-less "primitive" neighbor, the batakari indexed that distinction in Asante minds: as a sartorial marker of Muslim identity. However, as the nineteenth turned into the twentieth century, southern interest in northern magico-spiritual goods extended from what Muslim clerics offered to the shrines of deities of the stateless communities that Asante so disparagingly regarded. There is no certainty as to why. It may have been that the *ndonko* in the South advertised the powers of their northern gods to generate southerners' interest in perhaps more affordable magico-spiritual goods outside the purview of Islam. It may have been that the time-honored southern wish to thwart intractably malevolent spiritual forces found new expression in the problems and anxieties that colonial subjection/subjectivity presented in that period. Or it may have been that southern derogation of that culturally and ecologically exotic part of the North as primitive and uncivilized, ironically promoted it as a source of pure and potent ritual goods "unsullied by witchcraft and the malign forces" that colonialism unleashed.

Whatever it was that generated the expansion of southern interest to include ritual goods outside the talismanic creations of Muslim clerics, many southerners tried to travel North to consult non-Islamic shrines. It was an arduous pilgrimage North in search of exotic spiritual power.[29] With rising demand for that kind of power, acolytes of northern deities founded "franchises" of northern shrines South. Batakari was part of this development but, this time, as a non-specifically Muslim spiritual tool-kit. Because of its historic association with spiritual fortification batakari had developed an enduring image as a site (or at least an emblem) of spiritual power. So, fortified or not, it endowed its wearer with an impression of mystic power in the southern imaginations—an impression that prevails till today. This impression—this image of the batakari—made it worthwhile for non-Muslim priests/acolytes of the shrines in the South to wear batakari as a familiar stamp of spiritual efficacy. It seemed to matter less to these priests and acolytes that some northern shrines abhorred cloth and more that the batakari, with a longer-signified ritual identity, provided a desired stamp of efficacy. The result was a proliferation of batakari in the South, which detached the dress from a specifically Muslim identity per se and began to attach it to a more generic northern identity. The folk wit of the Asante people captured this transition in a proverbial lament: *batakari adooso ama yenhu kramo* (batakari has proliferated so much that now it is hard to tell who is genuinely a Muslim and who is not).

Between Colonialism and Independence: Batakari from Poor Man's Dress to Presidential Garb

Colonialism added more layers to the meaning of batakari over the first half of the twentieth century. British authorities were similar to the Asante and centralized states of the North in their ideas about the latter's cloth-less, state-less neighbors. George Ekem Ferguson, an agent of the colonial government sent to secure British influence in the North and who laid grounds for British military occupation of the area between 1890–7, distinguished between the northern societies "with organized government" on one hand, and the "barbarous tribes" who "live in village communities" under "a strong man" that has "arrogated to himself the position of a chief" on the other.[30] Also using dress as a marker of the barbarism he added that the "tribes" move about "in perfect nudity, their lips, noses, and ears … pierced, into which straws and beads are inserted as ornaments." Following Ferguson, the British Administration's first Annual Report on Northern Territories for 1898–9 echoed the distinction by saying of the stateless societies, that they are "composed of men whose naked savage-dom was a by-word of contempt among more civilized inhabitants" nearby. A British officer noted that he was typically "well received in Mahomedan [Islamic] towns" whereas people in the "bush village of fetish people" tended to turn out against him. In 1915, a British commissioner added, about a Talensi priest, that he is "dressed in nothing beyond a kilt of skin" and refuses to wear "a cover-cloth or robe of any kind."[31]

The British perpetuation of a spurious savage-civilized distinction between the northern peoples did not spare the entire North from its colonial labor exploitation.[32] Britain, which had overpowered the Asante, viewed the North mainly as a recruiting ground for labor in the colonial economy and coerced young northerners to serve labor needs in southern enclaves of mineral and agricultural exploitation. Notwithstanding British authorities' distinctions between savage and civilized of the North, they exploited labor across the entire span of the region. Colonialism also created "pull" factors for northerners' migration. The colonial project of turning the North into a labor zone closed once-vibrant trade routes and limited the market for key northern produce like shea butter and groundnuts. Stripped of economic prospect, the same young northerner who fled coercive colonial recruiters defied his parents to go eke a living in the South, arrived "raw and mostly naked from the bush" to "work as sanitary laborers, railway laborers, etc."[33] Colonialism thus facilitated the conflation of generic-ethnic identity (northerner) with class identity (migrant, menial laborer). The northern migrant now embodied a menial-laboring class in the southern imagination. Influenced by southern norms/fashion once cloth-less migrants sought to purchase imported cloths and European clothes, or at least batakari. By and large the northern migrant laborer could be seen in the batakari, particularly the street and work-convenient *densikyi*. In the result, Batakari became associated with the emergent, predominantly northern, laboring class. It was therefore remarkable that at independence in March 1957 Ghana's Prime-Minister-Elect Kwame Nkrumah, a southerner, wore the *densikyi* to address Ghanaians.

On March 5, 1957, a little after midnight signaled Ghana's independence from British colonial rule, Kwame Nkrumah stood on a podium at the Old Polo grounds across from Ghana's parliament to address a festive crowd. Under the glare of floodlights and flanked by members of his cabinet he addressed the crowd dressed in a sleeveless batakari. Why did Nkrumah choose batakari to address the country at independence? Ama Biney argues that Nkrumah wore batakari especially because it was associated with the North and the laboring class. She observes that, "batakari was the archetypal dress of the common man, particularly of the northerner," a "poor man's daily garment" as Elizabeth Harris describes it elsewhere. Biney explains that by wearing the batakari, Nkrumah "sent out an unambiguous symbolic image" of his "allegiance to the common man of the newly independent nation state."[34] Indeed, since the 1940s, Kwame Nkrumah had established his political identity by including the laboring classes in a broad-based independence-seeking constituency. One important basis of his successful leadership in the anti-colonial movement that led to Ghana's independence was the perception that he was close to the "masses," to the rank and file, and the less privileged. The batakari thus offered him a personalized dress with which, at a most visible and symbolic public level, and on a memorable occasion, he could express his affinity with the marginalized masses. By wearing a dress associated with a menially laboring class of northerners he articulated an inclusive policy that embraced the lower socio-economic strata of society and a region "deprived" by the colonial economy. His dress suggested that he would be more inclusive and not treat the North as an investment-deprived labor source.

Nkrumah's batakari was also a rejection of colonial cultural imperialism by turning what were once objects of colonial denigration into symbols of national culture and pride.[35] Nkrumah observed that colonialism denied Africans "knowledge of our ... past ... and taught us to regard our culture and traditions as barbarous and primitive."[36] Nkrumah was concerned that because of this hegemony, newly independent Africans would continue to articulate their selves-and-worlds in colonial terms unless there was an ontological revolution of sorts waged on the symbolic realm to combat any continued prostration to the discourse and representations of the colonizer. Nkrumah interpellated batakari as an emblem of national culture and, concomitantly, as a sartorial weapon in his ontological revolution against hardwearing colonial hegemony. Furthermore, British colonialism prompted African resistances to cultural impositions of western dress in public life: Africans nationalists who wore "native" dress to assert African culture tended to wear dresses from their own ethnic communities, thus (inadvertently or not) making those ethnicities stand-ins for the "nations" they imagined in their nationalism.[37] By wearing a dress outside his own Nzema-ethnicity—a dress associated with a deprived region and a derogated community at that—Nkrumah established that he saw independent Ghana in truly trans-ethnic national terms.

We can read acts of political legitimation in Nkrumah's use of the batakari to associate himself with the laboring poor and to assert a trans-ethnic national cultural identity. Acts of political legitimation seek to persuade political subjects to believe in a leader's right to govern. It is associated with the function of political representation wherein subjects want to feel that their leaders embody their best wishes and act in their best interests. In this regard it aims to mediate between brute power and the lawful sprit of a political community. Political legitimacy—what a leader seeks with their acts of legitimation—has been defined in both a narrow legal-procedural sense (as the subjects' belief that leaders exercise power in accordance with appropriate laws and customs) and in a larger social-moral sense (as the subjects' belief that the rulers conform to widely held principles).[38] However, there is another formulation of political legitimacy as, that which is accorded a leader on the basis of his/her special individual qualities or status.[39] Often leaders who seek to legitimize their authority on the basis of special individual qualities/status construct myths and symbols to project an image of unusual powers and personal characteristics with the aim of setting themselves apart from other human beings.[40] It is specifically this kind of political legitimation that I want to add to the discussion so far on the significance of Nkrumah's batakari.

A key ingredient in Nkrumah's legitimation strategies was his presentation of himself as a kind of spiritually ordained messianic leader. For instance, in his autobiography, he presented himself as a man gifted with supernatural vision/insight by relating an incident of his clairvoyance when he was a baby.[41] He (and his supporters) attributed magic, messianic, and god-like qualities to himself in various ways. He often said that "destiny" had assigned him a special duty. People reported that he appeared to them in dreams and visions. The League of Ghana Patriots called him "voice of the Son of Man … redeemer of the oppressed … apostle of peace and tranquility on earth" and "deliverer of mankind from the tortures of sinful imperialism." He had his own set of political beatitudes and an oath of allegiance to himself resembling the Apostle's Creed.[42] Rumor had it that his white handkerchief had magical powers that swooned followers to idolize him and could help him vanish in the face of danger. His rallies became personalized religious-symbolic forms of political legitimation whose emotional mystique emphasized Nkrumah's superordinate qualities. He recalled how, upon his release from the last of several colonial detentions, masses had persuaded him to lead them with a stirring rendition of the hymn, "Lead Kindly Light," implying that Nkrumah was identical with divine light.[43] The batakari served Nkrumah's efforts at this kind

Figure 3.1 President Jerry Rawlings gestures to a crowd of 60,000 people at the Accra Stadium as he campaigns for reelection to the presidency of Ghana, July 26, 1996. ISSOUF SANOGO/AFP via Getty Images.

of legitimation. Recall that the batakari, even without talismanic fortifications, endowed wearers with an aura of spiritual invincibility. Indeed, rumors abounded that Nkrumah had supernatural powers, including the ability to detect treachery or disappear upon sighting danger. His batakari—even without the talismans—could only enforce this particular belief. In short, wearing the batakari helped him to more or less set himself apart as supernatural or at least extraordinary: a destined and therefore somewhat exalted figure.

Batakari Days: Regional Development and Trans-Ethnic Fashion from the Presidential Stage

Nkrumah was overthrown in a military coup in 1966. Over the next twenty-five or so years, a period of successive military regimes in which military dress dominated the sartorial choices of Ghana's leaders, batakari did not enjoy as much prominence in the public political arena as it had during the Nkrumah years—not until 1998, when President Jerry John (J. J.) Rawlings wore the batakari to welcome US President Clinton on the latter's visit to Ghana. Before his overthrow, Nkrumah had worked to develop infrastructure and education by modernizing agriculture in the North. He had encouraged the substitution of imports with domestic production (a rice mills, meat plants, a tomato factory, etc.) to help the northerners with post-harvest income and security. He had also instituted a Northern Scholarship Scheme to provide subsidies and free tuition to students in the northern schools from basic through and beyond secondary school.[44] In the 1970s, the military government of General Acheampong promoted commercial agriculture in the North, including "cash crops" like cotton to feed local textile industries. However, these were not enough and by the 1980s the North-South development gap still remained, compelling many northerners to still seek economic opportunities in the South and therefore to perpetuate the derogation of the northerner. The Ghanaian playwright Mohammed Ben Abdallah captured this cycle of migration and derogation of the northerner, to and in the South, with the following lines from his play *The Verdict of the Cobra*. In the play, a northern chief observes,

> They [northerners] leave their people ... to the South. To work, they say. But what kind of work is this that yields so meager a reward for so much pain, suffering and insult? Laborers ... Latrine Boys ... Abongo Boys [low-ranked soldiers]! ... The North needs them. They run away to the South and the South spits on them.[45]

Rawlings first came to power in military coups before reinventing himself to be elected president of Ghana's constitutional democracy in 1992. One of his enduring efforts as a military leader and democratically elected president was at reducing the still-yawning development gap between North and South regions of Ghana. Under Rawlings's military (1980s) and, later, democratically elected (1990s) regimes, he was able to provide the North with some development infrastructure including roads, a university, and an electrification project to expand the national grid to unserved towns and villages in the region.[46] Rawlings observed about the North that it produced beautiful handmade crafts, including batakari, but could not market them. Therefore, he decided to draw national and international attention to the garment by wearing it to important state functions and foreign engagements, and by requesting newsreaders of Ghana's state television to present news in the dress.[47] His political opponents criticized him for "roaming foreign countries in batakari" and arriving "improperly attired in batakari" for a dinner with US corporate executives at Ghana's embassy in Washington, DC (Figure 3.1).[48] None of these dissuaded Rawlings who thumbed his nose at critics by wearing batakari to receive Clinton in Ghana.

Like Nkrumah, Rawlings wore his batakari over a dress shirt, although his was a long-sleeved shirt. However, the remarkable thing about his batakari was that it was brown in color and had a leopard skin attached from his right shoulder to his chest. I must point out my strong suspicion that his source of inspiration for that accessory was Hollywood—specifically Eddie Murphy's and James Earl Jones's characters in *Coming to America* (both have animal skins on the shoulders of their suits) rather than any practice in northern Ghana that I am aware of. Brown batakari, in northern traditions, are warrior-hunter tunics, dyed to camouflage the wearer in battle or hunt. Also, in those traditions the leopard is a totem, used in traditional healing practices. Indeed, animal skins are an important feature of material culture of northern politics but I have never seen it in the form Rawlings had on his batakari. I therefore read Rawlings dress for the Clinton visit as his high-fashion approach to marketing batakari on behalf of its northern producers on the political stage. High fashion is performance art in which spectacle drives consumer's eyeball and interest to a body of sartorial work. With *his* eye on the market—especially the international market—Rawlings took the opportunity that Clinton's visit offered for worldwide media attention, to model batakari with a King Jaffe-Joffer-like look. In other words, he deployed a rather contrived, nevertheless spectacular and Hollywood-made-globally-familiar picture of the fictional and commanding African leader with the skin of a dead feline on his shoulders, to market the less familiar batakari to the world.

Since the new millennium, batakari has become more commonplace in the dress choices of the average Ghanaian. Other public figures have joined late President Rawlings's pioneering public effort to market batakari in service of development in the still relatively deprived North. In 2013, King Ayisoba, a musician from the North, held the first Batakari Festival to highlight the dress as fashionable wear for all Ghanaians and a potential source of jobs for unemployed youth in northern Ghana. The festival is now an annual event featuring several Ghanaian musicians of international acclaim.[49] Then, in 2015, Savannah Accelerated Development Authority (SADA), a government agency coordinating development for the North, launched "Batakari Day" to be observed on the first Friday of every month.[50] The president of Ghana at this time, John Mahama, frequently wore batakari. It was a significant part of his sartorial repertoire at State of the Nation addresses, the United Nations, and in many other public appearances. Mahama *was* from the North, but in his era batakari enjoyed an unprecedented patronage as a pan-ethnic "traditional" fashion in the clothing market. Apart from government initiatives and marketing efforts of public figures like Rawlings, Mahama, and musician Ayisoba to help the North, fashion designers were drivers of batakari's popularity. An explosion of young designers unafraid to experiment with new, bold color combinations moved the look of batakari beyond the traditionally muted color combinations of white, black, red, and blue.[51] It is against the background of this complicated social and political history of the batakari, that in January 2019, President Akufo-Addo of Ghana arrived at the Yaa Naa's Palace in the Dagbon Kingdom wearing his batakari.

The Color of Peace: Batakari and the Performance of Presidential Neutrality

Online comments by the public, mostly in response to press reports about the president's outfit, were mixed. One comment congratulated and called him "Addo Show Boy," invoking a nickname that Ghanaians had given their first president Kwame Nkrumah for the highly performative character of his politics.[52] Another comment was that the president "looks nice." Yet another comment was that he "looked great" and was "dressed to suit their [Dagbon] culture."[53] The negative comments varied. One simply asked: "What is so spectacular about this dressing?" Another charged that the president's dressing at the investiture was a distraction from his administration's failure to solve the basic economic problems of the country. Many more of the negative comments were outbursts about the president's looks and diminutive height: one called his outfit an "idiotic dress" and compared him to a "log clad in a yellow sack" while another insisted that the dress wore the president, not the other way around.[54]

Generally, press reports about the dress were positive. They described the president's batakari as "a beautifully woven yellow," said he was "dressed to kill," that he "stole the show" and that the "swagger with which he strode around" in the dress was "a spectacle to behold." Most maintained that he was "perfectly" dressed for occasion: that it was typically the royal or person of means or high stature who added pantaloon and boots to their smock, and that yellow, though uncommon, represented peace and unity in Dagbon culture.[55] Only a couple were critical.[56] One of the two deemed his dress a "fashion disaster" because its mid-sectional floral flair did not suit the president's body type and noted that the bright yellow was "somewhat reminiscent of a school girl's outfit." The other was more abstruse. It faulted the president for not adding a traditional cap to his ensemble, yet seemed ignorant of (or perhaps it was making fun of) the president's boots by calling them "Wellington boots." What is more, this report echoed the social media descriptions of the outfit as "gringo-dressing" (and of the president as "Nana Gringo") in reference to the jocular parallels people drew between the president's boots and those worn by the Ghanaian Dance Hall musician Shatta Wale in his "American wild west" themed music video *Gringo*. Set in 1885 (and shot in Blanco, Texas), Gringo is the story of El Shatta, a foreigner who wins the heart of Jasmine, the beautiful girlfriend of a corrupt sheriff named Snake Eye. Beyond the comparison of footwear, there are parallels between the El Shatta and the president's batakari performance in the way they both draw from the trope of the stranger hero. After all, the president's presence at Yendi was also his way of claiming some personal credit, even as a southerner and therefore a "stranger" to Yendi, for the restoration of peace in Dagbon.

Ultimately it is in Akufo-Addo's own words that we find, perhaps, the most compelling explanation for his outfit. Two houses of the Dagbon royal family, Abudu and Andani, had been feuding over succession to the Dagbon rulership. In 2002, things got to a head when the reigning Yaa-Na was attacked and murdered. To complicate matters elites of the two families aligned themselves with the two main political parties in the country, turning the inter-communal conflict into a politically-partisan one. The result was seventeen years of a protracted dispute. A Peace Council of Eminent Chiefs from outside Dagbon was established in 2002 to address the conflict. Upon assumption of office Akufo-Addo's government decided to tackle the problem with new verve. On November 2018, the council presented a road map to peace to Akufo-Addo. That roadmap resulted in the restoration of peace and investiture of a new Yaa Naa in Dagbon. The story is that the president's ability to compellingly convey his commitment and neutrality to the feuding royal families was the secret formula for peace. The elaborate batakari was a declaration of his commitment to Dagbon as an "adopted" son of the kingdom.

Traditionally there is significance to some colors of the batakari. A chief may wear a one-color grey bath (*bienpenli*) pattern at their enskinment (installation) or at a funeral. Smock fabric with an interwoven mix of black and white colors (called *kpaankogbu* for their resemblance to guinea fowl feathers) is believed to wield spiritual powers to the benefit of the wearer and is a popular choice of traditional priests and priestesses. *Jaajekum* (a twin does not want death) is a smock that is sewn with alternating strips of plain white and strips with an interwoven mix of black and white. It is believed to protect the lives of twins and so may be found on that kind of sibling pair or twin dolls. Smocks with a combination of red and white warp stripes and red weft, or red and black stripes with black weft, are also deemed to have spiritual potency. Therefore, they may be used for sacrificial rituals to ward off evil. The solid yellow of Akufo-Addo's batakari is not something that is traditionally seen on Dagbon batakari. Nevertheless, it is a color that, as several reports explained, means peace to the Dagbon people. In this regard, the president's yellow batakari affirmed the neutrality needed of him in the conflict—it articulated that his interest was in peace and not with any faction of feuding royal houses. He reiterated this neutrality when he spoke at the Ya Naa's investiture, by declaring that he is "neither Andani nor Abudu" (names of formerly feuding but now reconciled royal houses of Dagon). My name is "Abudani" he added, adopting a combination of the names of the feuding houses to represent his mediational identity in the conflict and emphasizing that he stands for "unity and reconciliation."

In its journey through time and across diverse fields of power batakari has been many things, sometimes a number of them at once. It has been a Muslim dress, a mystic dress, a northern dress, the poor laborer's dress, a national dress, and a fashionable dress. Now, in the case of President Akufo-Addo's yellow batakari, it served as a conciliatory dress: an embodiment and expression of fervent hope that the peace that prevailed in the Gbaawe Palace of Dagbon would be long and lasting one.

Notes

1 Thomas Carlyle, *Sartor Resartus: The Life and Opinions of Herr Teufelsdrockh* (Urbana, Illinois: Project Gutenberg, [1831] 2012), https://gutenberg.org/files/1051/1051-h/1051-h.htm (accessed March 9, 2022).
2 Jeffrey Mensah, "Akufo-Addo Steals Show at Ya-Na's Coronation with Special Outfit," *Yen*, January 25, 2019, https://yen.com.gh/121779-akufo-addo-steals-show-ya-nas-coronation-special-outfit-photo.html (accessed March 9, 2022).
3 Batakari (a Hausa word meaning "outer gown") and fugu (a Mossi word meaning "cloth") have been uses interchangeably for this dress. See

Osuanyi Quaicoo Essel and Emmanual R. K. Amissah, "Smock Fashion Culture in Ghana's Dress Identity-Making," *Historical Research Letter* 18 (2015): 33. I shall use the former in this essay because it is more frequently found in the scholarly literature.

4 Jean Allman, ed., *Fashioning Africa: Power and the Politics of Dress* (Bloomington: Indiana University Press, 2004), 1.

5 Angela McRobbie, *British Fashion Design: Rag Trade or Image Industry* (London: Routledge, 1998), 15, see also Emma Tarlo, *Clothing Matters* (Chicago: University of Chicago Press, 1996).

6 Lou Taylor, *Studying Dress History* (Manchester: Manchester University Press, 2002), 2.

7 These include edited volumes such as Hildi Hendrickson, *Clothing and Difference: Embodied Identities in Colonial and Post-Colonial Africa* (Durham: Duke University Press 1996); Allman, *Fashioning Africa*; Heather Akou, JoAnn McGregor, and Nicola Stylianou, *Creating African Fashion Histories: Politics, Museums and Sartorial Practices* (Bloomington: Indiana University Press, 2022); and Karen Hansen and D. Soyini Madison, eds., *African Dress: Fashion, Agency, Performance* (New York: Bloomsbury, 2013). They also include monographs such as Heather Marie Akou, *The Politics of Dress in Somali Culture* (Bloomington: Indiana University Press, 2011); Vibeke Maria Viestad, *Dress as Social Relations: An Interpretation of Bushman Dress* (New York: New York University Press, 2018); Judith Perani and Norma H. Wolff, *Cloth, Dress and Art Patronage in Africa* (New York: Berg Publishers, 1999); Victoria Rovine, *African Fashion, Global Style: Histories, Innovations, and Ideas You Can Wear* (Bloomington: Indiana University Press, 2015); Okechukwu Nwafor, *Aso Ebi: Dress, Fashion, Visual Culture, and Urban Cosmopolitanism in West Africa* (Ann Arbor: University of Michigan Press, 2021); and Christopher Richards, *Cosmopolitanism and Women's Fashion in Ghana: History, Artistry and Nationalist Inspirations* (New York: Routledge, 2022).

8 Osuanyi Q. Essel, "Dress Fashion Politics of Ghanaian Presidential Inaguration Ceremonies from 1960 to 2017," *Fashion and Textiles Review* 1, no. 3 (2019): 35–55; Abena Dove Osseo-Asare, "Kwame Nkrumah's Suits: Sartorial Politics in Ghana at Independence," *Fashion Theory* 25, no. 5 (2021): 362–597; and Leslie Rabine, "Photography, Poetry and

the Dressed Body of Leopold Sedar Senghor," in *African Dress: Fashion, Agency, Performance*, ed. Karen Hansen and D. Soyini Madison, 171–85 (New York: Bloomsbury, 2013).

9 These included centers like Audaghost, a Berber town ten days march north of old Ghana in present-day southern Mauritania (there North African traders could buy gold from the kings of old Ghana); Koumbi Saleh the capital of old Ghana; Takrur, capital of a kingdom of the same name on the lower Senegal River; Gao, capital of the kingdom of the same name on the middle Niger River at the southern edge of the Sahara; and Tadmekka, lying northeast of Gao in present-day Mali.

10 See Peter Clarke, *West Africa and Islam* (London: Edward Arnold, 1982), 58–9. Mande languages are spoken in several countries in West Africa. The speakers are concentrated, above all, in Guinea and Mali.

11 Eleventh century Arab-Andalusian historian al-Bakri tells of an encounter between a Malian leader al-Musulmani and a Muslim guest. In al-Bakri's account the ruler "and his descendants after him as well as his nobles" became "sincerely attached to Islam" (Clarke, 41). Also, fourteenth century Malian leader Mansa Musa is said to have taken two Muslims with him on pilgrimage to Mecca, one of whom built the great mosque of Timbuktu and Mansa Musa's magnificent palace. In old Ghana Muslims lived under the auspices of a non-Muslim king who invited Muslim traders to the capital and employed them in his court (43–4).

12 al-Bakri's account of how Malian leader al-Musulmani became a Muslim, goes that after a year of drought that the Malians prayers and cattle sacrifices could not remedy, the leader's Muslim guest promised to pray for deliverance if al-Musulmani would convert to Islam. al-Musulmani converted to Islam, after which "God caused abundant rain to descend upon them. Upon that, the king ordered the idols to be broken and expelled the sorcerers from the country" (Clarke, 41; Nehemia Levtzion, "Islam in the Bilad-al-Sudan to 1800," in *History of Islam in Africa*, ed. Nehemia Levtzion and Randall L. Pouwels (Athens: Ohio University Press, 2000), 65)

13 Clarke, 45; Levtzion, "Islam in the Bilad-al Sudan," 67.

14 Nehemia Levtzion, *Ancient Ghana and Mali* (New York: Methuen and Company, 1973), 179.

15 Describing Timbuktu in the sixteenth century the Berber Andalusi diplomat Leo Africanus wrote that there, "fabrics are ... imported from

Europe to Timbuktu, borne by Berber merchants" but also that "shops of the artisans, the merchants, and especially weavers of cotton cloth are very numerous." See Leo Africanus, "Leo Africanus: Description of Timbuktu from 'The Description of Africa' (1526)," *Fordham University*, https://sourcebooks.fordham.edu/med/leo_afri.asp (accessed March 9, 2022); see also B. W. Hodder, "Indigenous Cloth Trade and Marketing in Africa," *Textile History* 11, no. 1 (1980): 203–7.

16 Levtzion, *Ancient Ghana and Mali*, 179.
17 Levtzion, *Ancient Ghana and Mali*, 109.
18 Esther Goody and Jack Goody, "The Naked and the Clothed," in *The Cloth of Many Colored Silks*, ed. John Hunwick and Nancy Lawler (Evanston: Northwestern University Press, 1996), 68–73.
19 For a more complete descriptions of all the batakari styles see Essel and Amissah, "Smock Fashion"; Samuel Acquaah, Emmanuel RK Amissah, and Patrique deGraft Yankson, "Dress Aesthetic of Smock in Northern Ghana: Form, Function and Context," *Journal of Textile Engineering and Fashion Technology* 1, no. 2 (1997): 68–77; Mumuni Zakari Fusheini, "The Dagomba Smock (Bim'Mangli) of Northern Ghana in the Light of Contextualism and Instrumentalism Theories of Aesthetics," *Africa Development and Resources Research Institute* 29, no. 1 (2021): 58–72; and Zakaria Mumuni Fusheini, Joe Adu-Agyem, and Eric Asante Appau, "Indigenous Aesthetic Qualities Inherent in the Dagomba Bim'Mangli (Smock) in Northern Region of Ghana," *International Journal of Research and Innovation in Social Science* 3, no. 4 (2019): 237–48.
20 For the Nana Kwaku Duah comment see Jean Allman and John Parker, *Tongnaab: The History of a West African God* (Bloomington: Indiana University Press, 2005), 31. For the Osei Bonsu comment see Enid Schildkrout, "The Ideology of Regionalism in Ghana," in *Strangers in African Societies*, ed. William A. Shack and Elliott P. Skinner (Berkeley: University of California Press, 1979), 191.
21 David Owusu-Ansah, *Islamic Talismanic Traditions in Nineteenth-Century Asante* (Lewiston: Edwin Mellen Press, 1991), 150.
22 For a fuller read of Asante cosmology see Owusu-Ansah, *Islamic Talismanic Traditions,* 113–19 and 124–30, and Allman and Parker, *Tongnaab*, 122–5.

23 T. C. McCaskie, "Innovational Eclecticism: The Asante Empire and Europe in the 19th Century," *Comparative Studies in Society and History* 14, no. 1 (1972): 32.
24 Owusu-Ansah, *Islamic Talismanic Tradition*, 119.
25 Owusu-Ansah, *Islamic Talismanic Tradition*, 126.
26 T. C. McCaskie, "Telling the Tale of Osei Bonsu: An Essay on the Making of Asante Oral History," *Africa* 84, no. 3 (2014): 365.
27 David Owusu-Ansah, "The Asante Kramo Imammate: Conflicting Traditions," in *The Cloth of Many Colored Silks*, ed. John Hunwick and Lawler Nancy (Evanston: Northwestern University Press, 1996), 355.
28 T. Edward Bowdich, *Mission from Cape Coast Castle to Ashantee, With a Statistical Account of that Kingdom, and Geographical Notices of Other Parts of the Interior of Africa* (London: John Murray, Albemarle-Street, 1819): 350. "Crambo" was Bowdich's mis-rendition of *karamogo,* Mende term for Islamic scholar-teacher from which the Asante word *kramo* for Muslim derives. H. N. Riis and J. G. Christaller's *Twi* (language of the Asante and other Akan people) dictionaries of 1854 and 1881 respectively, also describe batakari as a dress of "Mohammedans."
29 Allman and Parker, *Tongnaab*, 14.
30 Allman and Parker, *Tongnaab*, 56.
31 Allman and Parker, *Tongnaab*, 56–7, 76.
32 From the northwestern Sissala, Lobi, Wala, Kassena, and Dagaaba to Gambaga, Mamprusi, and Dagomba of the northeast, among others. Roger G. Thomas, "Forced Labor in British West Africa: The Case of the Northern Territories of the Gold Coast 1906–1927," *The Journal of African History* 14, no. 1 (1973): 84.
33 This got so predictable it was described as the "usual exodus of young men going south." In 1923 a checkpoint recorded the passage of 16, 816 voluntary migrants (Allman and Parker, *Tongnaab*, 92–4).
34 For Biney, see Ama Biney, *The Political and Social Thought of Kwame Nkrumah* (New York: Palgrave Macmillan, 2011), 77. For Harris, see Elizabeth Harris, *Ghana: A Travel Guide* (Aburi: Aburi Press, 1976), 137.
35 Kwame Botwe-Asamoah, *Kwame Nkrumah's Politico-Cultural Thought and Policies, Kwame Nkrumah's Politico-Cultural Thought and Politics* (New York: Routledge, 2005), 175.

36 A. B. Assensoh and Alex Assensoh, *Kwame Nkrumah's Political Kingdom and Pan-Africanism Reinterpreted, 1909–1972* (Lanham, MD: Lexington Books, 2022), 101.
37 The lawyer-nationalist Kobina Sekyi is an example. Sekyi captured his sartorial nationalism in a satiric play. See Kobina Sekyi, *Blinkards, a Comedy* (Oxford: Heinemann, 1977).
38 See my discussion of these ideas in David A. Donkor, *Spiders of the Market: Trickster Performance in a Web of Neoliberalism* (Bloomington: Indiana University Press, 2016), 12.
39 Fred M. Hayward and Ahmed R. Dumbuya, "Political Legitimacy, Political Symbols, and National Leadership in West Africa," *The Journal of Modern African Studies* 21, no. 4 (December 1983): 650.
40 Hayward and Dumbuya, "Political Legitimacy" 665–9.
41 Strapped to his mother's back while she waded through a stream he had suddenly cried out in excitement, "I am standing on the fish" and surprised his mother when she discovered she had actually trapped a fish with one of her feet. Several scholars have pointed to this narrative as Nkrumah's self-legitimation as a special, supernaturally gifted figure. See for instance, A. Rahman, *The Regime Change of Kwame Nkrumah: Epic Heroism in Africa and the Diaspora* (New York: Palgrave Macmillan, 2007), 21; Ebenezer Obiri Addo, *Kwame Nkrumah: A Case Study of Religion and Politics in Ghana* (Lanham, MD: University Press of America, 1999), 52; and Kwesi Yankah, *Beyond the Political Spider: Critical Issues in African Humanities* (Makhanda, RSA: African Books Collective, 2021), 240.
42 Barbara S. Monfils, "A Multifaceted Image: Kwame Nkrumah's Extrinsic Rhetorical Strategies," *Journal of Black Studies* 7, no. 3 (1977): 322–4.
43 Reeck, Darrell, "The Castle and the Umbrella: Some Religious Dimensions of Kwame Nkrumah's Leadership Role in Ghana," *Africa Today* 23, no. 4 (October–December 1976): 15.
44 Ali Yakubu Nyaaba and George M. Bob-Milliar, "The Economic Potentials of Northern Ghana: The Ambivalence of the Colonial and Postcolonial States to Develop the North," *African Economic History* 47, no. 2 (2019): 55–6.
45 Mohammed ben-Abdallah, *Verdict of the Cobra* (Alexander Street Press: Black Drama Database, 1987), 3. https://search.alexanderstreet.

com/view/work/bibliographic_entity%7Cbibliographic_details%7C3607961 (accessed March 9, 2022).
46 Nyaaba and Bob-Milliar, "The Economic Potentials," 55–6.
47 Ghana News Agency, "Rawlings, the Tribute: The Tenderness in His Toughness," *Joy Online*, January 24, 2021, https://www.myjoyonline.com/rawlings-the-tribute-the-tenderness-in-his-toughness/ (accessed March 9, 2022).
48 George Ayittey, "Ghana: On Kufuor's US Trip (2)," *AllAfrica*, July 11, 2001, https://allafrica.com/stories/200107100387.html.
49 Pilot Sedode, "King Ayisoba and Wiyaala Team Up to Promote Batakari in a New Music Video," *Kuulpeeps*, July 17, 2019, https://kuulpeeps.com/2019/07/17/king-ayisoba-and-wiyaala-team-up-to-promote-batakari-in-a-new-music-video/trending/news (accessed March 9, 2022).
50 Pius Amihere Aduku, "First Friday of Every Month to be Declared 'Batakari day'," *Citifmonline*, September 1, 2015, https://citifmonline.com/2015/09/first-friday-of-every-month-to-be-declared-batakari-day/ (accessed March 9, 2022).
51 Wunpini Fatimata Mohammed, "The Northern Smock," *Popula*, October 15, 2018, https://popula.com/2018/10/15/the-northern-smock/ (accessed March 9, 2022).
52 Linda Vicar (@vicarlinda), comment in response to "Akufo-Addo Steals Show with His Special Outfit as New Ya-Na is 1Installed," *Instagram*, January 25, 2019, https://www.instagram.com/p/BtDuGLfBK8X/?utm_source=ig_embed&ig_rid=888a8cfa-56fc-4a12-b059-7cfc38e77f79 (accessed March 9, 2022).
53 Ghpage.com, "Nana Addo's Gringo Dressing to Ya'Naa's Coronation Goes Viral on Internet," *GhanaWeb*, January 25, 2019, https://www.ghanaweb.com/GhanaHomePage/entertainment/Nana-Addo-s-Gringo-dressing-to-Ya-Na-s-coronation-goes-viral-on-internet-718216 (accessed March 9, 2022).
54 Ghpage.com, "Nana Addo's Gringo Dressing."
55 See, Abu Marik, "Everybody's Talking About Akufo-Addo's Yellow Smock and Boots at Yaa-Naa's Investiture," *Pulse.com.gh*, January 26, 2019, https://www.pulse.com.gh/news/local/everybodys-talking-about-akufo-addos-yellow-smock-and-boots-at-yaa-naas-investiture/x6zc2wz (accessed March 9, 2022); Editor Admin, "Akufo Addo's

Fugu Steals Show at Ya Na Installation," *Asempanews*, January 25, 2019, https://asempanews.com/akufo-addos-fugu-steals-show-at-ya-na-installation/ (accessed March 9, 2022); Mutala Yakubu, "Prez-Akufo-Addo Dazzles in Beautiful 'Batakari' at outdooring of Yaa Naa," *Prime News Ghana*, January 25, 2019, https://www.primenewsghana.com/lifestyle/photos-prez-akufo-addo-dazzles-in-beautiful-batakari-at-outdooring-of-yaa-naa.html (accessed March 9, 2022).

56 See Nana Tamakloe, "President Akufo Addo's Drop Crotch Batakari Style with Big Red Boots is a National Emergency and Ghanaians Know It," *Fashion Ghana*, January 25, 2019, https://www.fashionghana.com/site/president-akufo-addos-drop-crotch-batakari-style-is-a-national-emergency-and-ghanaians-know-it/ (accessed March 9, 2022) and Ghpage.com, "Nana Addo's Gringo Dressing."

4

Windrush Strikes Back: "Rivers of Blood," Performance, and Guerrilla Diplomacy

Mary Karen Dahl

Windrush Day, June 22, 2021, saw the unveiling of a commemorative blue plaque on the building where Enoch Powell once met with constituents and reportedly wrote what journalists christened the "Rivers of Blood" speech. One might assume that, like many others officially approved to designate sites where notable individuals lived or worked, this plaque acknowledges Powell's twenty-four years serving as MP for Wolverhampton South West. Instead, both the plaque and the day's ceremony honor long-time Wolverhampton resident Paulette Wilson, who in 1968 emigrated from Jamaica as a ten-year-old child.[1] Although a legal immigrant, after nearly fifty years of living and working in Britain, she had been caught up in the Tory government's "hostile environment" campaign against illegal immigrants, miscategorized as illegal, imprisoned and threatened with deportation. Persistent struggle won her not only citizenship and the right to remain in Britain, but national recognition as a champion fighting for other wrongly targeted members of the Windrush generation. That same year, 1968, Powell famously warned his fellow Britons that "we must be mad, literally mad, as a nation to be permitting the annual inflow of some fifty thousand dependents, who are for the most part the material of the future growth of the immigrant-descended population."[2] In 2021, the actions celebrating Wilson answered Powell. They proclaimed the Windrush campaigner's contribution to the nation—the significance of her presence. The ceremony ended, the plaque remains. Affixed to what was Powell's constituency office—now Wolverhampton's Heritage Centre serving the African and African Caribbean community—it symbolically initiates a dialogue between interwoven strands of Mike and Trevor Phillips's "wholesale reassessment" of British identity that came to a head in the Windrush scandal of April 2018.[3]

Setting the Stage

The year 2018 marked not only fifty years since Powell's speech, but seventy years since the *Empire Windrush* bearing 492 West Indian skilled workers[4] landed at Tilbury Docks on June 22, 1948. In the intervening years, these two events achieved mythic status. Each encodes a story of what it is to be British. When the abuses of the hostile environment policy came to light, the accident of this shared anniversary provoked vigorous analysis of the state of the nation both at home and in relation to the Commonwealth nations.[5] Commentators located the policy as part of a living, extended, and embodied negotiation to determine who belongs, how.

Among those who found significance in these intersecting anniversaries was Wolverhampton native Patrick Vernon, who led the campaign to establish a national Windrush Day and raised funds for Wilson's commemorative blue plaque. He saw the Windrush scandal as part of Powell's legacy: "He arguably was at the origin of the genealogy of the 'hostile environment' adopted by Theresa May, first as Home Secretary and then Prime Minster, whereby the Windrush generation and their children were seen as easy targets for deportation by the government."[6]

Guy Hewitt added an international perspective. High Commissioner of Barbados from September 2014 to October 2018, he represented the West Indian Commonwealth and the diaspora. In a speech marking the 184th anniversary of the abolition of slavery in the British Empire, this self-described "Caribritish" child of Windrush placed Powell's speech amidst other notable events that forced a national reassessment of what it meant to be British: "In 2018, on the 70th anniversary of the arrival [of] the Empire Windrush, on the 50th anniversary ... of Enoch Powell's odious 'rivers of blood' speech, on the 25th anniversary of the murder of Stephen Lawrence, the incontrovertible truth is that Britain appears ill at ease with matters of race and migration."[7] Now at last, he proposes, the scandal may heal this dis-ease: "Perhaps Windrush will provide the opportunity to finally bring this multicultural society together and eliminate the boundaries of intolerance, discrimination and cultural denigration that constitute the legacy of that horrific past, and in the process give birth to a truly united kingdom."[8]

Following their lead, I treat Powell's speech as a culturally productive moment containing the seeds of the 2018 scandal that repudiated his views. That April, H. C. Hewitt, intrigued by former Canadian diplomat Daryl Copeland's vision of a nimble "guerrilla diplomacy" unconstrained by the strict protocols of state-to-state relations, formed a coalition to contest government policy. Together, West Indian diplomats, British politicians, journalists, and civil society leaders staged acts of resistance: press conferences, media interviews, political speeches, and newspaper articles constituted an informal discursive field of official and extra-governmental cultural interventions that spoke back to Powell's legacy in institutionalized racism and called audience members to summon history, engage the action, reshape the plot, and transform Windrush victims into survivors. Like Paulette's blue plaque, these stagings in the discursive field depend on, yet shift how the (historical) constructs (buildings or ideas) they overwrite perform. Inspired by Judith Butler, I ask: "What is the performative power of calling for freedom ... when the one or the 'we' who calls has been radically *dis*enfranchised from making such a call, when the 'we' who makes the call reterritorializes the term from its operation within dominant discourse precisely in order to counter the effects of that group's marginalization?"[9] I suggest that the Windrush scandal coalition—with Windrush victims—engaged in just such a reterritorialization of Powell's legacy.

Sedimented Histories: The Territory

The Windrush Generation: Clear Sailing?

As the *Empire Windrush* steamed toward Tilbury, its passengers—like all subjects of the British crown—were secure in their legal right to enter and settle in the motherland. Officially, it was "the practice of the United Kingdom not to make any distinction between different races in British colonies as regards civil and political rights, or the right of entry into and residence in the United Kingdom."[10] This welcoming metropolitan vision of the imperial center shaped Britain's postwar policy even as dominance over its far-flung territories waned. In 1946, Canada created its own national citizenship; in 1947, India, Pakistan, and Ceylon won independence and followed suit. This harbinger of the end of Empire prompted the British to adapt: in order to maintain a global footprint, they reconfigured the Empire as the British Commonwealth and—through the 1948 British Nationality Act—created two categories of British citizenship: one for newly independent Commonwealth countries; one for the remaining colonies and the United Kingdom. All enjoyed the same rights.[11] Amelia Gentleman, the *Guardian* journalist who broke the story of Paulette Wilson, writes that between 1948 and 1958 "around 115,000 people, mostly single men ... arrived in London from the West Indies."[12] This first Windrush generation justifiably considered themselves to be British, as did the wives and children who came later.[13]

Crosswinds: Mixed Messages

From the start, the British Nationality Act generated controversy. The 1948 parliamentary debates that preceded its passage inaugurated an ongoing "trauma about citizenship, race and nationality which swiftly became associated with the arrival of Caribbean immigrants."[14] Home Secretary James Chuter Ede bluntly stated: "Some ... feel that it is wrong to have a citizenship of the United Kingdom and Colonies. Some people feel that it would be a bad thing to give the coloured races of the

Empire the idea that ... they are the equals of people in this country." Labour, he claimed, "do not subscribe to that view." Instead, Clement Atlee's government held that "the common citizenship of the United Kingdom and Colonies is an essential part of the development of the relationship between this Mother Country and the Colonies." They "recognise the right of the colonial peoples to be regarded as men and brothers with the people of this country." A few moments later, however, without evident irony, Ede invokes an imperialist paradigm to support this landmark change: Treating these "backward peoples" as citizens, he avers, will help Britain "raise" them to a level that justifies a "grant of full self-government."[15] But what if these "backward peoples," many of whom had enlisted to fight for Britain in the Second World War, rather than seeking advancement in the colonies, again answered the mother country's call—this time a call for workers to rebuild a country devastated by war? In 1948 and well after the Nationality Act became law, for those white Britons who viewed themselves as racially superior to non-white colonial subjects, an influx of Black immigrants, entitled by citizenship to equal rights, was unsettling.[16]

Indeed, anxiety about the West Indian presence dates from before the *Windrush* set sail. Amelia Gentleman describes the consternation news of its imminent arrival generated in official circles. West Indian passengers debarking at Tilbury noted the difference between their wartime reception as Royal Air Force (RAF) volunteers and as postwar immigrants. Racial tensions played out in everyday acts of discrimination that denied them housing or service.[17] They contributed essential labor and expertise to establishing London Transport, British Rail, and the National Health Service, but encountered hostility and violence when the economy and job market faltered. Within a decade, Hewitt observes, "anti-immigrant sentiment turned migration into a political issue."[18] That issue played out along the fault line Ede identified, dividing those who supported treating the "coloured races of the Empire" as "equals of people in this country" from those who did not. The politics were difficult: How could Britain resolve the contradiction between their openly celebrated promise of equality and fair play with the view—as historian David Adetayo Olusoga claims—"that Britishness is the same as whiteness":

> The great dilemma they faced was that any act that put limits on migration of British subjects from all parts of the empire would inevitably limit the movement of white people from the "white dominions" [Australia, Canada, New Zealand, South Africa]. Whereas draft legislation that overtly targeted the black and brown people would damage Britain's standing in the world and undermine the creation of the Commonwealth.[19]

The solution involved a complicated dance: According to political scientist Robert Ford, by the 1960s, the public was strongly against Black and Asian immigration. Policymakers were more liberal, or at least refrained from bringing race into national campaigns.[20] They tenuously balanced their constituencies' competing demands by passing a series of measures that sharply restricted non-white immigration while also enacting antidiscrimination protections for the Black and Asian immigrants already settled in Britain. Throughout, they scrupulously avoided open discussion of popular racial prejudice, in part, Ford concludes, to prevent offending the Commonwealth nations.[21] Into this relative silence, just as the Commons prepared to debate additional antidiscrimination legislation,[22] Enoch Powell launched his provocation.

Powell's Incitement Theatre

On April 20, 1968, MP Powell delivered what he called the "Birmingham Speech" to a meeting of West Midlands Conservatives at Birmingham's Midland Hotel. Its popular name, "Rivers of Blood," derives from its content—its substance and imagery—and its intent. Patrick Vernon distills Powell's message against uncontrolled immigration of permanent settlers: "There should be stringent targets for the numbers of black and brown people and a repatriation policy put in place: otherwise … the country [will] descend into a race/civil war."[23] A deliberately performative articulation of ethnonationalism, the speech captured the racial anxieties circulating through the populace, targeted Black British subjects, and opened the door to full-throated calls for their repatriation. The effects were widely distributed and enduring.

Despite his demurrals, Powell designed the speech to be incendiary. He prepared by asking family friend Clement Jones, editor of the Wolverhampton *Express & Star*, how to optimize press coverage. Using Clem's expert advice—provide an embargoed script to select outlets, highlight quotable passages, schedule the event on a Saturday afternoon so coverage will extend from Saturday through Monday morning—Powell elevated a 45-minute local address into a national event that sent shock waves through conversations on race and put immigration center stage. According to Jones family lore, although he refused to disclose the subject matter, he told Clem, "you know how a rocket goes up into the air, breaks up and explodes into lots of stars and then falls down to the ground. Well, this speech is going to go up like a rocket, and when it gets to the top, the stars are going to stay up."[24] It fulfilled that promise: "[It] was applauded by attendees and divided the nation."[25]

Powell did not escape unscathed: The speech rendered him persona non grata in some circles while elevating him to cultural icon in others. He was a prominent member of the Conservative Party, the defense secretary in Edward Heath's shadow cabinet. Heath stripped him of that role and issued a statement that recognized the performative effect of Powell's words: "I have told Mr. Powell that I consider the speech he made in Birmingham yesterday to have been racialist in tone, and liable to exacerbate racial tensions."[26] Heath's condemnation energized those who agreed with Powell. *Guardian* journalist Mark Sweney reports, "thousands of workers staged strikes and marches in support of Powell's views."[27] Some drafted petitions to protest his demotion. Others marched against him, but, overall, polls suggested that Powell had spoken for the white majority.[28] Over a decade later, Clement Jones encapsulated the speech's impact: "Powell struck the match which lit the fuse which caused the explosion which made racism acceptable to many people; crystallised the unspoken fear of many, and structured racism into British society."²⁹ Robert Ford confirms that "Powell's intervention was the first step in a lasting alignment on immigration and race."³⁰ Recognizing its persistent cultural/political importance, in 2018 the BBC curated a special event to mark the fiftieth anniversary: They would broadcast the speech in full on Radio 4—a first on UK radio— read by actor Ian McDiarmid who had played Powell in Christopher Hannan's play *What Shadows*. Pushback was immediate. The emotive power of the speech was too great. It was, Labour Peer Andrew Adonis protested, "the worst incitement to racial violence by a public figure in modern Britain."³¹ The presenter, however, BBC media editor Amol Rajan, argued that they had taken measures to defuse its presumed effects. They would disrupt the speech with commentary by scholars and the presenter himself.³² Like their critics, they assumed its potency if left to unroll unimpeded.

As the BBC fracas attests, "Rivers of Blood" did not simply describe a state of affairs. It transformed them, established a new paradigm, and restructured a discursive field that extends in its effects to the present day. Powell "struck a match" that set off a reaction that shifted ways of thinking and speaking. Patrick Vernon traces a direct line from the original address to attitudes that inform the policies that ensnared Paulette Wilson fifty years later.³³ If, as Jones asserts, the explosion Powell engineered "structured racism into British society," today the speech and its legacy call for multiple reciprocal interventions countering its effects. What might successful interventions look like? One way of answering that question goes through the speech itself. What is its appeal?

The Original Performance, April 20, 1968³⁴

As he begins his address, Powell takes care to position himself as a caring and farseeing representative of the people. In that role, he cues listeners to imagine situations his constituents describe in their letters. These scenes personalize harms to individuals (coded as white) from the working and lower classes and establish the narrative: Immigrants and immigration (coded as non-white) have negatively affected their neighborhoods, quality of life, and employment opportunities. The speech calls us to identify with anonymous little persons who are being disadvantaged and displaced by the alien other. Unable to affect governmental policies that privilege newcomers from foreign lands (current and former British colonies!), they are forced by poverty to live in close proximity to strangers whose cultural practices disrupt their own habits or offend their beliefs. Because these personages are anonymous, audience members can cast the roles by drawing from their own experiences or place themselves in Powell's scenarios. The technique relies on his selection of informants whose circumstances spark identification. Thus, words he attributes to an unnamed male constituent—"a decent, ordinary fellow Englishman"—activate fears that dominant culture (coded in racialized terms) is eroding. Worse, the balance of power is shifting: "In this country in 15 or 20 years' time the black man will have the whip hand over the white man."[35] The remedy, he argues, is to end immigration and encourage repatriation. Finally, in the oft-quoted passage that gives the speech its popular name, he assumes a new role, claiming classical authority to raise the specter of civil war: "Like the Roman, I seem to see 'the River Tiber foaming with much blood.'"[36]

Here, as throughout the speech, Powell's language prompts the audience to form a mental image of the action. "Foaming with much blood" evokes scenes of mass violence spilling into waterways, polluting the polity; "the black man will have the whip hand over the white man" signals physical dominance, degradation, and active violence. Zeroing in on tactics he believed had ensured Powell's words would "go over the heads of the liberal intellectuals" and strike home with the popular audience, cultural theorist Stuart Hall singled out images like "Piccaninnies" and "excrement through the letterboxes" as "deeply repugnant." Capturing the effect of what I've described as Powell's "incitement theatre," Hall adds: "His imagery is adapted to that base level appeal, it's not intended to be thought about rationally or intellectually."[37] A widely reported incident a day later confirmed that the tactic awakened empathy with the figures summoned through what historian Shirin Hirsch describes as "the ventriloquism of Powell's public voice."[38] As he left services at the Collegiate Church of St. Peter, Wolverhampton, another congregant affirmed his message: "Well done sir. It needed to be said."[39] Hirsch's astute description of Powell's technique as "ventriloquism" emphasizes its theatricality, the room it leaves open to his [mis]interpretation as he renders another's words. Even so, as this encounter reveals, that very ventriloquism produces real effects in real people. This relationship between the theatrical and the real emerges fully in the speech's wake. In her richly detailed account of the local scene, Hirsch observes that "in the weeks and months that followed … it seemed as if the racial contours, which had already been present within Wolverhampton, were suddenly strengthened through their reformulation."[40] Nationally, historian Robert Gildea comments, "the virulence of anti-immigration rhetoric was taken up in working-class communities and injected a new element of violence into local race relations."[41] For individual West Indians, the speech produced a visceral change as well: "I remember the sudden, shared feeling of fear, the huddling together against the impending violence," Stuart Hall writes, "the unspoken aggression in the streets as little groups of black men and women came together to discuss how to respond to the violence it seemed calculated to unleash."[42] That fear deeply marked its potential targets, as Mike Phillips attests in his obituary of Powell: "His memory will probably have me looking over my shoulder in the streets of my own city, London, for the rest of my life … I shall always think of him as part of my history and as part of my identity."[43]

Striking Back: Reterritorializing British Identity

I have argued that Powell's "Rivers of Blood" speech encoded the negative attitudes toward non-white immigration that haunted the Nationality Act in 1948 and divided Britain in 1968. Stuart Hall and Mike Phillips recognize their lasting effects on individuals; the Windrush scandal confirmed their virulence when enacted as government policy, their power to cast Black

Britons into a state of precarity, stripped of legitimately earned rights. The remedy, I suggest, was a strategy that treated the public as an audience to a discursive field that extends from the days of colonial slavery through 1948 and 1968 to the present. The Windrush coalition placed Paulette and others similarly targeted center field. In that scene, just as Judith Butler has proposed, "the word that wounds becomes an instrument of resistance in the redeployment that destroys the prior territory of its operation."[44] As a performance, their staging of the scandal played against Powell's speech and figuratively—that is, theatrically—redeployed words that wound to restore rights the state had wrongly denied.

Paulette Wilson joined the Windrush generation as a child, arriving by plane in 1968, the same year the representative for Wolverhampton South West, Enoch Powell, launched his attack on immigrants and urged repatriation. Her journey to becoming a nationally respected Windrush campaigner began more than forty years later with a brutally worded letter from the Home Office that declared her "a person who has failed to provide evidence of lawful entry to the United Kingdom" and warned that "if you do not leave the United Kingdom as required you will be liable to enforced removal to Jamaica … If you decide to stay then your life in the UK will become increasingly more difficult."[45] The threat was real; policies were in place to ensure dire outcomes. The letter, Paulette said, "made me feel like I didn't exist."[46]

In fact, Wendy Williams's official *Windrush Lessons Learned Review* determined that Paulette and others were caught in a trap of the government's making. The 1948 Nationality Act had assured citizens of the UK and Colonies of their welcome in the mother country. By 1962, that welcome had cooled. Despite worries over relations with Commonwealth nations, "successive rounds of immigration legislation in the 1960s, 70s and 80s, some of which have been recognized and were accepted at the time to have had racial motivations,"[47] had restricted Commonwealth citizens' rights to settle in Britain. In the process, these policies performatively produced changes in British identity. Only a few years after Powell prophesied the race war that would arise from Black settlement in the UK, the 1971 Immigration Act closed the door to additional large-scale non-white immigration. To do so, it ended what historian Ian R. G. Spencer calls the "old Empire-embracing concept of British subject or citizen," and introduced "essentially racially-defined categories of 'patrial' and 'non-patrial'" that weakened non-white and strengthened white rights to immigrate from the Commonwealth.[48] Looking forward, it appeared that Britishness would be reaffirmed as whiteness.

Even so, Mike and Trevor Phillips remind us that, just as Powell fueled anti-immigrant sentiment, he also inspired a burgeoning anti-racist resistance.[49] Moreover, the West Indian community was well-established and multigenerational. Consequently, at the second reading of the proposed 1971 Immigration Act, Home Secretary Reginald Maudling took pains to insist that the legislation achieved a balance between restricting future settlement while respecting the rights of the immigrant community. Williams reports: "The 1971 Immigration Act entitled people who had arrived from Commonwealth countries before January 1973 to the 'right of abode' or 'deemed leave' to remain in the UK. But the government gave them no documents to demonstrate this status. Nor did it keep records. This, in essence, set the trap for the Windrush generation."[50] Some had arrived as children traveling on a relative's passport; others lost their original paperwork. Not having an immediate need for proof of citizenship, others did not realize they could/should apply for documentation.[51] The trap waited, ready to snap shut. Like Paulette, many who qualified for the right to remain were unaware that their status was at risk until their employer fired them, their doctor refused to treat them under free NHS coverage, or the Home Office suddenly threatened them. Long after passage of the 1971 Immigration Act, they found that, absent government documentation, officialdom mis-recognized them, redefined them as illegal, not truly British. Mis-identified by the state, in order to "counter the effects,"[52] they would need to claim and redeploy their British citizenship against it.

Indeed, declaring that the Windrush migrants had the right of abode while failing to document all who were eligible to remain created the conditions for the misrecognition and misidentification that ensnared Paulette and others. Did this failure stem from incompetence? Inadequate resources? Ignorance of the constituency at risk? Institutional racism? Whatever the cause, failure to record their status thereby ensuring their inability to continue performing citizenship under the law created an opening for the state to performatively recast them as alien players in a long-running "state of the nation" drama. Wendy Williams's *Review* established the given circumstances: "Political pressure to deal with the perceived problem of immigration continued through the 1990s and into the 2000s, leading to the 'hostile environment' (later the 'compliant environment'), a set of measures that evolved under the Labour, Coalition and Conservative Governments. They aimed to make life as difficult as possible for people with no legal status in the UK to encourage them to leave."[53] The policy rhymes with Enoch Powell's 1968 demand that the Conservative Party encourage legal Black Commonwealth migrants to repatriate. Like Powell's intervention, it considers public opinion against immigration with an eye on electoral politics. But whereas Powell proposed that the government offer "generous assistance" to legal migrants who "would choose either to return to their countries of origin or to go to other countries anxious to receive the manpower and the skills they represent,"[54] May pledges "to create here in Britain a really hostile environment" not for legal, but for illegal migrants.[55] Both politicians engage an implicitly racialized discourse of belonging; however, their strategies—assistance versus hostility—reflect the difference between citizen and alien as the object of their action. Promising to reduce net migration to the UK, May and her colleagues devised a comprehensive system that transformed Britain into a barren landscape for illegal migrants—or for those misidentified as illegal.

The hostile environment deprived its targets of every means of surviving in Britain: Because its policies require employers, bankers, landlords, and medical professionals to verify legal status before hiring or providing services,[56] members of the Windrush generation who lacked adequate documentation lost jobs, pensions, housing, and access to free health care despite having worked and paid taxes for decades. Traps littered the landscape, ready to be sprung.[57] Once wrongly identified, they found themselves in a nightmare scenario, endlessly searching for documentation that would satisfy home office demands for proof of their legal presence under the terms of the 1971 Immigration Act. In this system, the state conscripts the public as its agents to carry out the everyday activity of defining the contours of the community. The state penetrates the civil domain. Society effectively polices itself, identifying and expelling putative outsiders. But while diverse social actors were enlisted in enforcing home office rules, the general public remained largely unaware of the way the policy was misfiring, destroying lives in the Windrush generation.[58]

For Paulette, the home office threats proved real: "Despite having worked and paid taxes for decades, she lost her state benefits and was no longer allowed to work in the UK. As a result, she was unable to buy food regularly and started eating meals at the homelessness centre where she had previously volunteered as a chef."[59] She was arrested twice, detained, and came perilously close to being deported. Her experience was not unique. She was the first, however, to go public: By raising her voice, she became the first to provide a reciprocal intervention repudiating Powell. On November 28, 2017, investigative journalist Amelia Gentleman published her story in the *Guardian*. It opened the floodgates. Others came forward, emboldened by the knowledge that they were not alone, someone would listen. The second story, Anthony Bryan's, appeared after his son convinced him to speak with Gentleman. Over the next few months, the public face of the problem literally took shape as Gentleman and the *Guardian* reported individual experiences—accompanied by professionally shot color portraits—in paper and virtually through worldwide access to its site. Paulette's action was the essential first step: "It is possible," Gentleman wrote, "that if Paulette had not overcome her reservations about talking to the media, the Windrush scandal would have continued to remain hidden."[60] Once begun, Paulette campaigned for justice until her death.[61]

Instruments of Resistance: Guerrilla Diplomats and Allies "Swim like Fish"

I set out to treat Powell's "Rivers of Blood" as a culturally productive moment that contained the seeds of its own repudiation. Fifty years later, I proposed, diverse social and political actors—like Paulette—rebutted Powell's legacy whether manifested in institutionalized racism or support for repatriation. Joining together in an informal coalition, they fomented what became known as the Windrush scandal. They answered Powell's fear-soaked evocation of a race-driven civil war with vivid narratives describing the Windrush generation's contributions to Britain. Against his emotionally charged ventriloquism, they set individuals telling their own stories. Keeping the audience to the discursive field in view, they relied on the theatricality of each appearance to focus attention on and valorize each person as a citizen of today's multiracial Britain. Critically, in a paradigm-shifting move, they borrowed a model of diplomacy from a former Canadian diplomat who argues that today's digital world requires a new "guerrilla" statecraft: "Guided by the principle of bringing the outside in and turning the inside out, our guerrilla diplomats would have to swim like fish in territorial waters as well as the high seas and engage energetically on the home front as well."[62]

And so, in a fitting reversal of power, representatives of Britain's former colonies initiated the crisis that—like Powell's 1968 speech—brought Britain's ambivalence toward its Black residents into sharp focus. The Windrush scandal broke on April 12, 2018. It was, H. C. Hewitt tells us, not accidental, but rather the result of a deliberate campaign. High commissioners and foreign ministers of the Caribbean nations had protested Britain's policies, without effect. They decided to raise the issue at the London meeting of the Commonwealth Heads of Government. Because appeals through traditional diplomatic channels had not borne fruit, H. C. Hewitt abandoned the strictly state-centric approach and moved toward civic engagement. He explains: "I was drawn to the work of Daryl Copeland on 'guerrilla diplomacy' that combined 'the sensibility and street smarts of a world traveller, the knowledge of a new age polymath, and the enterprising spirit of an entrepreneur [with] ... the practice of traditional diplomacy itself."[63] In that spirit, he worked with the former head of the Commission on Racial Equality (CRE), Lord Herman Ousley, to "form ... a 'coalition of the willing'" that included Commonwealth diplomats, British parliamentarians, *Guardian* journalists, and civil society leaders. They reached out to other Caribbean high commissioners and allies ranging from the Commissioner for Human Rights at the Council of Europe to the Church of England to "Caribbean students' associations"—each of them linked to the Windrush generation whether by their relation to the diaspora or by their concern with human rights, racial equality, or immigration and assimilation.[64] By enlisting state and non-state, international and domestic stakeholders in their cause, Hewitt and his colleagues not only added powerful advocates, but they freed discussions from the confines of traditional bilateral or even multilateral negotiations. That freedom allowed them to "engage energetically on the home front" by addressing the public directly.[65]

On April 12, just days before the 2018 Commonwealth Summit was to convene, Hewitt and his colleagues inaugurated a series of public-facing events. The campaign that ignited the scandal officially began with a press briefing that introduced Britain to the situation: "I am dismayed that people who gave their all to Britain could be discarded so matter-of-factly," Hewitt observed. "Seventy years after Windrush, we are again facing a new wave of hostility. This is about people saying, as they said seventy years ago, 'Go back home.' It's not good enough for people who gave their lives to this country to be treated like this."[66] Enoch Powell had "lit the fuse which caused the explosion that made racism acceptable to many people." Now the coalition identified the enemy, gathered its allies, and returned fire.

Media outlets—among them Channel 4 News, ITV, and the BBC—broadcast interviews with victims and coalition members. David Jessop credited Hewitt's appearance on BBC Radio's "Today" show with having "turned the issue into a front-page story for a week in every single British newspaper" and "the lead item on every radio and television news programme."[67] Worse followed. News that Prime Minister Theresa May had declined to meet with Caribbean leaders fueled the flames. By April 16, she had found time on her calendar. On April 17, a *Guardian* report that the home office had ordered the destruction of landing cards that would have confirmed when individuals of the Windrush generation had entered the country further undermined May's leadership.[68] All told, the affair resulted in the home secretary's resignation, repeated apologies from the prime minister, Wendy Williams's highly critical *Windrush Lessons Learned Review*, and commitments to compensate victims and put them on a pathway to citizenship. It also overwhelmed the Caribbean summit, swamping, then scuttling the British government's plans to use the meeting to strengthen its relations with Commonwealth nations as trading partners in anticipation of Britain's exit from the European Union.[69] The fear of offending Commonwealth members that long had haunted debates over immigration was realized in a foreign policy disaster.

Agents of Change: "Likkle but Tallawah"[70]

In their coauthored piece on the Windrush affair, H. C. Hewitt and his colleague, St. Kitts & Nevis High Commissioner Kevin M. Isaac, wrote that the scandal "showed that small Commonwealth states can also become their own agents of change."[71] In doing so, they implicitly addressed Powell's legacy and the message he delivered on April 20, 1968. Now, "facing a new wave of hostility," Hewitt asserted, the coalition successfully promoted what Mike and Trevor Phillips termed the "wholesale reassessment" of Britishness. As Powell intended, "Rivers of Blood" had reverberated throughout Britain: The rocket went up and the stars stayed up. Its message and phrases still circulate, sparking strong emotions, fit for use by political parties and activists. Fifty years later, the Windrush coalition deliberately engaged the deeply embedded, often denied, racism that the speech—in Clem Jones's words—"structured into British society." They entered the informally constituted discursive field to rewrite it. Whereas Powell's speech inflamed debate and divided the nation, Hewitt and his allies sought to unify the nation in supporting the Caribbean diaspora. Copeland's concept of guerilla diplomacy gave them the tools: it inspired them to look beyond state actors to forge partnerships that ensured wide distribution of their message throughout civil society. Most important, they addressed the nation directly through newspapers, media, personal appearances, and face-to-face advocacy in Westminster, fully exploiting what performance studies scholar James R. Ball describes as the "inherent theatricality" of each occasion to make it "legible, meaningful, and efficacious."[72] In their hands, guerrilla tactics awakened resistance to racist abuse and Powell's characterization of the victimized, "decent, ordinary Englishman." Instead, they demonstrated that decent, (extra)ordinary Paulette Wilson—like many others—was the victim.

Even before the Windrush coalition formed, Amelia Gentleman was mapping the territory. Between November 2017 and April 2018, the *Guardian* published interviews with Paulette and nearly twenty others. Their stories rendered the abstractions of the hostile environment into flesh and bone, actual harms perpetrated on specific individuals. They were not, as Powell purported, undeserving beneficiaries of British largesse, rude children, and thieves of working-class education and healthcare. Rather they were hardworking, taxpaying Britons. Their color portraits, each shot in a setting specific to them—perhaps in their home or yard—were especially effective in connecting the newspaper's vast online audience to each individual. Gentleman remembers, "the large photograph of Paulette, looking worried and vulnerable, made people want to reach out to support her."[73] By April 2018, when the *Guardian* published them as a group to coincide with the Windrush campaign, they told the distressing tale of an unresolved, still expanding, collective tragedy.[74]

As the Windrush scandal unfolded, its victims literally took the stage in the discursive field where belonging, race, and citizenship intersect. Powell had ventriloquized his anonymous letter writers, filtering their words to suit his purpose. He attributes only one word, "Racialist," to immigrants. Paulette Wilson, Anthony Bryan, and others speak for themselves. They articulate themselves as fully human subjects with family, friends, and a lifelong identity as British. Media interviews brought their profiles to life. When the scandal erupted, ITV's "Good Morning Britain" introduced viewers to two friends, Sonia Williams and Glenda Caesar, who lost jobs and were kept out of work, but were too embarrassed to confide in one another. They had done nothing wrong; they lacked paperwork and were told they were not British. When interviewers Piers Morgan and Susanna Reid ask how that made them feel, viewers may well join Morgan when he asserts, "You're as British as I am."[75] On another morning, Anthony Bryan's appearance with his son, Dijoun, rounded out his role within a multigenerational family. His troubles began because he needed a passport to visit his ailing mother in Jamaica. Dijoun asks how he can be British while his father is not. His care for Anthony invites onlookers to care as well.[76] More officially, Parliament's Human Rights Committee asked Paulette Wilson and Anthony Bryan to describe their experiences in a hearing that made national news and still lives on its website.[77] There Baroness Doreen Lawrence asked them whether they thought race had been a factor in their mistreatment. The answer—yes—closed the link between her son Stephen's murder and the Windrush scandal: In both instances, unacknowledged institutional racism deprived victims of their legal rights.[78] The scene draws power from its rootedness in a discursive field that interweaves present and past, where the Windrush scandal generates meanings both from and for Baroness Lawrence's unrelenting campaign for justice. Equally important, their very presence in this setting responds to the "base-level appeal" Stuart Hall identified in "Rivers of Blood" imagery. Powell conjured children intimidating a white neighbor; here two mature adults soberly recount their experiences. A family member who fought for them sits by their side. Each pair stages a longstanding, devoted partnership. Constellated with Baroness Lawrence, the group embodies the value the West Indian diaspora contributes to multiracial Britain.

As part of the larger guerrilla-inspired strategy of bringing the outside in and turning the inside out, placing Windrush victims in relation to Baroness Lawrence served the project of reterritorializing Powell's legacy and re-enfranchising Windrush victims. Former outsiders were welcomed to the halls of power. Victims became survivors became activists the media recognized and covered. Insiders, well-placed coalition members and their allies, turned their efforts outward. Parliamentarians, mobilizing the inherent theatricality of that platform, spoke to their colleagues, knowingly addressing a national and international audience through performances the internet and YouTube immortalize. The House of Commons became the stage for deposing the powerful. In a debate on immigration policy, Paulette Wilson's MP, the representative for Wolverhampton North East, Emma Reynolds, critiqued a home office that could not supply official records yet expected those it targets to document their lives after the fact.[79] The incompetence of government functionaries was evident. And from his position on the House of Commons back benches, MP for Tottenham David Lammy "shook the walls of Westminster"[80] with a succinct, impassioned speech that demanded an accounting of the rights violated under the hostile environment policy from Home Secretary Amber Rudd after reminding her and those assembled that, "despite slavery, despite colonization," West Indians had served Britain loyally in two world wars and the Windrush generation had migrated to Britain as citizens under the 1948 Nationality Act.[81] Lammy's words, coupled with his actions and stature as a Black British MP, forcefully rebutted Powell's message and legacy. He reinscribed the Windrush generation and their children in British history, insisting on their central role in defining national identity.

The scandal reverberates still. Resolution of individual cases has been slow. Windrush activists have called for an independent body to replace the home office as the adjudicator of individual citizenship claims and monetary compensation.[82] Although the struggle continues, the April scandal laid bare institutional abuses of power and succeeded in revitalizing discussions of Britain as a multiracial nation. Equally important, the Windrush coalition's implementation of guerrilla diplomacy provides welcome inspiration to those aiming to reverse the radical disenfranchisement of the marginalized. Here the record is mixed: Paulette Wilson died before the state compensated her for her suffering; Wolverhampton and the nation, however, honor her legacy. "Likkle but Tallawah" she entered British history, changed it, and calls others to that work by her example.

Notes

1 James Vukmirovic, "Paulette Wilson: Windrush Campaigner's Life Honoured with Ceremony and Plaque," *Express & Star,* June 22, 2021, https://www.expressandstar.com/news/local-hubs/wolverhampton/whitmore-reans/2021/06/22/paulette-wilson-windrush-campaigners-life-honoured-with-ceremony-and-plaque/ (accessed April 21, 2022).
2 Enoch Powell, "Enoch Powell's 'Rivers of Blood' Speech," April 20, 1968, https://anth1001.files.wordpress.com/2014/04/enoch-powell_speech.pdf (accessed April 21, 2022).
3 Mike Phillips and Trevor Phillips, *Windrush: The Irresistible Rise of Multi-Racial Britain* (London: HarperCollins, 1998), 6.
4 Sam King, Interview in Phillips and Phillips, *Windrush*, 59–60.
5 Guy Hewitt and Kevin M. Isaac, "Windrush: The Perfect Storm," *Social and Economic Studies,* 67, nos. 2, 3 (2018): 293+; link.gale.com/apps/doc/A568371835/AONE?u=tall85761&sid=bookmark-AONE&xid=a9aca4f2 (accessed April 23, 2022). Gale Academic onefile.
6 Patrick Vernon, "Many Rivers to Cross: The Legacy of Enoch Powell in Wolverhampton," in *Windrush (1948) and "Rivers of Blood" (1968): Legacy and Assessment*, ed. Trevor Harris (Milton Park: Routledge, 2019), 47, https://web-s-ebscohost-com.proxy.lib.fsu.edu/ehost/detail?sid=72d7072f-41f0-4fbf-8287-879465699d0e%40redis&vid=0&format=EB#AN=2279581&db=nlebk (accessed April 22, 2022).
7 Stephen Lawrence was a Black British teen killed in a racist attack in southeast London on April 22, 1993. Although an informant identified

his probable killers within days, and despite repeated efforts to bring them to justice, no one was convicted of the crime until 2012. The reasons for this failure were the subject of an official inquiry led by Sir William Macpherson. Issued in February 1999, *The Stephen Lawrence Inquiry* report identified "institutional racism" as a fundamental cause. The report defined the concept and recommended seventy actions to eradicate racist policies and practices not only in the Metropolitan Police force, but throughout government institutions. See Ben Quinn, "Macpherson Report: What Was It and What Impact Did It Have?" *Guardian*, UK Edition, February 22, 2019, https://www.theguardian.com/uk-news/2019/feb/22/macpherson-report-what-was-it-and-what-impact-did-it-have (accessed April 21, 2022).

8 Guy Hewitt, "Windrush Is a Chance to End British Intolerance Dating from Slavery," *Guardian*, UK Edition, August 1, 2018, https://www.theguardian.com/commentisfree/2018/aug/01/windrush-scandal-shows-britain-ill-ease-race-migration (accessed April 21, 2022).

9 Judith Butler, *Excitable Speech: A Politics of the Performative* (New York and London: Routledge, 1997), 158.

10 155 Parl. Deb., H. L. (5th Ser.) (1948) 795 (UK). Quoted without explicit attribution by Viscount [William Allen] Jowitt, then Lord Chancellor, in the British Nationality Act Debate, May 11, 1948, https://hansard.parliament.uk/lords/1948-05-11/debates/099d80fc-0cde-4e0c-956e-636dc7f86ac2/BritishNationalityBillHl#795 (accessed April 23, 2022). Ian R. G. Spencer attributes the statement to W. Ormsby-Gore at the 1937 League of Nations. See *British Immigration Policy Since 1939: The Making of Multiracial Britain* (London and New York: Routledge, 1997), 54, 172.

11 Phillips and Phillips, *Windrush*, 73–4.

12 Amelia Gentleman, *The Windrush Betrayal: Exposing the Hostile Environment* (London: Guardian Faber, 2019), 104. For annual numbers, 1948–71, see Guy Hewitt, "The Windrush Scandal: An Insider's Reflection," *Caribbean Quarterly* 66, no. 1 (2020): 113, doi: 10.1080/00086495.2020.1722378, https://web-s-ebscohost-com.proxy.lib.fsu.edu/ehost/pdfviewer/pdfviewer?vid=0&sid=3d68fd5e-132d-4f9e-86ff-e4a491962812%40redis (accessed April 23, 2022).

13 Although "Windrush generation" strictly applies to the first postwar West Indian arrivals, usage typically includes those who came after, including

their children, many of whom travelled on a relative's passport. Lacking their own passports, the latter—pensioners today—are the group often caught in the hostile environment trap. See Gentleman, *Betrayal*, 9.

14 Phillips, and Phillips, *Windrush*, 75. Parliament was debating passage in the Commons, July 7; *Windrush* docked on June 22.

15 453 Parl. Deb. H.C. (5th Ser.) (1948) 393–395, 398 (UK), https://api.parliament.uk/historic-hansard/commons/1948/jul/07/british-nationality-bill-lords#column_453 (accessed April 21, 2022).

16 Phillips, and Phillips, *Windrush*, 74.

17 Gentleman, *Betrayal*, 96–104; Hewitt, "Windrush Scandal," 113–14.

18 Hewitt, "Windrush Scandal," 115.

19 David Olusoga, "Windrush: Archived Documents Show the Long Betrayal," *Guardian*, UK Edition, June 16, 2019, https://www.theguardian.com/uk-news/2019/jun/16/windrush-scandal-the-long-betrayal-archived-documents-david-olusoga (accessed April 21, 2022).

20 Robert Ford, "Powell and After: Immigration, Race and Politics in Britain," in *Lives and Afterlives of Enoch Powell: The Undying Political Animal*, eds. Olivier Esteves and Stéphane Porion (Milton Park: Routledge, 2019), 13–14, https://web-p-ebscohost-com.proxy.lib.fsu.edu/ehost/ebookviewer/ebook?sid=da03c2c1-5eb1-40c6-a212-4d2994ed8b7a%40redis&vid=0&format=EB (accessed April 23, 2022).

21 Ford, "Powell and After," 13–14.

22 For details of the 1965 and 1968 Race Relations Acts, see Jason Rodrigues, "How the Guardian Covered the Introduction of the Race Relations Act" (1965), *Guardian*, UK Edition, December 8, 2015, https://www.theguardian.com/world/from-the-archive-blog/2015/dec/08/race-relations-act-50-years-ago-1965-uk (accessed April 21, 2022).

23 Vernon, "Many Rivers to Cross," 47.

24 Clement Jones, interview, in Nicholas Jones, "Powell and the Media: An Insider's Account," in *Lives and Afterlives*, 53.

25 Mark Sweney, "BBC Under Fire over Enoch Powell 'Rivers of Blood' Broadcast," *Guardian*, April 12, 2018, https://www.theguardian.com/media/2018/apr/12/bbc-to-air-reading-of-enoch-powells-rivers-of-blood-speech (accessed April 21, 2022).

26 Ian Aitken, "Enoch Powell Dismissed after 'Racialist Speech'–Archive 1968," *Guardian*, UK Edition, April 14, 2018, https://www.theguardian.

com/world/from-the-archive-blog/2018/apr/14/enoch-powell-dismissed-speech-1968 (accessed April 21, 2022).

27 Sweney, "BBC Under Fire."
28 Ford, "Powell and After," 17.
29 Clement Jones, *Race and the Media: Thirty Years' Misunderstanding* (London: Commission for Racial Equality, [UNESCO 1980] 1982), 9. Quoted by Jones's son, Nicholas Jones, in "Powell and the Media," 59.
30 Ford, "Powell and After," 14.
31 Sinead Baker, "BBC Defends Plans to Broadcast Enoch Powell's Rivers of Blood Speech for the First Time," *Thejournal.ie*, April 13, 2018, https://www.thejournal.ie/enoch-powell-bbc-rivers-of-blood-3956266-Apr2 018/ (accessed April 21, 2022). See also Yohannes Lowe, "Rivers of Blood Contributor Demands to be Removed from BBC Show as Backlash Intensifies," *Telegraph,* April 13, 2018, https://www.telegraph.co.uk/news/2018/04/13/rivers-blood-contributors-abandon-bbc-decides-air-divisive-speech/ (accessed April 21, 2022). Listen to the program curated by Amol Rajan, "Fifty Years On: Rivers of Blood," *BBC Radio*, Archive on 4, Broadcast on April 14, 2018, https://www.bbc.co.uk/sounds/play/b09z08w3 (accessed April 21, 2022).
32 Baker, "BBC Defends Plans."
33 Vernon, "Many Rivers to Cross," 51–3.
34 The original speech was not filmed in full. Reportedly, ITV central (then ATV) and the Wolverhampton *Express & Star* received the text in advance. For Powell's performance style, see ITV News, "'Rivers of Blood' speech, 50 Years On: Setting the Scene in 1968," https://www.youtube.com/watch?v=r3QC5_efQb0 (accessed April 21, 2022).
35 Powell, "Rivers of Blood."
36 Powell is voicing Virgil's Cumaean Sibyl (*Aeneid*, book 6), who is prophesying while possessed by the god Apollo. Powell recasts himself as an implicitly male Roman. Certainly, playing a "Roman" fits the image of an MP more than a god-maddened female prophetess. Baroness Lena M. Jeger also points out that Powell takes the passage out of context. See Porion's discussion in "Conclusion," *Lives and Afterlives*, 179–80.
37 Stuart Hall, Interview in Phillips and Phillips, *Windrush*, 242.
38 Shirin Hirsch, *In the Shadow of Enoch Powell: Race, Locality and Resistance* (Manchester: Manchester University Press, 2018), 1.

39 Aitken, "Enoch Powell Dismissed."
40 Hirsch, *In the Shadow of Enoch Powell*, 49.
41 Robert Gildea, *Empires of the Mind: The Colonial Past and the Politics of the Present* (Cambridge: Cambridge University Press, 2019), 128.
42 Stuart Hall, "A Torpedo Aimed at the Boiler-Room of Consensus." *New Statesman*, April 17, 1998. In Hirsch, *In the Shadow of Enoch Powell*, 6.
43 Norman Shrapnel and Mike Phillips, "Enoch Powell: An Enigma of Awkward Passions," *Guardian*, UK Edition, February 7, 2001, https://www.theguardian.com/politics/0098/feb/09/obituaries.mikephillips (accessed April 21, 2022).
44 Butler, *Excitable Speech*, 163.
45 Amelia Gentleman, "Without Paulette Wilson, Windrush Might Have Remained Hidden," *Guardian*, UK Edition, July 24, 2020, https://www.theguardian.com/uk-news/2020/jul/24/without-paulette-wilson-windrush-may-have-remained-hidden (accessed April 21, 2022).
46 Paulette Wilson, in Gentleman, *Betrayal*, 18.
47 Wendy Williams, *Windrush Lessons Learned Review*, HC-932020-21, [n. p.] [Online, Crown copyright, printed March 19, 2020], 9, https://assets.publishing.service.gov.uk/government/uploads/system/uploads/attachment_data/file/876336/6.5577_HO_Windrush_Lessons_Learned_Review_LoResFinal.pdf (accessed December 26, 2021).
48 Spencer, *British Immigration Policy,* 143–4. For Home Secretary Reginald Maulding's comments and the March 8, 1971, debate outlining goals and issues, see 813 Parl. Deb. H.C. (1971) 42–173 (UK), https://api.parliament.uk/historic-hansard/commons/1971/mar/08/immigration-bill#SSCV08813P0_HOC_267 (accessed May 23, 2022).
49 Phillips, and Phillips, *Windrush*, 254.
50 Williams, *Lessons Learned*, 9.
51 Gentleman, *Betrayal*, 132–4. Efforts in the 1980s to register members of the community as citizens appear to have been insufficiently aggressive. See *Betrayal*, 310–11.
52 Butler, *Excitable Speech*, 158.
53 Williams, *Lessons Learned*, 9. See also, Gentleman, *Betrayal*, 309–11.
54 Powell, "Rivers of Blood."
55 Gentleman, *Betrayal*, 117. For details of hostile environment, see 117–44.
56 Gentleman, *Betrayal*, 118; Hewitt, "Windrush Scandal," 111.

57 Gentleman, *Betrayal*, 52–60. Gentleman observed that passport applications appeared to trigger investigations. Anthony Bryan indicated that community members had become aware of this pattern and were wary of any contact with the state.
58 See Gentleman, *Betrayal*, 201–2.
59 Gentleman, "Without Paulette Wilson."
60 Gentleman, "Without Paulette Wilson." An appreciation of Paulette after her death, the article links to an article highlighting fifty Windrush victims: Amelia Gentleman, "'Lambs to Slaughter': 50 Lives Ruined by the Windrush Scandal," *Guardian*, UK Edition, March 19, 2020, https://www.theguardian.com/uk-news/2020/mar/19/lambs-to-the-slaughter-50-lives-ruined-by-the-windrush-scandal (accessed April 22, 2022). For Wilson's assessment, see Amelia Gentleman, "'I'm Glad We Spoke Out': Windrush Victim Who Shone a Light on the Scandal," *Guardian*, UK Edition, May 5, 2018, https://www.theguardian.com/uk-news/2018/may/05/im-glad-we-spoke-out-windrush-victim-who-shone-a-light-on-the-scandal (accessed April 21, 2022).
61 Amelia Gentleman, "Windrush Scandal Survivors Deliver Petition to No 10," *Guardian*, UK Edition, June 20, 2020, https://www.theguardian.com/uk-news/2020/jun/19/windrush-scandal-survivors-deliver-petition-to-no-10 (accessed April 21, 2022).
62 Daryl Copeland, "Guerrilla Diplomacy: Delivering International Diplomacy in a Digital World," *Canadian Foreign Policy* 11, no. 2 (Winter 2004), 174, http://doi.org/10.1080/11926422.2004.9673371 (accessed April 22, 2022). See also https://www.guerrhladiplomacy.com/ (accessed April 22, 2022).
63 Hewitt, "Windrush Scandal," 118, quoting Daryl Copeland, *Guerrilla Diplomacy: Rethinking International Relations* (Boulder, CO: Lynne Rienner, 2009), 33.
64 For details of the campaign, see Hewitt, "Windrush Scandal," 117–23.
65 Daryl Copeland, "Guerrilla Diplomacy," 174.
66 In Gentleman, *Betrayal*, 196.
67 David Jessop, "The Case of Guy Hewitt and the UK's Caribbean Windrush Generation," *News Americas*, April 23, 2018, https://www.newsamericasnow.com/the-case-of-guy-hewitt-and-the-uks-caribbean-windrush-generation/ (accessed April 22, 2022).

68 Hewitt, "Windrush Scandal," 123. The cards had been moved to the National Archives, inaccessible for proof of immigration status.
69 Guy Hewitt discusses in "Windrush Scandal," 123. Also see Gentleman, *Betrayal*, 196. For a perspective from the Americas: David Jessop, "The Case of Guy Hewitt." For another British perspective: Ian Jack, "Britain Sees the Commonwealth as Its Trading Empire. It Is Sadly Deluded," *Guardian*, UK Edition, April 7, 2018, https://www.theguardian.com/commentisfree/2018/apr/07/britain-commonwealth-trading-empire-brexit-eu-trade (accessed April 21, 2022)
70 "Little, but Powerful"—a Jamaican saying, inscribed on Paulette Wilson's blue plaque.
71 Guy Hewitt and Kevin M. Isaac, "Windrush: The Perfect Storm," 293.
72 James R. Ball III, *Theater of State: A Dramaturgy of the United Nations* (Evanston: Northwestern University Press, 2020), 5.
73 Gentleman, *Betrayal*, 40, 212.
74 *Guardian*, "'It's Inhumane': The Windrush Victims Who Have Lost Jobs, Homes and Loved Ones," *Guardian*, UK Edition, April 20, 2018, https://www.theguardian.com/uk-news/2018/apr/20/its-inhumane-the-windrush-victims-who-have-lost-jobs-homes-and-loved-ones (accessed April 21, 2022).
75 ITV Good Morning Britain, "The Windrush Women Who Are Fighting for Their British Citizenship," Interview, Sonia Williams and Glenda Caesar, April 18, 2018, https://www.youtube.com/watch?v=Ale49EpV8lo (accessed April 21, 2022).
76 ITV Good Morning Britain, "Piers Gets Passionate Over the Windrush Scandal," Interview, Anthony Bryan and son, Dijoun Bryan, April 24, 2018, https://www.youtube.com/watch?v=o8rx2MbyxhI (accessed April 21, 2022). See also novelist Stephen S. Thompson's award-winning film based on his brother Anthony's Struggle against deportation: Sitting in Limbo, produced by LEFT BANK Pictures, directed by Stella Corradi, aired on BBC1, June 8, 2020, http://netflix.com/title/81428086 (accessed May 18, 2022).
77 Paulette Wilson, with her daughter Natalie Barnes, and Anthony Bryan, with his partner, Janet McKay, gave evidence to the joint parliamentary committee on human rights. See Parliamentlive.tv, "Subject: Detention of Windrush Generation," *Human Rights Committee*, Video, 15:13:30, May

16, 2018, https://parliamentlive.tv/Event/Index/cdf5243e-3588-4248-becf-3cf07b9d89b0 (accessed April 21, 2022).

78 Nicola Slawson, "Race Was a Big Factor in Deportation Scandal, Windrush Citizens Say," *Guardian*, UK Edition, May 16, 2018, https://www.theguardian.com/uk-news/2018/may/16/race-was-big-factor-in-deportation-scandal-windrush-citizens-say (accessed April 21, 2022). See also Zubaida Haque, "The Windrush Review Is Unequivocal: Institutional Racism Played Its Part," *Guardian*, UK Edition, March 21, 2020, https://www.theguardian.com/commentisfree/2020/mar/21/windrush-institutional-racism-hostile-environment (accessed April 21, 2022). For a history of government efforts to restrict Black Caribbean immigration underlying "hostile environment" policies, see *The Unwanted: The Secret Windrush File*, directed by Tim Kirby and James Ross, written and presented by David Olusoga, featuring Anthony Bryan, aired June 24, 2019, on BBC Two, https://www.youtube.com/watch?v=f_rzJTNZSLM (accessed April 21, 2022).

79 Emma Reynolds, "Paulette Wilson 30 Westminster Hall 30 April 2018 01 05 2018 09 42 48," *YouTube Video*, May 2, 2018, youtube.com/watch?v=AriP3JbUb3U (accessed April 21, 2022).

80 Matt Kelly, "In Praise of David Lammy," *GQ*, April 19, 2018, https://www.gq-magazine.co.uk/article/david-lammy-speech-windrush (accessed April 21, 2022).

81 ITV News, David Lammy, MP for Tottenham. "Windrush Generation Being Subjected to 'Cruel and Inhumane Treatment by UK Government,'" *YouTube Video*, April 16, 2018, https://www.youtube.com/watch?v=Y2q2dQlsywY (accessed April 21, 2022).

82 Amelia Gentleman, "Independent Body Should Run Windrush Compensation Scheme, says Labour," *Guardian*, UK Edition, June 21, 2021, https://www.theguardian.com/uk-news/2021/jun/21/independent-body-should-run-windrush-compensation-scheme-labour-says (accessed April 21, 2022).

5

Organ Failure: Medicalized Torture During the Iraq War

Warren Kluber

December 15, 2003, the day after the capture of Saddam Hussein, news networks played a one-minute video looped on repeat.[1] Beginning in media res, we see a dirty, disheveled, and tired-looking man—barely recognizable as the former President of Iraq—getting checked for lice. Our gaze is aligned with the doctor, looking past his bald white head, latex gloves, and medical instruments to examine his patient. Ten seconds in, we get to the main act (Figure 5.1).[2] With flashlight in one hand and tongue depressor in the other, the doctor spotlights Saddam's mouth, and coaxes him, with gentle prodding, to open wider. The camera follows the beam of light into the dark maw of the deposed dictator.

Many critics have noted the bizarre and unprecedented nature of this video, which instantly became the most-watched medical exam of all time.[3] While it is standard procedure to give a basic physical exam to captured enemies, the exam is not typically filmed and released to the media. As many outraged doctors pointed out, it violated the oath of doctor–patient confidentiality, turning medicine into theatre. The scene's theatricality can be seen in two ways. First, there is an *unreality* in giving medical care to a man who will be executed; the act is evacuated of its normal telos of promoting the patient's long-term health, and becomes an acted-out charade. Acting it out, however, *makes real* an enabling metaphor for the United States' wars in Iraq and Afghanistan, and the more nebulous "War on Terror": war-as-medicine.

Figure 5.1 US Ambassador to Iraq, L. Paul Bremer, watches video of Saddam Hussein going through his medical examination shortly after his capture. The video presented at a briefing to the media gathered at the Iraqi Forum (formerly known as the Baghdad Convention Center) in Baghdad during Operation IRAQI FREEDOM. Courtesy of National Archives and Records Administration.

As the case for "preemptively"[4] attacking Iraq was debated in 2002, its proponents used a medical analogy that had been tested out during the first Iraq War. Saddam, as it was put in press releases in 1991, was a "tumor" that needed to be "excised" from Kuwait.[5] Now, a decade later, it seemed that the earlier operation had only driven him into remission. "Prophylactic" measures were needed to take him out before he metastasized and hurt the American body politic.[6] When the war did not bring the quick and easy cure that its planners had hoped for, a new policy for gathering "intelligence" was authorized, under the *nom de guerre* of "enhanced interrogation." Doctors, cognitive scientists, and psychiatrists were enlisted to design torture tactics that would inflict maximum pain without, ostensibly, doing long term harm to the detainee's health. As the infamous "Torture Memos" repeatedly reassure: each interrogation session is monitored by a medic.[7] At the same time, "surgery" became the watchword for both air and ground operations, with surgical strikes raining down from the sky, and surgical operations "cut[ting] out cancerous tissue while keeping the other vital organs intact."[8]

Saddam's doctor's office drama makes literal the war's medical metaphor, while also mixing its meaning. Saddam is cast as both *disease* (he is the cancer, surgically cut out of Iraq) and *diseased* (the lice check constructs him as dirty, crawling with bugs, before the tongue depressor and sanitary glove administer some American medicine). The first metaphor legitimates his arrest and execution as a life-saving act, and the second confuses exactly whose life is being saved.[9] Through the dissonant double metaphor, killing becomes curing.

In this essay, I argue that *performance* has been used to physically internalize the metaphor of war-as-medicine, patterning it into people's bodies.[10] James Ball writes in his introduction to this collection that, "the body often disappears from view in scholarship on global affairs," and he suggests that performance studies can bring it back into view.[11] This is what I attempt here. The performance of war-as-medicine disappears the bodies of individuals touched by war: enemy combatants are recast as inhuman pathogens, American military personnel are effaced by their technological instruments, and warzone civilians are subsumed within a larger body politic that is sick and needs saving. The untouched bodies of American civilians, by contrast, are made to feel fragile, fearful, and in need of protection.

To understand how this works, I first briefly recount the modern history of imagining war-as-medicine. I then examine a twenty-first-century permutation of this metaphor in the American military practice of enhanced interrogation, which rebrands torture as a medically safe means of "diagnosis" to identify pathogenic agents. I theorize how watching war-as-medicine induces "spectatorial anesthesia": numbing viewers to the pain that they witness, by promising that this violence will cure the fear and anxiety in their own bodies. I turn next to Frances Ya-Chu Cowhig's 2009 play *Lidless*, which dramatizes the impact of medicalized torture on victims, perpetrators, and tacitly complicit American civilians. At the same time, the play uses scenes of illness and medical care to enact an alternative model of health, in which life is sustained not by defending borders between self and other, but by making them porous. Finally, drawing on Resmaa Menakem's work in cultural somatics, I propose that "war is medicine" operates as a "wordless story" that we carry in our bodies, which infects us with the very illness that it purports to cure. I end by considering how theatre can help us purge this virulent story, and begin real healing.

War Is Medicine

While war-medicine metaphors can be found in writing going back for millennia, Lorenzo Servitje argues that it is during the nineteenth century that the metaphor becomes part of the Western "popular imagination."[12] Contagionism, miasma theory, and germ theory lent themselves to the metaphor of medicine-as-war against disease, which reciprocally stoked the metaphor of war-as-medicine, protecting the body politic against those deemed racially, culturally, and sexually Other. As bacterial "cultures" and "colonies" were imagined in terms of race, so were Britain's colonial subjects and racialized lower classes imagined in terms of germs. These changes accelerated during the First World War. On both sides of the conflict, medicine was seen as the key to military efficiency. Medical and military institutions became deeply entwined: financially, logistically, technologically, and metaphorically.[13] Doctors and surgeons adopted a military ethos to mark their profession as serious, masculine, and patriotic; and military propaganda incorporated medical metaphors to desensitize troops and civilians to violence, by couching killing in language of curing.[14] In the twenty-first century, Colleen Bell has shown how medical metaphors inform the strategy, ethics, and representation of American counterinsurgency warfare. Military intervention is legitimized as a therapeutic act, aiding a social body whose immune system is unable to protect itself from an insurgent "virus or bacteria."[15] This instills *"feelings* of confidence and preparedness," which make it possible to execute "brutal and indiscriminate violence against civilians," with "moral certainty."[16] The medical storyline both conceals and bolsters the precepts of "military orientalism" and "race war,"[17] constructing non-white bodies in the Global South as disease and as diseased.

This metaphor is implicit in the documents that have become known as the "Torture Memos." Completed by the Justice Department in July of 2002, the memos claim that the CIA's torture practices are not, in fact, torture. This is ensured by "medical personnel" who monitor each interrogation session to "watch for signs of physical distress or mental harm," and ostensibly to stop the procedure if it risks causing permanent damage.[18] Torture is made safe and humane by a watchful medical gaze.

Historian Alfred McCoy, a leading chronicler and critic of the American use of torture from the early Cold War to the current day, writes that American torture is characterized by a "theatricality," informed by medical, psychiatric, and cognitive science. In the 1970s, the CIA began to develop techniques of environmental and sensory manipulation, designed to destroy and remake the prisoner's perception of what is real—with regard to his or her world, self, and actions. These experiments, which located the "mind" not inside the skull, but distributed across one's living space, were instrumental in moving the field of cognitive science toward the "extended" and "enacted" mind hypothesis. And they guided the scripting and mise-en-scène of what McCoy calls a "psychological drama crueler than physical pain."[19] Here, the ontological uncertainty of theatricality, and the professed certainty of medical science, manipulate a reality/illusion dichotomy. The torture is real from the perspective of the tortured, and unreal from the perspective of the medic, who attests that the interrogation does no serious harm. This is the logic used to justify, for example, waterboarding: because the detainee only *imagines* he is drowning, and is not *really* drowning, no torture occurs.[20] As cognitive scientists and medical researchers were learning that no mind–body duality is possible in studying cognition, this very duality was used rhetorically to disavow the reality of the torture they perpetrated.

Diana Taylor has shown that the double consciousness of theatricality is not just a rhetorical tactic used to sell and hide torture, but it also enables normal people to commit atrocious violence. Shielded in the armor of a theatrical role, the torturer disidentifies with the act of torturing, which "makes the action 'safe'" for him.[21] However, in the recent American context, it is not just that torturers understand themselves as "actors"; rather, they act within an entirely different play than their victims. The "Torture Memos" legitimate the violence of enhanced interrogation on the grounds that it is an act of "self-defense."[22] The tortured logic of this legal rationale works through theatrical surrogation. The interrogator stands in for the United States (and any threat to the United States is a threat to his "self"), and the detainee, supposedly possessing information that could reveal terrorist plots, or the names and locations of other militants, is a sign pointing to an invisible threat.

Enhanced interrogation is thus imagined as a drama of "self-defense" in which both the "self" and the threat that it "defends" against are offstage. The literal scene could not be simpler: Two bodies are in a room, one is hurting the other. But the metaphorical scene is a diagnostic drama: The torturer is a doctor, performing a biopsy on cancerous tissue, excised from an ailing body politic. The detainee is not a human, but a specimen, tested and examined for signs of a dangerous disease. Thus, not only is torture framed and legitimized by medicine (monitored by a medic); in the metaphorical scene torture *is* medicine: An essential diagnostic tool that runs tests to identify the pathogenic agents that need to be cut out. The actual bodies in the room are effaced by abstract metaphorical bodies. Theatricality is used to make the medical metaphor feel real, and the violence unreal, to the torturer.

This medical metaphor, however obscene and absurd, helped make torture tolerable for a majority of American civilians. During the first years of the Iraq War, the public did not witness actual scenes of "enhanced interrogation," but they did see proliferating representations of torture in popular television and films. A number of cultural critics have argued that the Fox TV show *24*, and its epigones, were instrumental in normalizing torture as a policy option. Led by Jack Bauer, exuding the gritty confidence and authority of a TV doctor as he pumped terrorists with syringes filled with colorful liquids, enhanced interrogation took on a medical valence and scientific legitimacy in the public imaginary.[23] And it gave the American public permission to root for the torturer hero, secure in the conviction that he is doing no more harm than a doctor who submits his patient to a painful course of treatment.

On November 1, 2003, the Associated Press published a report on the tortures at the American Abu Ghraib prison in Iraq. There was nothing medical about it. Torture did not look like the sterile work of poised professionals using advanced technology. It looked like sadistic abuse, perpetrated by ill-trained military police barely out of high school. On December 15, before the story gained traction in the American media, network programs were interrupted to broadcast the footage of Saddam Hussein's medical exam. The spectacle returned viewers to watching war-as-medicine.

Spectatorial Anesthesia

In *Watching Babylon*, Nicholas Mirzoeff's study of American visual culture during the second Iraq War, Mirzoeff theorizes a kind of "watching" that is situated, interactive, and dependent on the spectator's embodied conditions. Just as important as the points of visual focus are the "moments of drift in which the attention is not fully engaged."[24] Partial images and scenes are retained as flashpoints and constellated into a drama we do not directly witness, nor see represented as a continuous story. Drawing on cognitive neuroscience, he writes, "seeing is not believing. It is something we do, a kind of performance."[25] Watching is a "multimedia site-specific performance of everyday life," and the "vision" we enact in turn produces and positions us as "visual subjects."[26] When watching war, medical metaphors affect both what we see and how our bodies react. For example, Mirzoeff notes the surge in sales of military-style SUVs and state-of-the-art home security systems, which guard the "fortified bod[ies]" of individuals, families, and the nation against "infectious diseases."[27] The "tinted windows" of SUVs, and elevated "height off the ground" give drivers a privileged viewpoint of seeing without being seen, while the armored sides ensure their invulnerability.[28] The "house becomes a body," with "eyes [that] are 'theatre'-style television screens," allowing residents to look out at the drama of a dangerous world that cannot get in.[29] The story of war-is-medicine is not just an external narrative that plays out on these screens; rather, it is interactively authored by our bodily sensations, comportment, and performances: how we armor ourselves to protect against injury or infection.

I call this emotional armoring "spectatorial anesthesia": an affective blend of fragility, anxiety, and numbness. As spectators dissociate from their agitated bodies, and fantasize about impermeable borders, they come to tolerate endless violence against imagined pathogenic threats. Crucially, American civilians are conscripted to wage war against their *own* bodies, fighting what they are unwilling to feel. Unfelt pain and grief leave an invisible festering wound, which is projected onto the very Others we are unable to grieve.

If mediatized performances pattern this way of feeling into our bodies, live theatre is uniquely able to expose it. Whereas screens put up a barrier between spectators' bodies and the bodies of pathologized Others, theatre can attune us to our mutual porosity and our ever-shifting somatic experiences. I turn now to one such play, that invites audiences to feel how the metaphor of war-as-medicine shapes our *own* bodies, thoughts, and relationships. Further, by denaturalizing this metaphor, the play opens up a space to rehearse different ways of feeling healthy and safe.

Organ Failure

Frances Ya-Chu Cowhig's *Lidless* (2009) is set in an imagined future, the year 2019, in which the Guantanamo Bay detention camp has been closed for nearly a decade. A former Guantanamo interrogator named Alice is tracked down by Bashir, a Pakistani-Canadian man whom she tortured. Bashir contracted hepatitis at Gitmo, and his liver is now failing. He remembered that during an interrogation session, Alice told him that they have the same blood type. He wants half her liver. Cowhig's dramatic focus on the fate of a failing organ is likely inspired by two revelations about the "enhanced interrogation" program that had recently been brought to light. The first was the stipulation that to qualify as "torture," the detainee must experience a level of pain equivalent to "organ failure."[30] The second, a rumor that Abu Ghraib detainees' organs were being harvested in operating rooms—apocryphal, but serving to inspire further terror in Iraqi combatants and civilians.[31] In the play, the ostensibly clean and medically safe torture stokes an insatiable desire for dominance, which discomposes the torturer's *own* body. In contrast to the epistemology of torture, which promises knowledge of the objectified Other through unilateral penetration, the play explores how we know others through the way they *get inside of our bodies*, changing our breathing, heartbeat, and gut sensations.

The first scene in *Lidless* flashes back to the year 2004. Riva, a Guantanamo Bay Army medic, steps into an orange spotlight, and mimes the medical examination of an invisible detainee. As she speaks into a recorder, we realize that he has been subjected to "clean tortures"—designed to leave minimal external signs of the "internal injuries" that Riva notes.[32] "Detainee complains of severe abdominal pain," she reports, "and should be tested for liver disease." Directing him to breathe in and out, Riva notices "problems in respiration," likely due to wearing a hood restricting his air supply. The play thus begins by evoking an absent body that has been penetrated without breaking the skin—the lack of "lacerations" belies his internal wounds. At the same time, he is claustrophobically confined within his body, to the point of suffocation. He is cut off from the outer world: his wounds invisible, and his breathing obstructed.[33]

For Alice, the interrogator, hurting the detainee in these "clean" ways has fueled a desire to dominate and degrade him more completely. She complains that the detainees still "can shut you out. Go anywhere in their heads."[34] She has not yet breached an interior space—mental, emotional, spiritual—which she is determined to enter, occupy, and own: to "make 'em stop believing."[35] A new interrogation tactic offers her an alternate, and theatrical, means of gaining entry. Termed "Invasion of Space by a Female," this tactic was based on supposed anthropological insights into the mind of Muslim men, and sought to exploit religious taboos in order to, as Alice puts it, "damn their souls."[36] Women interrogators were cast in a sexualized roleplay, costumed in skimpy dresses and made up with lipstick and blush, while using red paint as a prop to stand for menstrual blood. The "space" that is invaded, then, is at once physical and psychic—the inner sanctum that Alice failed to reach through pain alone. Smearing paint on her hand, Alice slinks into the interrogation chamber—signified abstractly by another spot of light—and she starts another session with the invisible detainee. Touching herself, she shows him the red on her hand, and then starts to caress him. She discovers that breathing lightly beneath his left ear gives him an erection. His involuntary bodily response makes him complicit in the roleplay: "You like this. Our heads and hearts try to trick us, but our bodies never lie."[37] Alice starts to veer off script. "I'm bleeding, and there's nothing shielding you from my twenty-five-year-old cunt."[38] She takes off her shirt, and straddles his erection, as the lights go out.

Sexual humiliation was a common tactic of the enhanced interrogation program, and it not infrequently led to rape. In all documented instances, however, it is the detainee who is penetrated by an interrogator—or forced to penetrate another detainee. But as Alice invades the detainee's space, he penetrates her. In this scene of domination, the torturer is not immune to the violence she inflicts: it gets into her body. And, we will see, it cannot be gotten out through martial and medical means.

Moving forward to the play's present of 2019, we learn that Alice has started a new civilian life as a florist in Minnesota. The psychiatric medications she took after returning from war seem to have wiped the worst abuses from her memory. Then one day, the detainee walks through the front door of Alice's flower shop, and introduces himself as "Bashir." After recounting his history and his illness, he asks for half her liver. Alice kicks him out of her shop, but on the threshold of the doorway, he turns to face her, pulls a *"black plastic bag over his head,"* and *"gasps and screams and wails."*[39] In the next scene, at home with her husband Lucas, and fourteen-year-old daughter Rhiannon, Alice relapses into Post Traumatic Stress Disorder (PTSD) symptoms that she hadn't experienced for years. Buried memories return to Alice's body, not as a conscious narrative, but as sensations, impulses, and pains. And their home world, structured by careful boundaries and containment, starts to come undone. Rhiannon becomes inquisitive about her mother's military service, after first discovering Alice's army jacket in the attic, and then receiving a package from Bashir, containing his orange jumpsuit from Guantanamo Bay. She upsets her mother by wearing the jacket around the house, and is upbraided by Lucas. "Remember when we talked about boundary violations? Wearing that jacket would be a violation of my boundaries."[40] To which Rhiannon retorts, "What if my boundary ends in your stomach?"[41] After being rebuffed by Alice a few more times, Bashir eventually shows up on her doorstep and lets himself in. Lucas tries to kick him out: "It's called a front door. It separates this family from the rest of the world, and if someone wants to cross that barrier, they knock."[42]

Behind the barrier of her front door, we see that Alice is still fighting her war. She confesses that when Rhiannon's pet chicken wouldn't stop squawking at night, she pulled out one of her feathers. "She didn't fight back, which made me furious. She sat on my palm, just watching, while I pulled out another feather, and another, until she was bloody and bald."[43] As when she tortured and interrogated Bashir, her total dominance makes her want more. And she seems to have passed her trauma on to her daughter.[44] Rhiannon meets Bashir when he comes looking for Alice, and she eventually asks him to be the subject of her oral history project for school. In their conversation, Rhiannon admits to "suffocating" a goldfish. "I was just holding it in my hand, watching it … Watching it try to breathe," studying the fish "gasping for breath like an idiot who can't control her own body."[45] "Sometimes I like killing crickets," she later blurts, to which Bashir responds, "You just want to understand how they sing."[46] This scenario of "watching" in order to "understand" engages a medical epistemology and an objectivist scientific gaze, anatomizing the crickets as she rips off their wings. But it quickly escalates to torture: scopic mastery leads to physical dominance and sadism. Rhiannon's desire for knowledge and control of others objectifies their bodies, and agitates her own body.

Bashir eventually guides Rhiannon to understand her bodily agitation not as the noise interfering with pure and total knowledge, but as itself a kind of knowledge. Rhiannon gets the hiccups when she first meets Bashir; he tells her that, "we get hiccups when our body knows something our mind doesn't understand," and then he frightens her to make them go away.[47] Hiccups are caused by involuntary contractions of the diaphragm, which briefly close the vocal cords. This motif of breath and blockage flows throughout the play. Lucas, a recovered heroin addict, practices tai chi with steady breathing in the living room. Rhiannon has asthma, which acts up in times of stress, making her breath shallow, wheezy, and choked off. In their interviews, Bashir reveals that he too had asthma as a child (our first hint that he is Rhiannon's biological father). The symptoms of Bashir's childhood asthma went away, he explains, when he changed the meanings that he gave it: "I made myself think: 'I want this. I love this. I'm happy.' My breath came back."[48] Rather than a disembodied mind controlling an objectified body, characters feel the feedback between their conscious thoughts and the unconscious knowledge of their internal organs—stomachs, hearts, and lungs.

One way in which bodily knowledges and desires manifest is through acts of theatre. In the opening torture scene, Alice performs a theatre of domination, wearing a costume and makeup as she violates Bashir. But later, Rhiannon instead playacts to take his place. Home alone, she puts on Bashir's orange jumpsuit and blackout goggles, handcuffs herself, and tries out a stress position. Acting out this scene triggers a sudden asthma attack. Unable to find the key to her inhaler, and unable to breathe, she dies. Through roleplay, something of Bashir gets into her, discomposing her internal organs. And something of Rhiannon subsequently gets into Bashir. We learn in the last scene that after Rhiannon died, Bashir received her liver, a perfect match (paternity hints confirmed). Alice visits Bashir in the hospital, and touches his incisions as she speaks to her daughter. She goes home, and finds Rhiannon's inflatable globe on the floor. "She's in here, still. This is her breath."[49] She pinches open the valve, and slowly, with pauses to breathe out, inhales her daughter's breath. In the last scene, Bashir is visited by his daughter, Zakiyah (played by the same actress as Rhiannon), who comforts him in his distress. "Soon your new liver will eliminate the toxins that have poisoned your body, and everything you're thinking will change."[50] Coming full circle, the physiological changes brought by his new organ will change his conscious thoughts, as he starts to heal.

Theatre Is Medicine

Mass media spectacles like Saddam's medical exam at once agitate our bodies and alienate us from our bodies, as we project our distress onto pathologized Others. It is thus not only the bodies of soldiers, insurgents, and warzone civilians who disappear in performances of military power. Watching the war, the bodies of American civilians also vanish from awareness, becoming both numb and reactive. As Alice's husband Lucas observes, "You know how you're supposed to act and react in every situation, but it's been lifetimes since something has moved you."[51] When we are dissociated from our own bodies, it is easier to disregard the bodies of others, and to deny a basic fact our bodies know: that war is violence, and that violence hurts.

The metaphor of war-as-medicine is encapsulated in the trope of immunity. Roberto Esposito and Donna Haraway have argued that modernity is marked by an immunity logic, which figures the immune system as a military force, defending the body's borders and policing its interior.[52] The drama of immunity—in medicine, politics, and aesthetics—spreads anxiety about something foreign "trespassing or violating borders ... and penetrat[ing] a body."[53] Esposito writes that, paradoxically, in order to defend ourselves against contamination and to safeguard "life," we numb ourselves to our own aliveness, and to the lives of others. "The preservation of life corresponds with a form of restriction that somehow separates it from itself. Its salvation thus depends on a wound that cannot heal."[54] I argue that this affects our day-to-day experience of embodiment: how our bodies open and settle, and how they constrict and grow agitated. A perennial defensiveness against an imagined pathogenic threat inflicts on our *own* bodies "a wound that cannot heal," which might manifest physically as muscular tension and shallow breathing, as we try to protect ourselves from what we are unwilling to feel. In *Lidless*, Bashir remarks that, "Societies are built around the avoidance of pain."[55] But avoided pain does not disappear; it is stored in the body, and wreaked on the bodies of others.

Resmaa Menakem, a leader in the field of cultural somatics, describes how racialized violence is held in our bodies, and reenacted by our bodies, often without conscious awareness. "Our bodies have a form of knowledge that is different from our cognitive brains. This knowledge is typically experienced as a felt sense of constriction or expansion, pain or ease, energy or numbness. Often this knowledge is stored in our bodies as *wordless stories* about what is safe and what is dangerous."[56] I suggest that "war is medicine" tells a "wordless story," in which racialized Others are inhuman pathogens who need to be controlled or eliminated, the US military is a team of benevolent doctors using sophisticated technologies to save lives, warzone civilians make up an ailing social body unable to heal itself, and US civilians are terrified of getting sick. While Menakem focuses on anti-Black racism within the United States, his description of the stories and sensations that incite violence in the name of protection is resonant here. US police departments, he writes, increasingly resemble "militarized ... occupying forces" that see themselves as "protective antibodies," guarding neighborhoods against dangerous darker bodies.[57] Black bodies are supposedly "impervious to pain,"[58] while white bodies are hypersensitive and ready to authorize violence to alleviate discomfort.

The first step toward mending racialized trauma and reducing violence, Menakem writes, is learning how to connect and listen to our *own* bodies. By observing our fluctuating sensations, we notice when we feel safe and open and when we feel threatened and closed off, and we see how these inner physical changes shape our perception of external reality. *Lidless* invites this kind of somatic reflectiveness in its audience, by modeling it on the stage. Theatre theorist Soyica Diggs Colbert writes that, "The perception of or desire for impermeability, for a static, fixed body, produces materiality and forms the imaginary borders of the body. But bodies are porous and, against all desires, nevertheless remain in motion and in common."[59] Cowhig's play exposes the imaginary borders built by the metaphor of war-as-medicine, which try to patch up our porousness, and freeze our perennial motion. Instead, the play's characters get inside of each other—whether or not they acknowledge it—and set off changes that are at once physical, mental, and emotional.

In so doing, the play enacts a deeper and older metaphor: theatre-as-medicine. Karelisa V. Hartigan reminds us that performing arts, in most cultures and times, have been a kind of medicine: healing bodies, minds, and souls through communal attunement.[60] As the play's audience notices their own bodily responses, they might feel their own dis-ease and woundedness, and sense what it takes to heal. Research in interpersonal neurobiology has shown that body awareness and shared attention, in which we *feel felt* by one another, regulates our bodily functions, boosts our immune systems, and promotes health.[61] While watching and listening to one another, our nervous systems co-regulate, and we experience "unconscious adaptations in muscles, connective tissue, breathing, heart rate, skin temperature, or even hormonal function."[62] In a sense, in-person empathic regard performs a metaphorical organ transplantation: syncing up our organ systems, as our breathing, skin response, and heartbeats entrain. Rhiannon says to Bashir, "You're holding your breath so that nothing affects you. Take a deep breath. I dare you."[63] When our bodies go numb, in a misguided attempt at self-defense, Cowhig reminds us that we can breathe them back.

Notes

1. CNN, "Iraq Saddam Captured," *YouTube Video*, 1:10, July 21, 2016, https://www.youtube.com/watch?v=WcveUNSzjZk (accessed June 1, 2018).
2. Department of Defense. Department of the Navy. Naval Imaging Command. "[US Ambassador to Iraq, L. Paul Bremer Watches Video of Saddam Hussein Going through His Medical Examination Shortly after His Capture. The Video Presented at a Briefing to the Media Gathered at the Iraqi Forum (Formerly Known as the Baghdad Convention Center) in Baghdad during Operation IRAQI FREEDOM.]" Photograph. Washington, DC: American Forces Information Service. Defense Visual Information Center, c2003. From National Archives Catalog: *Combined Military Service Digital Photographic Files, 1921–2008.* https://catalog.archives.gov/id/6659527 (accessed November 2, 2021).
3. A prominent queer studies reading interprets the scene as symbolically "sodomizing Saddam" by penetrating his orifices with phallic tools. See, e.g., W. J. T. Mitchell, *Cloning Terror: The War of Images, 9/11 to the Present* (Chicago: University of Chicago Press, 2011); Nicholas Mirzoeff, *Watching Babylon: The War in Iraq and Global Visual Culture* (London: Routledge, 2005).
4. The war was not preemptive, as Iraq had neither the intent nor the capacity to launch an attack on the United States. By some estimates, it was a "preventive war" (which assumes that Iraq would *eventually* attack the United States, some years down the line). More likely, it was a war of aggression, invading a country that posed no threat to US security. The rhetoric of preemption, however, and its medical correlates were crucial to legitimizing the campaign as a "just war." For definitions of preemptive, preventive, and aggressive war, from the perspective of just war theory, see Michael Walzer, *Just and Unjust Wars* (New York: Basic Books, 1977), 74–85.
5. Rob Nixon, *Slow Violence and the Environmentalism of the Poor*, Paperback Edition (Cambridge, MA: Harvard University Press, 2013), 207.

6 The rationale for the new US doctrine of "pre-emptive" strikes was vigorously defended in a book by Alan Dershowitz, whose legal analysis is built on the metaphor of war-as-medicine. He quotes Machiavelli, writing that it is easier to cure "the disease [before it] is too far advanced." Alan Dershowitz, *Preemption: A Knife That Cuts Both Ways* (New York: W. W. Norton, 2006), 63.

7 David Cole, ed., *The Torture Memos: Rationalizing the Unthinkable* (New York: New Press, 2009), 28.

8 United States. Department of the Army. *The U.S. Army/Marine Corps Counterinsurgency Field Manual: U.S. Army Field Manual No. 3–24. Marine Corps Warfighting Publication No. 3–33.5.* (Chicago: University of Chicago Press, 2007), 1–23.

9 His later trial and execution were carried out by the new Iraqi government installed by the US military, with no cameras allowed and much less media attention in the United States.

10 Sociologist Michael Kimmel uses the term "retrojection" to describe how cultural metaphors are mapped into the body, and "discourse goes under the skin," influencing how we feel, move, and react to the bodies of others. Michael Kimmel, "Properties of Cultural Embodiment: Lessons From the Anthropology of the Body," *Sociocultural Situatedness* 2 (2008): 77–108.

11 James R. Ball III, ed. *Performing Statecraft: The Postdiplomatic Theatre of Sovereigns, Citizens, and States* (London: Methuen Drama, 2022), 17–18.

12 Lorenzo Servitje, *Medicine Is War: The Martial Metaphor in Victorian Literature and Culture* (Albany: State University of New York Press, 2021), 32.

13 Fiona Reid, *Medicine in First World War Europe: Soldiers, Medics, Pacifists* (London: Bloomsbury Academic, 2017), 5, 10.

14 Roger Cooter, "Medicine and the Goodness of War," *Canadian Bulletin of Medical History* 7, no. 2 (October 1990): 147–59. Mark Harrison, "Medicine and the Management of Modern Warfare," *History of Science* 34, no. 4 (Winter 1996): 379–410.

15 Colleen Bell, "Hybrid Warfare and Its Metaphors," *Humanity: An International Journal of Human Rights, Humanitarianism, and Development* 3, no. 2 (Summer 2012): 225–47, 234.

16 Bell, "Hybrid," 228; Colleen Bell, "War and the Allegory of Medical Intervention: Why Metaphors Matter," *International Political Sociology* 6, no. 3 (September 2012): 325–8.
17 Bell, "Hybrid," 226.
18 Cole, *Torture Memos*, 28.
19 Cole, *Torture Memos*, 127.
20 This is not to say that those who authorized waterboarding believed it was medically safe. To the contrary, before the practice was started in the Iraq and Afghanistan Wars, the CIA's medical office issued a memo stating that: "waterboarding is neither efficacious nor medically safe." Cole, *Torture Memos*, 26.
21 Diana Taylor, *Disappearing Acts: Spectacles of Gender and Nationalism in Argentina's "Dirty War"* (Durham: Duke University Press, 1997), 129.
22 Cole, *Torture Memos*, 23.
23 See, e.g., Michael Richardson, *Gestures of Testimony: Torture, Trauma, and Affect in Literature* (New York: Bloomsbury, 2016), 14.
24 Mirzoeff, *Watching*, 30.
25 Nicholas Mirzoeff, *How to See the World: An Introduction to Images, from Self-Portraits to Selfies, Maps to Movies, and More* (New York: Basic Books, 2016), 14.
26 Mirzoeff, *Watching*, 31.
27 Mirzoeff, *Watching*, 51.
28 Mirzoeff, *Watching*, 36.
29 Mirzoeff, *Watching*, 50, 52.
30 Cole, *Torture Memos*, 47.
31 Mitchell, *Cloning Terror*, 36.
32 Frances Ya-Chu Cowhig, *Lidless* (New Haven: Yale University Press, 2010), 5.
33 The "Torture Memos" mandate a strategy that alternates between extremes of containment (confining the detainee in a small box with a restricted air supply), and exposure (stretched out and strapped in place, helpless to resist bodily penetration). Cole, *Torture Memos*, 5; Mitchell, *Cloning Terror*, 114.
34 Cowhig, *Lidless*, 8.
35 Cowhig, *Lidless*, 8.
36 Cowhig, *Lidless*, 8.

37 Cowhig, *Lidless*, 10.
38 Cowhig, *Lidless*, 11.
39 Cowhig, *Lidless*, 22.
40 Cowhig, *Lidless*, 51.
41 Cowhig, *Lidless*, 51.
42 Cowhig, *Lidless*, 58.
43 Cowhig, *Lidless*, 24.
44 Research in epigenetics has shown how traumatic life events cause changes in gene expression, which can be inherited by one's offspring. Bessel A. Van der Kolk, *The Body Keeps the Score: Brain, Mind, and Body in the Healing of Trauma* (New York: Viking, 2014), 154.
45 Cowhig, *Lidless*, 28.
46 Cowhig, *Lidless*, 46.
47 Cowhig, *Lidless*, 27.
48 Cowhig, *Lidless*, 29.
49 Cowhig, *Lidless*, 71.
50 Cowhig, *Lidless*, 73.
51 Cowhig, *Lidless*, 57.
52 Roberto Esposito, *Immunitas: The Protection and Negations of Life* (Cambridge, UK: Polity Press, 2011) and Donna Haraway, "The Biopolitics of Postmodern Bodies: Constitutions of Self in Immune System Discourse," in *Simians, Cyborgs, and Women: The Reinvention of Nature*, 225–52 (New York: Routledge, 1990).
53 Esposito, *Immunitas*, 2.
54 Esposito, *Immunitas*, 8.
55 Cowhig, *Lidless*, 71.
56 Resmaa Menakem, *My Grandmother's Hands: Racialized Trauma and the Pathway to Mending Our Hearts and Bodies* (Las Vegas, NV: Central Recovery Press, 2017), 5; emphasis added.
57 Menakem, *My Grandmother's Hands*, 116.
58 Menakem, *My Grandmother's Hands*, 27.
59 Soyica Diggs Colbert, *Theory for Theatre Studies: Bodies* (New York: Methuen Drama, 2022), 50–1.
60 Karelisa Hartigan, *Performance and Cure: Drama and Healing in Ancient Greece and Contemporary America* (Classical Inter/Faces Series. London: Duckworth, 2009).

61 Daniel J Siegel, *Pocket Guide to Interpersonal Neurobiology: An Integrative Handbook of the Mind* (New York: W. W. Norton & Company, 2012), 34–5.
62 Christina Shewell, "Poetry, Voice, Brain, and Body," *Voice and Speech Review* 14, no. 2 (May 3, 2020): 143–66.
63 Cowhig, *Lidless*, 47.

6

Viral Diplomacy: Music, Masks, and Maritime Borders Between China and the Philippines

Adam Kielman

As the global severity of the Covid-19 pandemic became clear in April 2020, the Chinese Embassy in the Philippines released a music video that quickly went viral. With parallel lyrics in Mandarin and Filipino penned by the Chinese ambassador to the Philippines, "Iisang Dagat" ("One Sea") features Chinese and Filipino pop stars and politicians. Images of boxes of medical supplies being off-loaded from Chinese commercial airliners are intercut with videos of frontline workers in Manila including a team of Chinese doctors, set to a soft-rock ballad: "You and I are in the same one sea, looking after each other with love. I will not let go of your hand as we look toward a bright future." Resembling widely popular Chinese music videos circulated on domestic social media offering encouragement in a difficult time and celebrating China's success in mitigating the spread of the pandemic within its borders, the song builds upon a longer history in China of the political mobilization of music. But, on the international stage, it backfired. Social media users in the Philippines immediately reacted with indignation to this musical staging of China's "mask diplomacy" (*kouzhao waijiao*), and took the "one sea" to be an implicit reference to the South China Sea (often referred to in the Philippines as the West Philippine Sea), where ongoing territorial disputes between China and its Southeast Asian neighbors have become flashpoints for broader discomfort with China's increasingly assertive posturing in the region.

This chapter explores the production and circulation of "Iisang Dagat" within these contexts with several aims. First, it attends to the musical dimensions of theatres of diplomacy, and offers an acoustically tuned perspective on international relations that builds upon accounts discussed by musicologists and scholars in other fields. By considering this example within a broader history of music and statecraft in China and theorizing it with reference to the Confucian conceptual pair of music (*yue*) and ritual (*li*), it furthermore nuances understandings of music and diplomacy that are largely grounded in Western histories and practices. Second, it considers the chaotic public sphere of transnational social media as a stage where public diplomacy takes place, and explores how diverse voices challenge, complicate, and even circumvent the official channels through which diplomacy traditionally operates. Finally, by focusing not only on the music, lyrics, and images of the music video, but also on the activities it memorializes, the online discussions it brought about—as well as intersections of all three—I examine the ways musical performance is intertwined with other performative dimensions of diplomacy.

Music and Diplomacy

Music is ubiquitous in theatres of diplomacy. From the carefully choreographed musical entertainment at state dinners to public concerts staged by consulates as part of their public diplomacy initiatives, music is more than just background to the machinations of power; rather, it reflects, shapes, and contributes to the exercise of power, and is an acoustic element of broader performative negotiations between states. Scholars in diverse disciplines have attended to the roles of music in diplomatic ceremony, from hidden court musicians in early modern Europe,[1] to transnational hip hop collaborations in South Asia, Eastern Europe, and Africa.[2] As James R. Ball III's extended description of French president Nicolas Sarkozy's state visit to the United States in the introduction to this edited volume demonstrates, no diplomatic ceremony is complete without musical performance.[3] In the context of formal diplomatic ceremonies, music serves many functions; as Damien Mahiet summarizes, music may be employed "to emphasize cooperation between parties … , honor guests … , highlight national differences … , or underscore transnational identities."[4]

At the same time, music often serves to make publicly audible the ideologies and agendas that diplomats are charged with promoting on an international stage. As an important component of public diplomacy, music thus often serves as part of "a government's process of communicating with foreign publics in an attempt to bring about understanding for its nation's ideas and ideals, its institutions and culture, as well as its national goals and current policies."[5] The US Jazz Ambassadors program, and the deployment of jazz and improvisation as metaphors for democracy, egalitarianism, and freedom—as well as the problematic foundations of such metaphors when considered in light of racial injustice in the United States—are particularly good examples of the complex political fields that public diplomacy involving music navigates. In a discussion of American musical diplomacy during the Cold War, Danielle Fosler-Lussier reminds us that deployments of music in the service of diplomacy are far from monolithic top-down efforts, involve the agencies of many players, and are subject to complex processes of reception.[6]

These multileveled, multisited, and sometimes unpredictable processes of negotiation and engagement are key to thinking about music as part of "postdiplomatic theatre," and attending to such processes furthers an understanding of the performativity of statecraft that this book is proposing. As Ball summarizes, postdiplomatic theatres are "sites of struggle, as states perform to distinguish themselves from one another, articulating visions that invite opposition from within and without."[7] This chapter thus means to bring attention to what Stuart Hall would call the "negotiated readings" of music as part of public diplomacy,[8] and to advocate for an understanding of musical diplomacy as encompassing a wide range of activities, mediums, and forms of engagement.

In addition to dovetailing with the wide scope of political performance that this book takes as its focus, such an approach also follows recent and related interdisciplinary scholarship on musical diplomacy that extends its focus well beyond the confines of formal diplomatic ceremony and public diplomacy efforts. Drawing on what they call an "acoustic turn in international relations," Ramel and Prévost-Thomas put Erving Goffman's notion of scene (in an intertwined theatrical and social sense)[9] in dialogue with William Straw's notion of *musical* scene (as a form of community and musical sociality)[10] in order to interrogate how "musical and diplomatic scenes, local and international scenes actually articulate."[11] In *Resounding International Relations: On Music, Culture, and Politics*, Franklin and others connect perspectives and approaches from sound studies, media studies, and international relations in order to propose approaches to the study of music and diplomacy that decenter state actors and consider a wide range of musical and sonic fields.[12]

While this chapter extends these discussions, considering "Iisang Dagat" within the context of the diplomatic relationship between China and the Philippines also invites nuancing broader Western-grounded understandings of musical diplomacy. Contextualizing this music video within the particular historical legacy of the political deployment of music in China not only reveals how that history resonates through contemporary practices, but also offers insights into the ways musical performance relates to other tools of diplomacy.

Rethinking Musical Diplomacy Outside the West

Discussions of musical diplomacy in Western contexts often pay tribute to Baldassare Castiglione's *The Courtier* (1528) as an early acknowledgement of—and call for—the political and diplomatic power of music.[13] Castiglione draws on ancient Greek notions of the "harmony of the spheres" that related musical vibrations to heavenly ones. Newly in vogue and reformulated in Renaissance Europe, these Pythagorean theorizations of music were deployed as evidence of music's universal power, and thus of its subtle power of persuasion. Contemporary historians often trace the development of practices and understandings of musical diplomacy to this Renaissance European reformulation of a Greek idea; grounding an understanding of musical diplomacy in this history foregrounds a passive process where musical sounds generate subtle changes in human experiences of and views toward the exercise of political power.

One could just as easily begin a theorization of the political and diplomatic power of music by bridging early Chinese sources and twenty-first-century practices. The *Yue Ji* ("Record of Music") is a treatise on music generally understood to preserve Confucian thinking on the political and social dimensions of music in early China.[14] While an extended discussion of the text is beyond the scope of this chapter, several ideas found in it resonate through later intersections of sound and statecraft in China and East Asia more broadly.

First is an understanding of music as reflective of human nature, local distinction, and individuals' reactions to the society, time, and political climate in which they live.[15] The text proposes music as a way for the state to understand the inner lives of its citizens; music reflects not only the people who inhabit a particular territory, but also the effectiveness of the government that rules them. Second is an understanding of a particular realm of music as a tool that may be used by the state to exhibit and promote virtuous behavior. As Cook summarizes, music "turns from a mere carrier of the people's sentiments into one of the supreme tools of the superior man used to unite the people and bring about a sense of order throughout the kingdom."[16]

Perhaps most significant for thinking about musical diplomacy, though, is the conceptual pair of music (*yue*) and ritual (*li*) central to Confucian thinking about music. Put simply, while music harmonizes, ritual serves to distinguish; they thus function together to mediate relationships. As James Garrison summarizes, "li are more than rituals … . On the one hand, li deals with ceremony writ large … . However, li also include much more subtle forms of etiquette and comportment, in daily life"[17] that serve to "establish hierarchical and deferential relationships"[18] and contribute to "the continual and stratified co-emergence of the singular and plural, of self and society."[19] Such an understanding of ritual prefigures theorizations of performativity; ritual is both ceremony (performance) as well as the relationships and social roles that such performances manifest. Furthermore, music is not just ornamentation upon ritual, but rather crucial to its effective functioning,[20] as recent scholarship on the ways the political efficacy of music was understood and utilized in early China demonstrates.[21] This offers an entryway into understanding musical performance as intersecting with other performative dimensions of statecraft.

These early Confucian theorizations of music's political dimensions offer an alternative backdrop to Castiglione's *The Courtier* for understanding the political power of music. More broadly, such a historical perspective would illustrate the extent to which "theaters of state"[22] are often *musical* theatres—from imperial performances of Confucian ritual music in early China to the 2008 Olympic opening ceremony drawing on these traditions, from revolutionary songs broadcast in the early days of the PRC to contemporary large-scale celebrations such as the National Day Galas that restage the same songs,[23] and even to the ways personal and business relationships are mediated through musical performances of "toasting,"[24] music has long played a central role in statecraft and mediating relationships on various scales. Contemporary musical diplomacy in China is most productively read against these contexts, and these contexts in turn offer alternative perspectives for theorizing musical diplomacy more broadly.

Having laid some conceptual groundwork for an analysis, I now turn to a discussion of the production, circulation, and reception of "Iisang Dagat."

The Players

"Iisang Dagat" was produced as a collaboration between the Chinese Embassy in the Philippines, Guizhou Xinpai Media Company (a

Chinese television and radio production company), and Chinatown TV (a Manila-based weekly television program that bills itself as a "Filipino-Chinese lifestyle show"). Chinese lyrics were first written by Ambassador to the Philippines Huang Xilian, who has served in senior roles in the Ministry of Foreign Affairs of the PRC since the 1990s. The lyrics were translated into Filipino by a team including one of the singers, and the music was composed and produced by Hui Yuanqiong, a singer, producer and recording engineer who works with many prominent artists in China. The song features four singers, including pop stars, television personalities, and most interestingly, politicians and diplomats.

Yu Bin, the most recognizable participant from China, was born in 1991 and came to fame in 2013 as one of four members of M4M, a Mandopop boy band formed and promoted by a major South Korean K-pop agency and record label. He later branched out to acting, and in 2019, starred in two widely popular television dramas, *The Untamed* (*Chenqing Ling*) and *Return the World to You* (*Guihuan Shijie Gei Ni*). Yu Bin's role in these dramas made him a household name and widely recognizable face in China in 2020.

Filipino singer and politician Imelda Papin brings further star power to the video. Born in 1956, her breakout hit "Bakit" ("Why") was released in 1978. Since then, she has had an active career in the Philippines, where she has released many chart-topping hits, and in the United States, where she has toured widely, had long residencies in Las Vegas, and has hosted television and radio programs. In the 1990s, she went into politics, serving as vice governor of her native Camarines Sur Province from 1998–2004; she was elected to the position once again in 2019, resuming an active role in the political life of the Philippines.

Jhonvid Bangayan is a Filipino Chinese singer who has participated in several segments on Chinatown TV in which he speaks Filipino, Mandarin, and English. He was second runner up in a 2018 singing competition produced by Chinatown TV and Quanzhou Radio Broadcast and Television Station. As part of the "2018 Philippine-Fujian (Quanzhou) Television Week,"[25] the event was described by the Philippines Consul General as a "platform to promote cultural exchanges" between Hokkien-speaking regions of China and the significant Filipino Chinese population with roots in the area; thus, although primarily a singer, Bangayan has regularly been featured in diplomatic efforts connecting China and the Philippines.

The fourth featured singer is Xia Wenxin, an early-career diplomat in the Embassy of the People's Republic of China in the Philippines who has worked at the Ministry of Foreign Affairs since 2016. Despite being the only non-professional actor or singer among the four performers, she has a polished and distinctive singing voice.

While other chapters in this book explore the actions of diplomats and politicians through the lens of performance, or the performances of actors through the lens of diplomacy, it is notable in this example that diplomats and politicians are performing in a quite traditional sense as singers alongside professionals, delivering in song a message of cooperation and hope conceived musically by the Chinese ambassador himself. In fact, several of the participants have careers that span both politics and performance. This slippage between notions of performance brings attention to the performativity of diplomacy more broadly.

"Iisang Dagat"

A long shot of an expansive harbor with urban skyline in the background and an empty container ship in the foreground fades to a close-up of a traditional three-hulled small wooden fishing vessel with two men looking at the camera, recapitulating common visual juxtapositions that invoke binaries of modernity/tradition, development/underdevelopment, and global/local. The Chinese title in handwritten calligraphy "Hai de Nabian" (Across the Sea) is superimposed first, soon joined by the Filipino title "Iisang Dagat" (One Sea).

The instrumental underpinning of the verse—a common I-IV-I-V chord progression in Eb utilizing several chord inversions—forms a musical introduction. In the upper register, a syncopated four note figure—Eb F Ab Bb—played by a piano-like synth stays constant, overseeing the movement below. The tempo is a slow 72 bpm, outlined by a simple and unadorned rock drum figure featuring only a synth bass drum and reverb-saturated snare sound. In the "aesthetic cosmopolitan" conventions of pop rock,[26] the accompaniment utilizes common musical tropes of soft rock ballads, with both harmonic movement and rhythm signifying melancholy, hope, forward motion, and contemplation.

Moving drone shots of subdued Metro Manila neighborhoods lead to a close-up of a sign printed on A4 paper taped to a closed storefront gate: "Please be informed that the clinic will be CLOSED starting tomorrow, March 16, 2020 until further notice to make way for Community Quarantine in Metro Manila, for COVID-2019." Close-ups of public signage about masks and hand hygiene are intercut with footage of bus employees taking temperatures of passengers and local police directing traffic while wearing masks.

Yu Bin begins to sing in Mandarin, with subtitles in Chinese on the right and Filipino on the left. He holds common earbud headphones to his ears, and we do not see a microphone. A tightly framed close-up of Yu's face against a plain white wall evokes a webcam view, mimicking the visual perspective that became so common through the rise of video communications software during the pandemic. While this appears visually similar to the socially distanced musical collaborations that became common in 2020 in China and elsewhere, the high quality of the vocal recording and audible post-production are inconsistent with a DIY recording made on one's laptop.

Imelda Papin takes over, singing in Filipino. Unlike Yu, she wears studio monitor headphones, and is notably less casual in dress and appearance. Lyrics describe a cold winter shrouded in dark clouds while looking forward to spring with hope, and still images show various groups—schoolchildren, a minor league football team, aid workers—holding signs that read "Zhongguo jiayou, Wuhan jiayou" (Go China, Go Wuhan!) and occasionally holding PRC flags.

Xia Wenxin and Jhonvid Bangayan sing the next verse in turns. Lyrics describing support, friendship, and love are set to images of

Binondo, Manila's Chinatown neighborhood. We see several "Chinese Filipino Friendship" arches, built in Binondo in the 1970s to celebrate the establishment of diplomatic relations between the Philippines and PRC. While such arches are a common sight in Chinatowns throughout the world, one of the arches stands out for its size and magnificence. The largest Chinatown arch in the world, it was built in 2015 and funded by the China Energy Fund Committee (CEFC), a "non-governmental, non-profit civil society organization" that aims "to promote international cooperation and mutual respect through public diplomacy."[27] Rather than the messages of Chinese-Filipino friendship that are seen on other arches in Chinese, Filipino, and English, it reads simply *"Zhongguo Cheng,"* literally "Chinatown," but a wording that is less commonly used than other terms *"Tangren Jie"* or *"Huaren Qu."* This arch met with resistance from some residents for foregrounding the Chinese nation (Zhongguo) rather than Chinese ethnicity or Sinophone identity formations that decenter the PRC state (e.g., *Tangren* or *Huaren*), and like the music video it is featured in, is emblematic of broader political maneuvering and controversy.[28]

As Bangayan sings the final line of the first verse, the musical accompaniment lands on the dominant, setting up the triumphant-sounding chorus. Yu and Xia are now shown in split screen, and sing the chorus in Mandarin that contains the phrasing that caused controversy:

You and I are in the same one sea,
Looking after each other with love.

Papin and Bangayan take over in Filipino, once again with two voices in unity as metonym for the partnership the lyrics describe, contrasting with the single voices featured in the verse:

I will not let go of your hand,
As we look toward a bright future.

With the lyrics set to an energetic and hopeful melody in a higher register, images of Chinese aid to the Philippines are shown: A photograph of a large check for 120,000,000 pesos (approximately US$2.4 million) being presented at the Federation of Filipino Chinese Chambers of Commerce and Industry, Inc.; boxes being unloaded from a Xiamen Air flight, cartons of PPE emblazoned with the logo of "China Aid" (*Zhongguo Yuanzhu*) and slogan ("For shared future"), and medical supplies and food being unloaded, sorted, and distributed.

The next section of the video features the activities of the team of Chinese doctors. All wear uniforms that read "China Health" (*Zhongguo Weisheng*). Doctors are shown arriving on the airport tarmac, holding meetings in person and by video conference, overseeing the distribution of medical supplies, and seeing patients. The lyrics then allude back to the winter and dark clouds that began the song, with a metaphor of blossoming flowers and spring that will come through cooperative actions aimed at ending the epidemic.

As this verse comes to a close, the volume of the music lowers, and several Philippine officials are shown addressing the camera directly in clips excerpted from television news coverage. Philippine Foreign Secretary Teodoro Locsin Jr. first says, "We are so grateful. Deeply appreciated, never will be forgotten. Thank you from the bottom of our hearts." Carlito Galvez, Jr., described in the caption as "chief implementer of government's national policy on COVID-19," is then shown addressing a series of reporters' microphones from international news networks, acknowledging receipt of medical equipment and commenting on its high quality. Two other senior government officials are shown delivering public messages of gratitude in media interviews. Finally, we see president of the Philippines Rodrigo Duterte, who personally thanks Chinese President Xi Jinping by name for China's aid.

With this, the music returns at full volume for the chorus once again. Members of the Chinese Medical Experts Team are shown one by one, removing their masks, and giving a thumbs up. We see various groups and individuals that have been featured throughout the video, including both the doctors, aid workers, diplomats, and singers reciting "*Zhongguo jiayou, Feilübin jiayou!*" (Go China, Go Philippines!) and "*Laban Pilipinas!*" (Fight Philippines!).

Finally, there is a fade to a shot of several sailboats on the ocean at sunset, with words superimposed: "*Zhouwang xiangzhu. Tong yipian hai.*" ("Mutual help and protection. Together in one sea.")

Mask Diplomacy

"Iisang Dagat" explicitly memorializes Chinese medical aid to the Philippines that began weeks before the song was released. The aid consisted of a "12-member Chinese anti-epidemic medical expert team [comprising] medical experts in the fields of infectious disease prevention and control, clinic treatment, and laboratory testing," as well as medical equipment including "300,000 surgical masks, 30,000 medical N95 masks, 5,000 medical protective suits, 5,000 medical face shields, and 30 non-invasive ventilators."[29]

This aid to the Philippines was one of the first efforts of what came to be known as "mask diplomacy" (*kouzhao waijiao*) by the PRC that later extended into Europe, Africa, and the Americas. Under a global shortage of medical and personal protective equipment, China maintained a large production capacity and was an important global source for masks, ventilators, and other items essential to combatting the pandemic. At the same time, especially in these early months of the pandemic, China was perceived as uniquely experienced and knowledgeable about the virus and methods of combatting it. As Philippine Foreign Secretary Teodoro Locsin Jr. is quoted saying in the Xinhua news report, "the only ones who can really tell us how to handle it are those who fought it on the ground and those are the experts in China."[30]

Discussing medical aid efforts by the PRC during the Covid-19 pandemic more broadly, Bartosz Kowalski argues that "mask diplomacy can be viewed as serving external but also domestic political ends."[31] Mask diplomacy aims to performatively manifest China's global leadership, competence, and the advantages of a one-party state compared to fractured democracies that struggled to provide crucial medical supplies and control local outbreaks. Such a performance serves to bolster party legitimacy both domestically and abroad, and many forms and levels of performativity mutually constitute this performance. Kowalski further discusses the "donation ceremonies" that took place on airport tarmacs upon arrivals of Chinese planes carrying medical supplies, featuring politicians, diplomats, and medical personnel, and consisting of speeches thanking China, and in one case, even the Serbian President kissing a Chinese national flag on live television.[32] Like these standardized donation ceremonies, "Iisang Dagat" was part of a broader performance of Chinese regional and global leadership, even featuring President Rodrigo Duterte explicitly thanking Xi Jinping by name. Invoking the Confucian concept of *li* (ritual, propriety) discussed earlier, these ceremonies both enact and regulate a particular hierarchical relationship between a global power and its beneficiaries. The musical performance thus cannot be extricated from the performance of the aid it memorializes, as well as the diplomatic relationships that such aid mediates.

However, public reception in the Philippines focused on an entirely different perceived message.

Public Reactions to the Video

When "Iisang Dagat" was posted on Youtube and shared on the Chinese Embassy's Facebook page on April 24, 2020, it quickly went viral on various social media, and was often shared under the hashtag "#chexitph," a play on "Brexit" and an abbreviation for "China exit the Philippines." Three days later, it had had garnered 2,000 "likes," 146,000 "dislikes," and 20,000 comments. Though the video was also posted on Chinese social media and video sharing sites, it attracted little attention from Chinese audiences, and seemed to fade into a sea of similar songs being produced at the time. One of the most responded to comments on the Chinese Embassy's Facebook post, quoted in National Public Radio (NPR) and other media coverage of the controversy,[33] succinctly summarizes many other posts that often employed more vitriolic language:

> Excuse me but the West Philippine Sea has always been and will always be rightfully ours. Kindly stop exploiting our seas and building on our islands and shoals. Leave our fishermen alone and let them make a living from it as they have always done. We don't need this song. We need you to respect our claim, the ruling of the international tribunal and leave.

Like many commenters, this Facebook user does not mention the message of cooperation or the context of the Covid-19 pandemic, and instead focuses entirely on the title of the song, which she perceives as an expression of Chinese claims in the South China Sea.

The South China Sea is a resource-rich and strategically important body of water bordered on the North by China, and on the West and South by Vietnam, Malaysia, Brunei, Indonesia, and the Philippines. Half of the world's merchant shipping and one third of its oil passes through its waters. China asserts sovereignty over much of its waters according to a "nine-dash-line" included in Chinese maps since 1947. Such claims are disputed by Southeast Asian nations, and in 2016, the United Nations Convention on the Law of the Sea ruled against China's claims. China, however, did not participate in the arbitration, and does not recognize its authority. In recent years, conflicts have frequently erupted over China's land reclamation efforts in the disputed Spratly Islands, and over fishing and oil drilling rights in the region. Summarizing the stakes of such disputes while putting the conflict in a longer historical perspective stretching back to the sixteenth century, Hayton observes that "the South China Sea is both the fulcrum of world trade and a crucible of conflict."[34] Events during the Covid-19 pandemic—both those directly related to the pandemic, and unrelated—brought the conflict to the forefront, and risked further eroding China's position.[35]

Under these contexts, it is perhaps not surprising that the phrase "One Sea" was heard with reference to these military machinations that bitterly divide China and the Philippines. Even generous commenters on the Facebook post acknowledged the insensitivity of the name:

> Uhm … maybe naming the song "Iisang Dagat" isn't a very good idea considering the current issues we have rn [right now] … but nonetheless, I'd like to believe that this song simply wishes to highlight the friendship China had with the Philippines throughout the years, and the help both countries are giving each other, putting aside our differences during these trying times. Also, Yu Bin ILY~ [I love you.]

A news story in the *Philippine Daily Inquirer* brought the song to wider public attention, and seemed to echo and amplify the negative reactions of many Filipinos:

> What mainly set netizens off was the song's titular "sea" being a body of water supposedly shared by China and the Philippines—Asian neighbors locked in a longstanding dispute and on-and-off diplomatic spats over maritime claims in the West Philippine Sea.[36]

The *Manila Times* responded directly to the *Inquirer* article in an opinion piece by Mauro Gia Samonte provocatively titled "Inquirer's Masterful Journalistic Sleight of Hand," criticizing the *Inquirer*'s coverage as biased, irresponsible, and promoting an anti-China and pro-US agenda:

> With the above lyrics, how could the Inquirer ever have thought of deducing that what is being alluded to in the video is the South China Sea, err, as America would term it and as the Inquirer would repeat after it time and again, the West Philippine Sea?[37]

The contrasting interpretations of the video by these two newspaper columnists illustrate how the debate over this maritime border articulates with internal divisions in the Philippines over the country's complicated relationships with both the United States and China, relationships which have been dramatically and continually recalibrated in recent years. President Rodrigo Duterte's goal of a political realignment with China and distancing from the United States beginning in 2016 was domestically controversial; by the time this video was released, the Philippines was already retreating from its full embrace of China, in part due to unsuccessful negotiations over the South China Sea.[38] Allusion to the political alliances of the two newspapers, as well as to reactions to the video by the online public illustrates the extent to which interpretations of this song are inherently theatres of diplomacy, and how public perceptions of diplomatic relationships intersect with media portrayals of them, both shaping and being shaped in a dynamic and multi-vocal process.

Given the extent to which public reactions to the video focused nearly entirely on its title, it is very interesting to note a discrepancy in the meanings of the titles in Chinese and Filipino. The Filipino title of the song, "Iisang Dagat" is drawn from the first line of the chorus:

> Ikaw at ako ay nasa **iisang dagat**
> Ang iyong pagmamahal aking kasama.
> (You and I are in **one sea**
> Your love is my companion.) (emphasis added)

This chorus is not actually sung in Filipino, but rather in Mandarin as follows, with the Filipino text as subtitles on the left of the screen.

> 我和你 在 在 在 同一片海
> 守望的 爱 爱 爱 陪伴
>
> Wo he ni zai, zai, zai, **tong yipian hai**.
> Shouwang de ai, ai, ai peiban.
> (You and I are in the same one sea,
> Looking after each other with love.) (emphasis added)

The equivalent term in Chinese, "Tong yipian hai" (The Same One Sea) is not used as the Chinese title. Instead, "Hai de nabian" (Across the Sea) is used, drawn from the following verse:

> 等一个春天 那样的遥远
> 海的那边 千岛之国 共度患难

Deng yi ge chuntian nayang de yaoyuan,
Hai de nabian qian dao zhi guo gong du huannan.
(Waiting for a spring so distant,
Sharing adversity with a nation of a thousand islands just **across the sea.**) (emphasis added)

The lyrics of this verse in the Filipino translation are quite different:

Pagdating ng liwanag na ating minimithi
Ito'y magbibigay ng pag-asa sa bawat bansa.
(When the light we desire comes,
It will give hope to every nation.)

While one can only speculate on the discussions and considerations that led to the different titles in the two languages, as well as the discrepancies in the original Chinese lyrics and the Filipino translation, they bring attention to the bifurcation of reception by intended domestic Chinese and international audiences. More broadly, they highlight processes of listening and reception, and bring attention to the ways hearings and mis-hearings are inherent to both the power and unpredictability of musical diplomacy. While the Filipino title was widely understood as promoting Chinese claims in this disputed "one sea," the Chinese title foregrounded Chinese aid delivered "across the sea." For many Filipino audiences, the context of conflict over maritime borders overwhelmed any other meaning of the song. Public discussions of these "oppositional readings"[39] by influential public writers in major newspapers, and by regular citizens on social media form an inseparable part of the performance as a whole, alongside the sounds, images, and mask diplomacy they celebrate.

Only two days before the music video was released, Philippines Foreign Secretary Teodoro Locsin Jr. (who appears in newsreel footage included in the music video) lodged two formal diplomatic complaints with the Chinese Embassy relating to recent events in the South China Sea.[40] While one can also only speculate on the strategy behind releasing a music video titled "One Sea" that begins with an image of a fishing boat in the Manila Bay at such a time, it is reasonable to assume that the issue of the South China Sea was understood by diplomats on both sides—as it was by ordinary citizens—as an important context for seemingly unrelated interactions between the countries. Perhaps, then, the intention of the Chinese Embassy was to project a message of unity, looking beyond political differences by subtly alluding to the disputed sea: "Even if we can't agree on who owns it, we're in it together."

On the other hand, the negative reactions to the video could be understood as a byproduct of a poorly chosen metaphor or diplomatic blunder. Filipino Chinese newspaper columnist Wilson Lee Flores was quoted in a *South China Morning Post* news article about the song, explaining people's negative reactions, and suggesting "one sea" was a

> wrong metaphor because there is a dispute over these islands, there should not be a metaphor about the sea ... you discuss things that are common to you ... If you have a best friend and you always argue over basketball, you don't discuss this when you want to promote harmony.[41]

Rather than speculate about the exact intentions of the Chinese Embassy however, it is more productive to simply note that it is through this ambiguity and controversy that the music video served to mediate Filipino public opinion. Through its explicit content, the video tied the delivery of medical aid to the uneven power relationship between benefactor and recipient that it mimics. Through its implicit subtext, it brought the evolving relationship between China and the Philippines to the center of public discussion, performatively enacting the importance of China in domestic affairs in the Philippines. That is, even if "One Sea" was just a poorly chosen metaphor (which seems unlikely), it had the effect of instigating public debate and reinscribing China into the center of Filipino affairs.

Musical Diplomacy in the Era of Social Media

The controversy generated by "Iisang Dagat" brings attention to some of the ways the power of music wielded by the state is both amplified and complicated by the unwieldy and chaotic public sphere of the contemporary networked world. Theorizations of musical diplomacy—regardless of the histories they are grounded in—must be reconsidered in the context of the heightened importance of online worlds, video telecommunications, and networked relations, changes vastly accelerated by the absence of face-to-face musical interaction since the Covid-19 pandemic.

The rise of social media in the past two decades has altered practices of diplomacy and created new forms of interactive debate surrounding international relations.[42] Social media has brought about an increase in the speed of information dissemination, the decentralization of information sources, new possibilities for direct engagement with citizens, and a crowded public sphere that "talks back" to public diplomacy initiatives in new ways. Focusing primarily on the Arab Spring, but touching on many other case studies, Philip Seib summarizes these shifts in *Real-Time Diplomacy: Politics and Power in the Social Media Era* as a "displacement of traditional hierarchies by networks,"[43] and argues that "crafting successful foreign policy in the years ahead will depend on governments' willingness to accept the transformative combination of new politics, new technologies, and new participation."[44] These changes are also transforming musical diplomacy.

The PRC state no doubt recognizes the power of social media; this is attested to in the domestic sphere by the significant amount of ideological content created and promoted by the state, as well as by the strict monitoring of social media content by state regulators who are charged with guiding public discussion and prioritizing stability over dissonance. In recent years, China has also turned to international social media in the service of public diplomacy; as Bradshaw and Howard observe, "beyond domestically bound platforms, the growing sophistication and use of global social networking technologies demonstrates how China is also turning to these technologies as a tool of geopolitical power and influence."[45]

These new uses of social media both build upon and transform longer histories of the political and diplomatic mobilization of music in China. Han Li examines some of the ways that the Chinese state is "actively re-inventing its propaganda apparatus to appeal to a younger, highly mobile, and global audience,"[46] and focuses on a series of short music videos shared to international social media produced by Fuxing Road Studios. Li explores the ways that "uplifting tunes, catchy lyrics, and even cartoon characters ... signify a stark contrast from previously established CCP propaganda,"[47] and furthermore point to "the complex dynamics of new media, popular nationalism, and state intervention."[48]

As "Iisang Dagat" demonstrates however, the reception of such musical diplomacy delivered by social media may be unpredictable. But even instigating debate is a performance of power, foregrounding China's role as a key global player, projecting a Chinese perspective on international relations, and shaping public discussions that, wherever they lead, begin with the assumption of China's strength and international influence.

Musical Diplomacy as State Ritual

One of the most significant insights in Confucian thought about music and statecraft that can contribute to a broader understanding of musical diplomacy is that music is a political tool inseparable from other practices of governance. As the *Yue Ji* summarizes, "Ritual regulates the people's hearts; Music harmonizes the people's voices. Administration is used to carry them out; Punishment is used to prevent [transgressions against] them. If the four develop and go unopposed, then the kingly Way is complete."[49]

As the analysis in this chapter has aimed to demonstrate, musical performance is often intertwined with other performative dimensions of diplomacy. In this case, music ("Iisang Dagat") is inseparable from state ritual (mask diplomacy), and is further entwined with the practicalities of statecraft (publicly mediating a complex and unequal power dynamic that frequently hinges on a disputed maritime border).

Such a perspective also, as Ball summarizes in his articulation of the concept of postdiplomatic theatre in the introduction to this volume, "re-centers diplomacy on the moments in which it is performed, recognizing that the content it putatively transmits is inseparable from the times and spaces in which it operates, the forces it deploys, the affects and atmospheres it generates, and the ways it is embodied."[50] Refracted through contemporary practices, this offers a ground on which to conceptualize how in the case of "Iisang Dagat," a music video circulated through social media, online discourse surrounding it, ceremonies celebrating diplomatic aid efforts, and the delivery of aid itself are all intertwined layers of diplomatic performance.

Notes

1 Arne Spohr, "Concealed Music in Early Modern Diplomatic Ceremonial," in *Music and Diplomacy from the Early Modern Era to the Present*, eds. Rebekah Ahrendt, Mark Ferraguto, and Damien Mahiet (New York: Palgrave Macmillan, 2014), 19–44.

2 Kendra Salois, "The Ethics and Politics of Empathy in US Hip-Hop Dipolomacy: The Case of the Next Level Program," in *Popular Music and Public Diplomacy*, ed. Mario Dunkel and Sina Nitzsche (Bielefeld: Transcript Verlag, 2018), 233–53.

3 James R. Ball III, ed., *Performing Statecraft: The Postdiplomatic Theatre of Sovereigns, Citizens, and States* (London: Methuen Drama, 2022), 3–4.

4 Damien Mahiet, "The Diplomat's Music Test: Branding New and Old Diplomacy at the Beginning of the Nineteenth and Twenty-First Centuries," in *International Relations, Music and Diplomacy: Sounds and Voices on the International Stage*, eds. Frédéric Ramel and Cécile Prévost-Thomas (Cham: Springer, 2018), 124.

5 Hans N. Tuch, *Communicating with the World: U. S. Public Diplomacy Overseas* (New York: Palgrave Macmillan, 1990), 3.

6 Danielle Fosler-Lussier, *Music in America's Cold War Diplomacy* (Oakland: University of California Press, 2015).

7 Ball, *Performing Statecraft*, 17.

8 Stuart Hall, "Encoding/Decoding," in *Media and Cultural Studies: Keyworks*, ed. Meenakshi Gigi Durham and Douglas Kellner (Malden, MA: Blackwell Publishers, 2001), 128–38.
9 Erving Goffman, *The Presentation of Self in Everyday Life* (Woodstock, NY: Overlook Press, 1973).
10 Will Straw, "Systems of Articulation, Logics of Change: Communities and Scenes in Popular Music," *Cultural Studies* 5, no. 3 (1991): 368–88.
11 Frédéric Ramel and Cécile Prévost-Thomas, eds., *International Relations, Music and Diplomacy: Sounds and Voices on the International Stage* (Cham: Springer, 2018), 7.
12 M. I. Franklin, ed., *Resounding International Relations: On Music, Culture, and Politics* (New York: Palgrave Macmillan).
13 Rebekah Ahrendt, Mark Ferraguto, and Damien Mahiet, eds., *Music and Diplomacy from the Early Modern Era to the Present* (New York: Palgrave Macmillan, 2014), 5; Ramel and Prévost-Thomas, *International Relations, Music, and Diplomacy*, 1.
14 Authored by a second-generation disciple of Confucius around the fifth century BCE or compiled by Confucian scholars early in the Han Dynasty (202 BCE–220 CE), some sections were lost, and others persisted in fragments in other works such as the *Li Ji* ("Book of Rites") and *Shi Ji* ("Records of the Grand Historian Sima Qian").
15 *Yue Ji* 1.3, in Scott Cook, "'Yue Ji' 樂記 — Record of Music: Introduction, Translation, Notes, and Commentary," *Asian Music* 26, no. 2 (April 1, 1995): 29.
16 Cook, "Yue Ji," 41.
17 James Garrison, "The Social Value of Ritual and Music in Classical Chinese Thought," *Teorema* 31, no. 3 (2012): 211.
18 Garrison, "The Social Value," 213.
19 Garrison, "The Social Value," 214.
20 Bell Yung, Evelyn Sakakida Rawski, and Rubie S. Watson, *Harmony and Counterpoint: Ritual Music in Chinese Context* (Stanford: Stanford University Press, 1996).
21 Lothar von Falkenhausen, *Suspended Music: Chime-Bells in the Culture of Bronze Age China* (Berkeley: University of California Press, 1993); Erica Fox Brindley, *Music, Cosmology, and the Politics of Harmony in Early China* (Albany: State University of New York Press, 2012); Daobin

Fu, "Village People, Village Music and the Theoretical Significance of the Concept That Poetry Can Harmonize People," *Frontiers of Literary Studies in China* 2, no. 3 (2008): 321–48.

22 James R. Ball III, *Theater of State: A Dramaturgy of the United Nations* (Evanston: Northwestern University Press, 2020).

23 Adam Kielman, "Sites and Sounds of National Memory: Performing the Nation in China's Decennial National Day Celebrations," *International Communication of Chinese Culture* 7, no. 2 (June 1, 2020): 147–68.

24 Levi S. Gibbs, "Improvised Songs of Praise and Group Sociality in Contemporary Chinese Banquet Culture," *International Communication of Chinese Culture* 7, no. 2 (June 1, 2020): 133–46.

25 Philippine Consulate General, "2 Filipino-Chinese Young Singers Triumph in the 2018 Philippine-Fujian (Quanzhou) Television Week— Singing Competition Finals," *News Release*, January 18, 2019, https://xiamenpcg.dfa.gov.ph/news-room/news-press-releases/733-2-filipino-chinese-young-singers-triumph-in-the-2018-philippine-fujian-quanzhou-television-week-singing-competition-finals (accessed July 15, 2021).

26 Motti Regev, *Pop-Rock Music: Aesthetic Cosmopolitanism in Late Modernity* (Cambridge, UK: Polity, 2013).

27 "China Energy Fund Committee," China Development Forum, https://en.cdf.org.cn/cdf2017en/jgjs/3170.htm (accessed July 15, 2021).

28 Kimberly Go, "World's Largest Chinatown Arch Unveiled," *Rappler*, July 7, 2015, https://www.rappler.com/moveph/largest-chinatown-arch-binondo-history (accessed July 15, 2021).

29 "China's Medical Expert Team Arrives in Philippines to Help Fight Covid-19," *Xinhua*, April 5, 2020, http://www.xinhuanet.com/english/asiapacific/2020-04/05/c_138949480.htm (accessed July 15, 2021).

30 "China's Medical Expert Team Arrives in Philippines to Help Fight Covid-19."

31 Bartosz Kowalski, "China's Mask Diplomacy in Europe: Seeking Foreign Gratitude and Domestic Stability," *Journal of Current Chinese Affairs*, April 8, 2021, 5.

32 Kowalski, "China's Mask Diplomacy," 7.

33 Scott Neuman, "Chinese Song Expressing Friendship During Pandemic Backfires with Wary Filipinos," *NPR*, April 28, 2020, https://www.npr.org/sections/coronavirus-live-updates/2020/04/28/846888880/chin

ese-song-expressing-friendship-during-pandemic-backfires-with-wary-filipinos (accessed July 15, 2021).

34 Bill Hayton, *The South China Sea: The Struggle for Power in Asia* (New Haven: Yale University Press, 2014), xvi.

35 James Char, "Contesting for Supremacy in the Asia-Pacific in the Time of COVID-19: How the Pandemic May Have Already Unravelled China's Long-Term Strategy in Southeast Asia," *Prospect and Exploration* 18, no. 9 (September 2020): 134.

36 Pocholo Concepcion and Rey Anthony Ostria, "Chinese Embassy's 'One Sea' Video Draws Wave of Anger," *The Philippine Daily Inquirer*, April 26, 2020, https://newsinfo.inquirer.net/1264816/chinese-embassys-one-sea-video-draws-wave-of-anger (accessed July 15, 2021).

37 Mauro Gia Samonte, "Inquirer's Masterful Journalistic Sleight of Hand," *The Manila Times*, May 2, 2020, https://www.manilatimes.net/2020/05/02/opinion/columnists/inquirers-masterful-journalistic-sleight-of-hand/721449 (accessed July 15, 2021).

38 Derek Grossman, "Duterte's Dalliance With China Is Over," *Foreign Policy*, November 2, 2021, https://foreignpolicy.com/2021/11/02/duterte-china-philippines-united-states-defense-military-geopolitics/ (accessed July 15, 2021).

39 Hall, "Encoding/Decoding," 138.

40 Jim Gomez, "Philippines Protests China's Sea Claim, Weapon Pointing," *Associated Press News*, April 22, 2020, https://apnews.com/article/dfa2fabb14f91a8b2780b6faab93f509 (accessed July 15, 2021).

41 Alan Robles, "'Laughable': Filipinos Pan Covid-19 Music Video as Chinese Propaganda," *South China Morning Post*, April 27, 2020. https://www.scmp.com/week-asia/politics/article/3081796/laughable-cynical-filipinos-pan-chinese-coronavirus-music-video (accessed July 15, 2021).

42 Corneliu Bjola and Marcus Holmes, *Digital Diplomacy: Theory and Practice* (London: Routledge, 2015); Britney Harris, "Diplomacy 2.0: The Future of Social Media in Nation Branding," *Journal of Public Diplomacy* 4, no. 1 (2013).

43 Philip Seib, *Real-Time Diplomacy: Politics and Power in the Social Media Era* (New York: Palgrave Macmillan, 2012), 9.

44 Seib, *Real-Time Diplomacy*, 173.

45 Samantha Bradshaw and Philip N. Howard, *The Global Disinformation Order: 2019 Global Inventory of Organised Social Media Manipulation* (Oxford, UK: Project on Computational Propaganda, 2019), 2.
46 Han Li, "From Red to 'Pink': Propaganda Rap, New Media, and China's Soft Power Pursuit," *American Journal of Chinese Studies* 25, no. 2 (2018): 90.
47 Han Li, "From Red to Pink," 90.
48 Han Li, "From Red to Pink," 105.
49 *Yue Ji* 1.8, in Cook, "Yue Ji," 40.
50 Ball, *Performing Statecraft*, 16.

7

The President Makes a Play: Putin and Erdoğan's Sporting Statecraft

Sean Bartley and Jared Strange

You learn more about a guy after one round of golf than you'd learn doing business with him for a month. I didn't vote for him, but now I'm a big fan.
     O.J. Simpson on Bill Clinton, as quoted in *The American Spectator*, September 1996.[1]

Political leaders often use the arena of sport to powerfully stage their authority. Some even take to the field themselves, usually in low-stakes exhibitions designed to inflate their aptitude and reinforce their populist credentials. In this chapter, we examine two leaders who have used sports performances to burnish their personas and expand their influence: Russia's Vladimir Putin and Turkey's Recep Tayyip Erdoğan. As part of a carefully cultivated image as a rugged outdoorsman, Putin annually performs in a hockey exhibition alongside his oligarchs and famous heroes of the Soviet and Russian Federation Olympic teams. Putin always wins, and his opponents comically contrive ways to let their president score. Erdoğan, meanwhile, has close ties to the Turkish soccer establishment, thanks in part to his career as an amateur player, his affiliation with an Istanbul club (which he consummated with a conveniently excellent performance in a friendly match), and his overt courting of established stars in the Turkish diaspora. Though both men have mobilized sport for their political aims, their forays into the arena have engendered resistance and revealed their foibles, illustrating that sport is as much a stage for political contestation as it is for promotion.

American media outlets often explicitly connect Putin and Erdoğan's staged events to those of far-off dictatorial rulers as a way to poke fun. For these dictators, such displays are par for the course. As Jack Holmes put it in *Esquire*, "Because so much depends on a cult of personality, a common feature of any authoritarian state is that The Leader himself feels compelled to perform public displays of strength and virility to reassure the public he's the man for the job."[2] In 1966, Chinese Communist Party officials claimed that Chairman Mao Zedong had swum 15 kilometers along the Yangtze River in just 65 minutes, far faster than the world record for such a distance. *Time* magazine would later call the alleged swim "one of his greatest acts of political theater."[3] According to North Korean state media, in 1994 Kim Jong-Il shot eleven holes-in-one and scored an unimaginably low 38 on the first day he held a golf club (for comparison's sake, the lowest PGA score ever was a 58 and no professional golfer has ever shot more than three holes-in-one in a single round). But the autocrat most commonly invoked in Western stories about Putin and Erdoğan's efforts is Turkmenistan's president, Gurbanguly Berdymukhamedov. An avowed equestrian, Berdymukhamedov fell off his horse and violently hit the ground in a 2013 racing event. According to a BBC reporter in attendance, fans wept in near silence for 40 minutes before Berdymukhamedov emerged from the ambulance that rushed to help him.[4] After using the public address system to instruct audience members to delete any video recordings of the fall, Turkmen officials doctored the video, broadcast the race on state television that night without the incident, and declared Berdymukhamedov the winner. Western media outlets posted the unedited video of his accident as they would later do when Putin suffered a fall of his own.

As outlandish and obviously contrived as these particular feats are, it is worth remembering that robust displays of physical strength and skill are praised in leaders all over the globe, including in comparatively more democratic countries. US presidents, for example, are often called upon to throw the first pitch of the Major League Baseball season, while recent presidents Barack Obama and Donald Trump have drawn attention, and sometimes derision, for their love of basketball and golf, respectively. What distinguishes Putin and Erdoğan from most others is that their sporting performances are part of larger political projects that combine the powers of their offices with the legitimating powers of the sports-industrial complex. Throughout this chapter, we will refer to this conjoining of political and sporting power as "sports-as-politics." We offer this shorthand as a way to identify personal or institutional projects that incorporate sport in the use of, expansion of, or, in some cases, resistance to governmental powers. The term comes out of the widespread recognition of sport's national role in "enhancing prestige, securing legitimacy, compensating for other aspects of life within [national] boundaries, and pursuing international rivalries by peaceful means,"[5] as well as the broad, inclusive notion of "sports politics" that can cover any manner of definitions of both terms it contains.[6] However, we use it here to consider the expansion and contestation of state power, specifically. While leaders like Putin and Erdoğan obviously foreground their ties to sport, the level at which their sporting and political power is conjoined is not always clear; in fact, it often finds greater purchase when conducted in the murky spaces between institutions. This very murkiness requires us to consider not only the ways sport is used to further state projects, but the ways in which sport serves as a site for contesting and wielding institutional powers. In short, the realms of sport and politics are tightly intertwined, but they can work at cross-purposes with one another, such that leaders employing sports-as-politics can rig sporting institutions to their own devices, whereas sporting governments can prove to be far more stubborn than some leaders are equipped to deal with.

Before reading Putin and Erdoğan's projects more closely, it is important to consider one of the key features of sporting events as performance. Vital to our understanding is the notion of a hockey game or soccer match as a "scenario." In Diana Taylor's conception, scenarios allow for prearranged enactments with agreed upon rules to serve a number of social functions through performance. Thus, a soccer match or hockey game can simulate combat between groups that are themselves represented by avatars in the form of players and teams. Though the match or game is ultimately a scenario and therefore not "real," the sensations and symbols it traffics in can be potent stimulants for identity-formation, community-building, and, unfortunately, as the history of sports will attest, violence. As Taylor warns us, however, a scenario often says "more about the 'us' envisioning them than about the 'other' they try to model."[7] In other words, it is not just the players who deserve the lion's share of the scrutiny, nor even just the fans, but rather the "sports-industrial complex,"[8] the enormous entity that brings together distinct yet overlapping economic and political interests in the form of governments, corporate sponsors, mass media, medicine, and biotechnology. Thus, conceiving of the sporting event as a scenario allows us not simply to investigate what is performed on the pitch or ice and how it is received, but to theorize how that performance is framed and claimed—indeed, how the game itself "performs" for the forces that invest in it. Putin and Erdoğan depend on these scenarios in similar ways, albeit with certain distinctions. Therefore, we offer up these case studies in dialogue with one another, taking into account their performances, the media coverage and political entanglements that greeted them, and the ways they illuminate the political powers available through (and to) sport.

Scenario 1: Vladimir Putin

Dressed in his signature red number eleven jersey, Russian leader Vladimir Putin skated into the Bolshoi Ice Arena in 2019 to play his part in an annual tradition: his appearance in a gala exhibition for the Night Hockey League, a nationwide amateur organization he founded in 2011. His teammates? A panoply of Russian hockey legends, including two-time Stanley Cup winner and Olympic hero

Viacheslav Festisov and the famed "Russian Rocket," Pavel Bure. His opposition? A group of amateurs and bureaucrats, including billionaire oligarch Vladimir Potanin and Putin's closest childhood friend Gennady Timchenko, an energy magnate under sanctions in the West for his role in the Russian Federation's invasion and annexation of Crimea in 2014. The 2019 exhibition sticks out from previous competitions for two principal reasons. First, the reporting discrepancy in Putin's offensive performance (somewhere between eight and ten goals). Second, in a video clip that quickly went viral in the West, Putin tripped on a carpet while making a postgame celebratory lap, tumbling face-first onto his hands and knees as his teammates looked on helplessly. In this brief moment, the arena itself momentarily seized control of the scenario's narrative from Putin and the Russian State.

Founded by Putin and former Soviet hockey player Alexander Yakushev, star of the famous "Summit Series" between the USSR and Canada in 1972, the Night Hockey League is a massive umbrella organization for local amateur teams in thousands of municipalities across nine geographic regions. Unlike pickup leagues and adult amateur leagues in the West, Night League games feature paid officials, on-site medical support, and video crews who broadcast games on local television and stream them on the internet. Since it was built for the 2014 Olympic Winter Games, Sochi's Bolshoi Ice Arena annually hosts 160 plus teams in the finals of each division (men eighteen–thirty-nine, men over forty, and the so-called Amazon women's division) as well as the celebratory exhibition featuring Putin. In these annual spectacles, the Russian president had netted at least forty-one goals by 2019 (according to the TASS, the official Russian state news agency, that year's ten goals would make a total of forty-three). Even at age sixty-nine, the president of the hockey-obsessed country seems to dominate the exhibitions despite the fact that he only learned to ice skate in his late fifties. According to the "Interests" section of his official Kremlin website, Putin "spent two months training under famous hockey player Alexei Kasatonov" after promising a Russian youth team he would learn.⁹ Just weeks after allegedly putting on skates for the first time, he scored five goals in the first Night League exhibition.

Putin's annual hockey heroics are just part of his ongoing series of public physical and athletic performances. His pursuits, detailed by the Kremlin's web pages, include skiing (the website features quotes by Soviet skiing champion Leonid Tyagachev complimenting his technique), fishing, horseback riding, and whitewater rafting. In 2015, he joined officers of the Russian Geographical Society on a deep-sea diving expedition to investigate abandoned vessels at the bottom of the Black Sea. In 2012, he dressed in a white flight suit and piloted a hang glider across the Yamal Peninsula in Northwest Siberia, hoping to teach a stranded group of White Siberian Cranes how to migrate. Later that year, RT, a Kremlin-controlled press outlet that publishes pro-Russian coverage in English and other Western languages, ran a news report about Putin saving the lives of a documentary television crew by shooting an endangered Amur Tiger with a tranquilizer gun, supposedly kissing the stunned animal before tagging it with a GPS collar. When the International Fund for Animal Welfare and World Wildlife Fund accused Russian authorities of not only staging the rescue, but killing the animal in the process, RT deleted text and video versions of their coverage online.

But perhaps most famously in the West, the Kremlin regularly publishes pictures of Putin fishing and horseback riding while shirtless. In 2018, Austrian journalist Armin Wolf asked Putin bluntly if the official photographs were a publicity attempt:

WOLF: There are many photos of you half-naked, which is rather unusual for a head of state. These photos were not taken by paparazzi or tourists. They were published by the Kremlin. What is the story behind these photos?

PUTIN: You said "half-naked" not "naked," thank God. When I am on vacation I see no need to hide behind the bushes, and there is nothing wrong with that.¹⁰

Months later, Megyn Kelly (formerly of NBC News) attempted a similar line of questioning:

KELLY: One of the images that we see of you in the United States is without the shirt on a horse. What is that about?
PUTIN: You know, I have seen photos of me riding a bear. I have not ridden a bear yet, but there are such photos already.[11]

Indeed, a 2017 YouTube clip featuring a badly Photoshopped Putin cruising shirtlessly down a river atop an enormous brown bear has garnered over 430,000 views. Commenters on the video assure viewers that it is "beary beary real."

As the Kremlin is also quick to advertise, the former KGB operative has practiced Judo since childhood and in 2010 received an honorary doctorate in the martial art from Yong In University in South Korea.[12] In recent years, international outlets have proposed that Kremlin coverage of Putin's Judo training is as doctored as the ridiculous bear video. Criticizing the scores of YouTube videos released by the Kremlin and RT featuring fawning descriptions such as "Putin has taken another step to boost his charisma by holding a wrestling session with members of Russia's national teams," Benjamin Wittes, martial artist and editor of the legal and national security outlet *Lawfare*, questioned the veracity of Putin's Judo claims:

> But for all his displays of the crudest forms of masculinity, Putin only fights people who are in his power, whom he can have arrested, whose lives he can ruin. And I think they're all taking falls for him. In fact, they're not really fighting him at all. I don't pretend to have seen all of Putin's martial arts videos, but I've watched a bunch of them, and they seem to follow a similar pattern: they involve some shots of Putin and others doing warm-ups, and then they involve a sequence of short clips, in each of which Putin throws someone who is prepared to take the throw; then there are warm handshakes and photo ops. At least in the videos I have seen, there are no committed attacks on Putin, and I see no evidence that his opponents are ever trying to get the better of him. The videos are demonstrations in which he shows off

his masculine prowess with them taking what the Japanese call *ukemi* (defensive falls) for him.[13]

In a tweet publicized and shared by scores of Putin critics (including former US Ambassador to Russia Michael McFaul and Soviet chess prodigy Gary Kasparov), Wittes challenged Putin to a fight: "I will meet him any time and any place where he lacks legal authority to have me locked up. #brookingsfightclub."[14] Neither the Kremlin nor President Putin have responded to Wittes's 2015 invitation.

Different audiences will inevitably interpret Putin's game playing through their own lenses and biases, but Putin also carefully directs his performances toward this multiplicity of viewers. In *The Presentation of Self in Everyday Life*, Erving Goffman offers the term "audience segregation" to describe the ways in which we all adjust and recalibrate our performances of self to present a desired character to those around us. Putin offers three very different iterations to different audiences. For the Russian people, Putin performs the confident, hypermasculine athlete in the Night League hockey exhibition and the selective video and press accounts from Kremlin-controlled sources. For journalists like Wolf and Kelly, he plays the clever troll, making light of their questions and dodging their importance while nevertheless appearing open to Western scrutiny and journalistic investigation. For political critics like Wittig, McFaul, and Kasparov, he refuses recognition and offers only silence.

Scenario 2: Recep Tayyip Erdoğan

At sixty years of age, Recep Tayyip Erdoğan may not have seemed the most formidable athlete when he trotted out onto the soccer pitch to play for Turkish club Başakşehir in the summer of 2014. Nevertheless, the Turkish Prime Minister, then on his way to becoming president, managed to bag a hat-trick (three goals in one game) in a 9–4 victory in front of a crowd dotted with celebrities and dignitaries. One of his goals was an especially impressive curling effort delivered with the outside of his left foot, an audacious show of skill made possible by the significant distance afforded to him by the opposition defense. Erdoğan's conveniently virtuoso display was a fitting flourish to the commemorative opening of Başakşehir's new stadium and to his own imminent inauguration as Turkey's twelfth president, an achievement he relished by donning the number 12 jersey.[15] Unusual though his excursion may seem, Erdoğan's brief foray onto the pitch is well in keeping with his personal history and political branding.

In addition to being a pseudo-benefactor of the game with an Istanbul stadium named in his honor, Erdoğan is also a former semi-professional player who has long been part of the fabric of Turkish soccer. His most notable playing stint was with the club IETT Spor in the Istanbul Amateur One Championship, with whom he lifted the championship trophy in 1977. While there, he supposedly earned the nickname "Imam Beckenbauer," a reference both to his religious piety and his resemblance, in skill and physique, to legendary German defender Franz Beckenbauer.[16] Despite playing at the amateur level, Erdoğan insists his future would have been bright had the military coup not happened: allegedly, he was twice offered a chance to sign for Fenerbahçe, one of the three leading clubs in Istanbul.[17] Erdoğan eventually left IETT Spor after it was taken over by a military figure following the 1980 military-led coup, claiming his departure was in protest of a new rule requiring the men to be clean-shaven, which was interpreted as an anti-Muslim measure.[18] While the accuracy of these claims is difficult to determine, they advance a vision of the past in which Erdoğan appears not only as a skilled sportsman with untapped potential but also a devout believer whose career was adversely affected by the machinations of Turkey's secular military establishment. As it happens, that 1980 coup resulted in the embrace of neoliberal policies in Turkey, which in turn spurred political investments into Turkish soccer.[19] With the help of state intervention, new corporate money was injected into the Turkish game, reshaping it over the next few decades into a middle-class clientele that largely, if superficially, adhered to government messaging or remained ostensibly apolitical.[20] This tenuous connection between the state and the Turkish soccer establishment, partly enabled by growing corporate investments in sport and politics, helped the Justice and Development Party (AKP) connect with its conservative, middle-class powerbase and disrupt the secular politics typically associated with Turkish clubs, particularly in Istanbul. It also allowed Erdoğan to leverage his ties to the sport on his way to the top of the AKP pyramid.

In most ways, Başakşehir is not a club readily associated with a leader as ambitious as Erdoğan. Named after the conservative enclave on the edges of Istanbul in which it is located, the club was only created in 1990 and promoted to the Turkish Super Lig in 2007, and just recently won its first league title in 2020 after play was resumed following the Covid-19 outbreak. Compare that to the Istanbul triumvirate of Galatasaray, Fenerbahçe, and Beşiktaş, all of which are over 110 years old and boast numerous trophies between them, not to mention much larger fanbases. Nevertheless, that 2020 championship, rewarded the following season with a debut in the lucrative European Champions League, is evidence of how much Başakşehir's fortunes have improved since it was acquired by owners affiliated with the AKP. With that new ownership came new funding, which in turn resulted in the acquisition of pedigreed players from superior European leagues and the opening of a new stadium. That stadium has hosted pre-match spectacles of militaristic power and conservative values, including video images of fighter jets striking their targets, child mascots parading around dressed as Ottoman soldiers, and chants of "God is great" from a hardcore group of roughly five hundred fans. For all its comparative lack of history, Başakşehir has proven to be Erdoğan loyalists' most successful attempt yet to create an appropriately neo-Ottomanist, "pro government" club.[21] As such, Erdoğan's appearance on Başakşehir's behalf, accentuated by his conveniently excellent performance and framed by the conservative, neo-Ottomanist messaging practiced by the club, effectively consummated the union between state and sporting institutions he has overseen and embodied. Unlike Putin, whose machismo supports various athletic adventures, Erdoğan is very much embedded in the fabric of Turkish soccer, which has, over time, been positioned to suit the AKP's political endeavors. Considering the breadth of the game's reach in Europe, this ensures Erdoğan's sporting presence is felt not only across the nation but across the continent.

Coverage and Context I: Vladimir Putin

Media outlets in the West focused their coverage of Putin's 2019 exhibition on his tumble to the ice, emphasizing the symbolism of the accident as a central way to understand the exhibition. The *New York Times*, in an article by Palko Karasz entitled "Putin Shoots, Scores and Falls Face First on Hockey Ice," gets to his "faceplant" just two sentences into their coverage.[22] A piece in the *Guardian*, "Vladimir Putin Scores at Least Eight Goals in Hockey Exhibition, Then Falls on Face," dubs the incident a "face-first spill" in the opening sentence.[23] The digital version of these articles, like dozens of others in English-language press outlets, both feature an embedded video clip of the fall just beneath the headline and before the actual body text, ensuring that audiences have already seen (and, presumably, chuckled at) Putin's misfortune before they begin to read. A quick search on YouTube reveals clips of the fall posted by dozens of Western media outlets, including ABC News, the *Washington Post,* NBC News, *CBS This Morning,* and BBC News. As of this writing, the *Guardian*'s clip has been viewed over 1,130,000 times.[24] The *Independent*'s YouTube clip actually graphically superimposes a rectangular box around Putin, making sure the viewer can distinguish him from the other players in uniform just before he trips and falls.

But in Russian publications, those in both English and Russian, from state outlets and more independent sources, evidence of Putin's stumble is harder to find. The Kremlin's official press release listed the top players on each team and even included the complete transcript of Putin's pre-game remarks, but made no mention of the accident.[25] RT led with the headline "Putin Scores 10 Goals in Night Hockey League Match in

Sochi," but left out the president's fall. Their YouTube clip, unlike the dozens of others, shows Putin skating on to the rink to the cheers of the Sochi audience, scoring one of his goals, and posing for photographs at center ice.[26] Even the *Moscow Times*, an independent English-language outlet that is often fiercely critical of Russian state policy, buried the details of the fall that generated so much interest elsewhere, mentioning the exhibition in the tenth paragraph of a weekend news roundup and stressing that Putin "appeared in good spirits" after the stumble. Unless they were in the arena for the game or happened to read English and seek out just one line in the *Moscow Times*, everyday Russians would be wholly unaware of the story as the outside world was experiencing it.[27]

Coverage and Context II: Recep Tayyip Erdoğan

Like Putin, Erdoğan stages his sports-as-politics appearances knowing he will receive full deference from Turkey's loyal media outlets. The *Daily Sabah*, a notably pro-government newspaper, likened one of his goals in the friendly match to the work of Barcelona and Argentina superstar Lionel Messi.[28] He has also worked diligently to court Turkish celebrities, ensuring his influence in Turkish media is enriched by their associations. However, he has found, just as Putin had with his hunting trips, deep-sea dives, and wildlife conservation efforts, a media landscape abroad that is much more prone to ridicule and controversy. On May 13, 2018, Erdoğan was photographed at an event in London alongside Mesut Özil, Ilkay Gündoğan, and Cenk Tosun, all players in the English Premier League. All three gave the President signed shirts in their club colors; Gündoğan, who plays for Manchester City, handed his over with the inscription "to my president, with my respects."[29] That sentiment is striking considering Gündoğan and Özil are German-born players of Turkish descent who, at the time, were key members of the German national team preparing for the 2018 World Cup in Russia. Despite their attempts to downplay the meeting, the photo op generated a furor in Germany that renewed xenophobic sentiments about immigrants and their descendants, damaging the tolerant self-image the country had been carefully constructing with help from the men's national team. Özil eventually quit the German team, joined Fenerbahçe, and maintained his public ties with Erdoğan; Erdoğan even served as the best man at his wedding, taking the opportunity to give a speech that reaffirmed his conservative credentials.[30]

In addition to complicating the public personas of athletes through association, Erdoğan's union of state and sport has faced challenges from sporting institutions. On October 11, 2019, the Turkish national team secured a 1-0 win over Albania in their EURO 2020 qualifying campaign thanks to a goal from striker Tosun, who later posted a picture of himself and several other players saluting during their goal celebration to his Instagram account with the caption "For our nation, especially for the ones who are risking their lives for our nation."[31] The entire Turkish team was subsequently photographed giving the salute in the dressing room; the picture was posted to the official Turkish Football Association's Instagram account with a similar message of support for the troops. The salute coincided with the Turkish military's anti-Kurdish incursion into Syria and immediately prompted scrutiny thanks to UEFA's stance against overt political expression within the stadium. The gesture was later revived in a 1–1 draw with France, after which calls for recrimination intensified.[32] Ultimately, UEFA settled on a fine for the Turkish FA rather than the more severe punishment argued for by France, namely the retraction of Istanbul's lucrative hosting rights for the 2020 UEFA Champions League Final[33] (which was eventually moved to Portugal after Covid-19 lockdown).

Nevertheless, in addition to illustrating the Turkish team's role as a national avatar in the sporting arena worthy of Erdoğan's sports-as-politics project, the incident also demonstrated the power of the sport's governing bodies to levy sanctions of their own, albeit under the guise of a dubious anti-political ethos. Indeed, the fact that the Turkish FA escaped serious recriminations should not be an indicator of UEFA's ineffectuality. Such sporting bodies are significant entities in their own right, capable of leveraging enormous material power through corporate sponsorship, government subsidies, and cultural capital of the highest order. Organizations such as FIFA are especially formidable, to the point that when the 2018 World Cup hosting rights were controversially awarded to Russia, there was little opposition from contesting nations such as England, despite compelling evidence of wrongdoing. Choosing to allocate or withdraw lucrative hosting rights and sanctioning teams who exhibit inappropriate behavior by, among other things, levying fines or banning fans from the stands are among the ways these sporting governments can curb unwanted political activity and, in effect, flex their own political muscle.

In addition to encountering obstacles abroad, Erdoğan has also faced soccer-based opposition at home. Resistance has been especially potent among left-leaning fans of Istanbul club Beşiktaş, some of whom vociferously decried him from their home stadium and engaged in anti-AKP, pro-democracy activism during the 2013 Gezi protests that resulted in governmental crackdowns.[34] Subsequent government moves to stifle further organizing, whether by adopting stricter crowd-control policies or setting up a controversial ticket managing scheme connected to an AKP-affiliated bank, have also garnered widespread criticism among fan groups.[35] While the capacity to leverage fan engagement with politics into coherent organization is limited, any effort on behalf of elite powers to mold the social components of sport into compliance is limited by the dynamism and complexity inherent in fandom. Thus, while Erdoğan's sports-as-politics project has found a degree of success, it must contend with structural and social forces that utilize sport for their own purposes. The enormous sporting governments that hold so much power within the sports-industrial complex have their commercial interests and agendas to protect against insurgent politics. Fan communities, meanwhile, can use their clubs as sites for building consensus and levying criticisms. Add these to the burgeoning economic crisis in Turkey, spurred by Erdoğan's own faulty policies,[36] and the path toward political power and economic prosperity through sport is perhaps less sure than it once was.

The "It Effect"

Whereas Özil, Gündoğan, and Tosun each assumed political risk by associating themselves rhetorically, photographically, and sartorially with Erdoğan, other players, such as Turkish midfielder Arda Turan, have benefitted from his attention and even actively campaigned on his behalf. Past Soviet hockey stars and present-day Russian superstar athletes, meanwhile, confidently ally themselves to Putin in public without fear. Of course, fear can help authoritarian leaders marshal a degree of public support while they remake the rule of law to suit their purposes. Putin has held office and solidified his rule for over two decades, arresting and assassinating up-and-coming political rivals and manipulating the rules of the State Duma and Federal Assembly of Russia, the country's two parliamentary houses.[37] In 2018, Putin won reelection with 77 percent of the popular vote. In January 2020, Putin's entire cabinet resigned en masse, empowering him to make sweeping constitutional changes that will ensure lifetime rule. Not only does a Russian athlete incur little risk by appearing publicly with Putin, they avoid the life-and-death consequences that often come with openly rebuking him. Erdoğan, too, has successfully punished many of his critics in and out of sports while gradually eroding the checks and balances in the Turkish legislature and judicial system. After Turkish-born Enes Kanter (now going by Enes Kanter Freedom), former center for the Boston Celtics and star of the Turkish National Basketball Team, began criticizing Erdoğan via Twitter in 2013, Turkish officials canceled his passport. They branded Kanter and his father as terrorists, issued an extradition request with Interpol for the athlete, and imprisoned his father for five days. For years, Freedom did not travel to Canada with the Celtics when they played road games against the Toronto Raptors for fear of being extradited. He has since become a United States citizen and remains a vocal critic of Erdoğan.[38]

By aligning themselves with famous athletes (or threatening them with censure), Putin and Erdoğan access the powers of celebrity to boost their own public images. Joseph Roach uses the term "public intimacy" to describe "the illusion of proximity to the tantalizing apparition" of a celebrity figure who possesses the "It-Effect," that intangible draw that in turn inspires "craving for greater intimacy with the ultimately unavailable icon."[39] Here, Roach is describing the imagined intimacy between a member of the public and a celebrity whom they do not know personally, but we might extend the notion of proximity to describe how some figures might access the It-Effect of others by affiliation, or even compound the powers of their own It-Effect by sharing the stage. Putin and Erdoğan's credentials as charismatic, populist figures to their admirers are already assured, but they can both conceivably benefit from proximity to global superstars who share an ethnicity or nationality, ties to a profession, and, perhaps implicitly, a pride in one's nation. If nothing else, Putin and Erdoğan appreciate the value of the It-Effect and of sports celebrity as a currency that circulates in a wide public—in fact, Putin's accidental tumble or Erdoğan's playing the role of fan in front of Özil by collecting jerseys may lend them both a certain humility that invites onlookers to imagine themselves in their shoes. Of course, their own It-Effects are burnished by the deference shown to them by these players, even if that deference sometimes comes with hasty disavowals. Ultimately, these leaders understand that playing the role of sportsmen in public, especially with "fellow" sportsmen, means tapping into an aura that is maximized by the media spheres in which sports imagery circulates.

Nevertheless, it is worth reiterating that all sports, never mind the world's most lucrative and popular, are discourses in and of themselves and are thus open to contestation. The scenarios they generate, whether within the arena itself or in the political realms that invest in them, can activate as much political resistance as consolidation. Putin and Erdoğan understood this before coming to public office, though they may have underestimated the degree to which different "publics" would start to pose challenges to their sports-as-politics endeavors. In the post-Habermasian sense pioneered by Michael Warner, publics are "constitutive of a social imaginary"[40]: they are reflexive realms in which a circulation of texts, experiences, and practices creates bonds through the shared act of exchange. Hockey and soccer may trade on transcendency thanks to their (near-)ubiquity in the respective countries, but that "transcendency" is actually a shared fascination that can be iterated and reiterated in countless different ways. Hence why Putin's hockey career and other adventures play so well to factions of the Russian public, but are derided in the West, or why some of Turkey's soccer fans are courted by powerful elites while others use their club affiliations to argue for alternative politics. Even in its most varied states, sport is ultimately about opposition and competition, about scenarios that yield results, even if those results are manipulated by powerful actors or debated by pundits and fans; that, in and of itself, ensures that sport as a discourse is never really about consensus. Thus, by checking into matches and games with a distinctive allegiance in a sporting discourse already marked by overt political divisions, Putin and Erdoğan ensure that their sports-as-politics will inspire a potentially equal and opposite counter-project united in the real and symbolic realm. In short, the very nature of Putin and Erdoğan's sports-as-politics projects, entangled as they are in the machinations of sporting governments and the complexities of public perception and fan engagement, often sow at least as many seeds of dissent as they do of advancement.

Conclusion: Soft Power?

The focus of this chapter has been on two of Europe's hardliners and the ways in which they mobilize sports-as-politics to consolidate their powers and burnish their credentials in the public eye. However, it is worth reiterating that sports have also been key components of the personas constructed by US Presidents. For example, Dwight Eisenhower and Gerald Ford often described their exploits as American football players at West Point and Michigan on the campaign trail, while former Yale pitcher and Texas Rangers owner George W. Bush experienced his highest approval ratings after an inspired ceremonial pitch at the first World Series game in New York City following the September 11 attacks. And yet, sports performances have not always yielded positive press. Bill Clinton was mocked mercilessly for his various cheating methods on the golf course. Richard Nixon, often ridiculed for having sat on the bench throughout his football career, once called his friend George Allen, head coach of the team now known as the Washington Commanders,[41] during the halftime break of an NFL game to suggest a play. As the press gleefully pointed out the next day, the play backfired and resulted in a 13-yard loss. Whether authoritarian or ostensibly democratic, many political leaders recognize the value of performing well in the sporting arena (and the embarrassment of performing poorly).

Where men like Putin and Erdoğan differ from their American counterparts is the degree to which they have engineered sporting performances to suit their success. Whether in the contrived spectacles designed to inflate their accomplishments, the courting or condemnation of major athletes, or the backroom machinations that have tied politics and sports together through the mediation of neoliberal economics, Erdoğan and Putin have demonstrated that the traditional "soft" power of sport can have a hard edge. The fact that this particular form of soft power already comes with a firm edge—that sports are "real" and consequential in the sense that, say, the performing arts are not, and that they are so often used to define and test the foundations of conservative masculinity—makes it especially appropriate for two leaders with established authoritarian credentials. That sense of authority is what distinguishes their sports-as-politics from the first pitch of the baseball season: in their arenas, the pitch is almost always good because it has to be. That they have invested so heavily in accessing and controlling the economic components of sport and all the political clout that comes with that only increases the chances that they will, one way or another, win the game. However, as their efforts illustrate, there is still ample opportunity to lose. Putin's slip and Erdoğan's cold receptions demonstrate both the fragility of contrived sporting spectacle and the contestation automatically generated by any venture into the world of "real" sports. Their entanglements with transnational endeavors in the Olympics and global soccer also prove that elite sport can exercise a hard edge of its own. As in the theatre, sport may entertain a variety of audiences and agendas, sometimes under political duress, but its own internal mechanics can shape a narrative on their own terms. After all, even men like Erdoğan and Putin have to play by *some* of the rules.

Notes

1 Byron York, "Bill's Big Lie," *The American Spectator,* September 1996, 38.
2 Jack Holmes, "Vladimir Putin's 8-Goal Hockey Game Is a Glimpse into Our Possible Future," *Esquire Online,* May 10, 2019, https://www.esquire.com/news-politics/a27435491/vladimir-putin-hockey-8-goals-donald-trump/ (accessed April 25, 2022).
3 Richard H. Solomon, "The Chairman's Historic Swim," *Time Online,* September 27, 1999, http://content.time.com/time/world/article/0,8599,2054250,00.html (accessed April 25, 2022).
4 "Turkmen President Escapes Injury in Riding Accident," *BBC News Online,* April 30 2013, https://www.bbc.com/news/world-asia-22352281 (accessed April 25, 2022).
5 Alan Bairner, *Sport, Nationalism, and Globalization: European and North American Perspectives* (Albany: State University of New York Press, 2001), 18.
6 See Jonathan Grix, *Sports Politics: An Introduction* (London: Palgrave Macmillan, 2016) for an expansive look at the many ways sports and politics, in their many definitions, intersect and overlap.
7 Diana Taylor, *Performance* (Durham: Duke University Press, 2016), 141.
8 Joseph Maguire, "The Sports-Industrial Complex: Sports Sciences, Social Developments, and Images of Humankind," in *Power and Global Sport: Zones of Prestige, Emulation, and Resistance,* ed. Joseph Maguire (Abingdon: Routledge, 2005), 159–76.
9 "Vladimir Putin's Interests: Sport," *Kremlin.ru* (n.d.), http://en.putin.kremlin.ru/interests (accessed December 12, 2020).

10 "Vladimir Putin Interview With Armin Wolf," *ORF*, June 15, 2018, https://www.youtube.com/watch?v=77_jB4yJYaA (accessed April 25, 2022).
11 "Interview to American TV Channel NBC," *Kremlin.ru*, March 10, 2018, http://en.kremlin.ru/events/president/news/57027 (accessed April 25, 2022). Putin is certainly skilled at trolling American journalists and celebrities. In 2005, New England Patriots owner Robert Kraft met with Putin during a business trip to Russia, removing one of his Super Bowl rings and offering it to Putin to try on. According to Kraft, Putin remarked that he "could kill someone with this" and absconded with the ring. Kraft contends that officials from George W. Bush's State Department urged him to downplay the theft of the ring and to pretend that he had intentionally given it to Putin as a way to preserve positive relations between the countries.
12 In March 2022, the International Judo Federation stripped Putin of his honorary presidency of the organization following the Russian Federation's invasion of Ukraine.
13 Benjamin Wittes, "I'll Fight Putin Any Time, Any Place He Can't Have Me Arrested," *Lawfare*, October 21, 2015, https://www.lawfareblog.com/ill-fight-putin-any-time-any-place-he-cant-have-me-arrested (accessed April 25, 2022).
14 Wittes, "I'll Fight Putin Any Time."
15 Shamoon Hafez, "Istanbul: Two Days, Two Derbies, Two Continents, One New Football Power Emerging," *BBC Sport Online*, April 15, 2019, https://www.bbc.com/sport/football/47830726 (accessed September 13, 2019).
16 Patrick Keddie, "Understanding Authoritarianism Through Soccer," *The New Republic Online*, May 7, 2018, https://newrepublic.com/article/148313/understanding-authoritarianism-soccer (accessed September 13, 2019).
17 Keddie, "Understanding Authoritarianism Through Soccer."
18 Keddie, "Understanding Authoritarianism Through Soccer." As Keddie argues in his book *The Passion: Football and the Story of Modern Turkey* (London: I.B. Tauris, 2018), these accusations make for a convenient myth.
19 Dağhan Irak, "Turkish Football, Match-Fixing, and the Fan's Media: A Case Study of Fenerbahçe Fans," in *Sports Events, Society and Culture*,

ed. Katherine Dashper, Thomas Fletcher, and Nicola McCullough (Abingdon: Routledge, 2015), 115–28.

20 Dağhan Irak, "'Shoot Some Pepper Gas at Me!' Football Fans vs. Erdoğan: Organized Politicization or Reactive Politics?" *Soccer & Society* 19, no. 3 (2018): 404–5.

21 For comments on the club's pro-government stance, see Laura Pitel, "This Turkish Soccer Club May Help Erdoğan Stay in Power," *Ozy*, April 29, 2018, https://www.ozy.com/the-huddle/this-turkish-soccer-club-may-help-erdogan-stay-in-power/86473/ (accessed September 20, 2019). For more on neo-Ottomanism and how it intersects with Turkish soccer, see Daghan Irak, "Football in Turkey During the Erdoğan Regime," *Soccer & Society* 21, no. 6 (2020): 680–91.

22 Palko Karasz, "Putin Shoots, Scores and Falls Face First on Hockey Ice," *The New York Times,* May 11, 2019, https://www.nytimes.com/2019/05/11/world/europe/putin-hockey-falls.html (accessed April 25, 2022).

23 "Vladimir Putin Scores At Least Eight Goals in Hockey Exhibition, Then Falls on Face," *The Guardian*, May 10, 2019, https://www.theguardian.com/sport/2019/may/10/vladimir-putin-hockey-fall-hockey-exhibition (accessed April 25, 2022).

24 "Vladimir Putin Scores Eight Goals in Ice Hockey Match Then Falls Over on Victory Lap," *Guardian Sport*, May 10, 2019, https://www.youtube.com/watch?v=cgbI55HdqQs (accessed April 25, 2022).

25 "Night Hockey League Gala Match," *Kremlin.ru*, May 10, 2019, http://en.kremlin.ru/events/president/news/60500 (accessed April 25, 2022).

26 "Putin Scores Ten Goals in Night Hockey Match in Sochi," *RT*, May 10, 2019, https://www.youtube.com/watch?v=hIQFzE2uhTA (accessed December 12, 2020).

27 The emphasis by Western outlets on how false, flat, and humiliating these displays by Putin, Kim Jong Il, and other autocrats are implies that American presidents are somehow less choreographed and more authentic. Which, of course, they are not. Examples abound: Clinton playing Sax on Arsenio Hall's late-night TV show, Obama "Slow Jamming the News" with Jimmy Fallon, and the multiple staged photo opportunities showing Trump and Biden driving trucks.

28 "Turkish PM Erdoğan Scores a Hat Trick," *Daily Sabah*, 28 July 2014, https://www.dailysabah.com/football/2014/07/28/turkish-pm-erdogan-scores-a-hat-trick (accessed December 13, 2019).
29 Philip Oltermann, "Özil and Gündoğan's Erdoğan Pictures Causes Anger in Germany," *The Guardian*, 16 May 2018, https://www.theguardian.com/world/2018/may/16/mesut-ozil-ilkay-gundogan-recep-tayyip-erdogan-picture (accessed September 20, 2019).
30 Christopher F. Schuetze, "German Soccer Star Is the Groom. Turkey's President Is the Best Man," *New York Times*, https://www.nytimes.com/2019/06/08/world/europe/erdogan-mesut-ozil-wedding.html (accessed September 20, 2019).
31 "Euro 2020: Uefa Probes Turkey Footballers' Military Salute," *BBC News*, October 14, 2019, https://www.bbc.com/news/world-europe-50041529 (accessed October 24, 2019).
32 Ece Toksabay "Turkey Players Salute Syria Operation After Goal Against France," *Reuters*, 15 October 2019, https://www.reuters.com/article/us-syria-security-turkey-soccer/turkey-players-salute-syria-operation-after-goal-against-france-idUSKBN1WU1HU (accessed October 24, 2019).
33 Roger Gonzales, "UEFA Asked to Change Site of Champions League Final Due to Turkey–Syria Military Conflict," *CBS Sports*, October 16, 2019, https://www.cbssports.com/soccer/news/uefa-asked-to-change-site-of-champions-league-final-due-to-turkey-syria-military-conflict/ (accessed October 24, 2019).
34 Dağhan Irak, "Football in Turkey During the Erdoğan Regime," *Soccer & Society* 21, no. 6 (2020): 683.
35 Irak, "Football in Turkey During the Erdoğan Regime," 683.
36 Jared Maslin, "As Turkey's Currency Collapses, Erdoğan's Support Sinks Even in His Hometown," *Wall Street Journal Online*,13 December 2021, https://www.wsj.com/articles/as-turkeys-currency-collapses-erdogans-support-sinks-even-in-his-hometown-11639403803?reflink=desktopwebshare_permalink (accessed February 7, 2022).
37 Putin technically stepped down from 2008–12, but he maintained the office of prime minister, elevated his close political ally Dmitry Medvedev to the presidency, and maintained total control of state and military decisions.

38 Isaac Chotiner, "Enes Kanter Freedom's Political Awakening," *The New Yorker Online*, December 9, 2021, https://www.newyorker.com/news/q-and-a/enes-kanter-freedoms-political-awakening (accessed February 7, 2022).
39 Joseph Roach, *It* (Ann Arbor: University of Michigan Press, 2007), 44.
40 Michael Warner, *Publics and Counterpublics* (New York: Zone Books, 2012), 12.
41 The American football team in Washington, DC, temporarily changed its name to the Washington Football Team in 2020 and later, permanently, to the Washington Commanders in 2022, following years of public pressure and activism by Native American groups and others opposed to the team's original name, a racial slur commonly used against Native Americans.

8

Statecraft and Revolution: Remaking Bolívar for an Anti-Imperialist Transnational Alliance[1]

Angela Marino

One of the most lauded figures of the American wars of independence, Simón Bolívar has been revered by successive governments throughout the hemisphere since the mid-nineteenth century. His profile, typically outfitted in gold tasseled epaulettes, is printed on paper and coin currency, stamps, billboards, playing cards, brochures, posters, and mural art with thousands of theatrical and cinematic reembodiments in school assemblies, on plazas, and on national stages. As a two-century long meme, Bolívar is perhaps best known for his unrequited dream of a united Southern hemisphere. He is also the namesake of the Bolivarian Revolution of Venezuela, a socialist turn that took place through democratic elections and that has now been targeted by US cold-war aggression for nearly twenty-five years.

Over the last decade of an ongoing revolutionary process, artists and activists in Venezuela have taken up the figure of Bolívar for a deeper kind of diplomacy, both within the country and globally.[2] Graffiti artists at the 2013 Venice Biennale, for example, remade the famous portrait of Bolívar with dark shades next to his famous white horse zigzagged across the wall with brilliant colors streaming through its mane. Amidst sometimes rancorous controversy and never short of debate, Bolívar's example shows us the instability of states and the staying power of performance, where the performing icon of Bolívar today clings on to new expressions of revolutionary state power.

This chapter is about how popular mobilizations remake the state—and the struggle that continues to craft it anew. With the example of Simón Bolívar in the twenty-first century, cultural producers in Venezuela appropriate, remake, and in some cases, move beyond this figure to challenge a top-down order of statecraft ultimately to horizontalize, or equalize, what scholar and activist Jesús 'Chucho' García called the "paladins of liberty." I argue this by referring to what in Venezuela is called popular power, or a kind of statecraft by non-state actors, where groups including the Biennale artists, see themselves as agential in shaping the revolutionary state. So much so that an opposition post published in Miami in 2012 lamented the "thunderous" movement of pro-Chávez street art, suggesting that these murals should be sanctioned.[3] I first discuss recent mobilizations in the national assembly, and then return to examples in which activists and artists have worked through the figure of Bolívar to extend demands for racial equality, sovereignty, and transnationalism. Along the way, cultural symbols like Simón Bolívar are dialectically remade through a process of historical recovery and policy debate in which popular power is recrafting the state from the inside.

To offer more specifics on what I mean by popular power, I turn to scholar and activist Meyby Soraya Ugueto-Ponce of the Venezuelan Institute of Scientific Research (IVIC) who described, in a recent conference, how Black women's collectives alongside broad-based support including teachers, community leaders, artists, farmworkers, and students are currently pushing forward a platform of anti-racism legislation through the highest levels of government.[4] In her presentation, Dr. Ugueto-Ponce, who is also a founding member of the Afro-Venezuelan and Afro-descendant women's collective, Trenzas Insurgentes (Insurgent Braids),[5] introduced a video of elected Deputy Casimira Monasterio's speech to the national assembly celebrating the successful passing of the International Day of Afro-descendant Peoples on September 1, 2021.[6] The approval process, Ugueto-Ponce explained, further opens the way toward a deeper set of policy reinforcements for the Law Against Racial Discrimination (originally passed under

Hugo Chávez Frías in 2011) including a nationwide education project and other initiatives to comprehensively advance anti-racist activism throughout the country.

Watching the video of this speech by Monasterio, and one can see that the two images of Bolívar and former president Hugo Chávez are placed side by side on tripods on the lower level of the stage. In the footsteps of leaders like the late Argelia Laya (1926–1997), the moment Monasterio took the podium was, for Ugueto-Ponce, "to occupy the power constituted within the influence of popular power, with intersectional awareness. It was also a performance within an ancestral and collective lineage of struggle."[7] During the early years of the revolutionary process, the presence of the white statesman reportedly served to appease mainstream interests beholden to the time immemorial bust of Bolívar.[8] Decades later Bolívar's image hung to the lower left corner of the stage, a crucial part of the cast, but not the star.

These momentary visual cues on the stage of the national assembly offer a glimpse into what can be considered two phases of revolutionary state transformation. The first is constructed out of what Partha Chatterjee describes as "popular politics"[9] where in the first decade of the revolution, Hugo Chávez established a quasi-state expansion of civil society within and parallel to the Venezuelan government including a communal bank and a structure for tens of thousands of communal cooperatives and participatory projects of the "grassroots" throughout the country.[10] The second can be considered the appropriation of the state by a broader influence of popular politics, in which new policy enables activist collectives to define and shape the state's investments in legislation and enforcement.

While right-wing movements around the world appeal to increasingly nativist or anti-globalist fronts, these state formations in Latin America today suggest a very different relationship to the global order. It is both local and global, in which socialist revolutionary alliances in Latin America, through partnerships with other global superpowers and grassroots organizations, are building alternative futures outside of the backyard diplomacy of the United States and the

Organization of American States (OAS). This is where we can turn to Bolívar to make sense of why he is still potentially useful to this process of state transformation.

As monumental as Bolívar's petite frame could appear (he was 5'3"), rising above plazas across the Americas (including in San Francisco and New York City) to perform "statehood," Simón Bolívar, especially in the last twenty years in Venezuela, has been transformed by popular culture into something broadly and profoundly transnational. Since Chávez won his first election, an education campaign recirculated his writings and speeches through tiny booklets to make a powerful appeal for national neighbors (Colombia, Bolivia, and Panama among others) to reconsider Bolívar's ideas of a unified America to defend itself against military and economic intervention by the United States.[11]

Such was the significance of Bolívar's life story, in 2010 Hugo Chávez led a widely publicized exhumation of Bolívar's grave in order to determine if there was foul play in his death. The exhumation was a spectacular moment of state performance with soldiers standing guard, and a play-by-play narration as the coffin was opened on national television. A new facial reconstruction of Bolívar was produced a short time later by a highly respected French forensics team, depicting the statesman with a strikingly more prominent jaw and protruding forehead. These official performances and renderings, as spectacular as they were, are part of a long history of remaking Bolívar.

Rather than a fixed symbol, however, consider how popular reconstitution of a figure like Bolívar remixes representations of Bolívar to activate ideas of both sovereignty and hemispheric alliance through its symbolic power. Venezuelan anthropologist Yolanda Salas de Lecuna, explained this proliferation of Bolívar's symbolic power through popular religiosity. She wrote, "[Bolívar] is not so much about a character that lived in a moment of historical time in the world of memory, of what was, and of his glories, rather his powers and forces are actualized by people who pray to him, who call him and who ask from him."[12] The same kind of religiosity was frequently attributed to Chávez by opposition media, projecting a messianic obsession that obscured the ideas, the analysis, and the policy that undergird his popularity. Rather than under spell, or unwittingly compelled to remake Bolívar for state funds, many activists and artists express that they see Bolívar as potentially useful for popular education, regional expansion, and anti-imperialism. Moreover, this diplomacy asserts a broader platform of regional unification within the African diaspora and among indigenous communities of the hemisphere with its networks and ongoing debates and connections in the past and present.

Jean Graham-Jones might call Bolívar a performing icon, as "cultural agent and cultural product."[13] As an agent, Bolívar enacts a particular set of ideals in the social and political environment toward unification and transnational solidarity. As a product, Bolívar appears on street murals, in enactments onstage, in film, and in active debates, "collectively made, unmade and remade."[14] Artists at the Venice Biennale spoke of Bolívar as still alert, alive, and watchful, "a spirit that lives in all of us."[15] In so far as the icon of Bolívar is dynamic and malleable, it is also collectively being undone and ultimately, challenged as a singular "liberator" in order to raise up other leaders and in some ways, question the primacy of Bolívar that still prevails through government discourse.

Debates over Bolívar present a crossroads of two major revolutions: one of the nineteenth century and the other of the twenty-first century that has far-reaching repercussions for who claims the state, whom it serves, and what new futures of racial equity in the Americas may be achieved. As Jesús 'Chucho' García, a Venezuelan historian and founder of the Afro-Venezuelan network *La Red de Organizaciones Afrovenezolanas*, argues, "long before the French decreed liberté, egalité, et fraternité, Africans imprisoned in cacao, sugarcane, and cotton fields in the Americas were already revolting against their exploitation."[16] For García, José Leonardo Chirinos's rebellion in 1795 began the revolutionary wars for independence, a battle that was, for many, defined as much by emancipation from slave society as that of tax and property levies that tied Venezuela to Spain.

For mestizos and Afro-descendants of Venezuela, García writes that "reconstructing this other history," a history of Afro-descendant struggle in the revolutionary period, "also meant elaborating strategies to demystify the erasure of the Africanity of Venezuela's national formation."[17] Both within and outside the country, as García explains, "Eurocentric notions of Venezuela's white creole 'paladins of liberty' could not accept the insurgent and more complete ideal of liberty contributed by the African and Afro-descendant rebels whose quests for freedom had helped to destabilize and defeat the Spanish colonial regime."[18] More than arguing for a corrective to the historicity of revolution, García and a wide network of other activists in Venezuela point to a lineage of Black emancipation to raise foundational debates in the nation and throughout the Caribbean about accepted narratives from both then and now.[19] As told through oral historians in the region around the independence wars, these discredited histories include stories of healers such as Cocofío, who inspired José Chirinos's rebellion in 1791, broadening networks through his council among *cumbes* (self-liberated spaces) and other villages on the coast.

As Ugueto-Ponce emphasizes, "Although Bolívar and Chávez are central in Black discourse, our voice extends beyond the era of the Republic to reach the colonial moment, from Miguel and Guiomar of Buría in 1552.[20] It is this much wider vision of the anti-imperialist and anti-colonialist struggle of more than 500 years."[21] To realize a 'dream' of a united America, one of the tasks at hand, according to activists, is to recognize the lineage of struggle that led to liberation, and the many forms of knowledge production that were absented from or continuously discredited or devalued in a state effort to deny it. This includes the arts in songs, music, poems, and dance that transmit these histories collectively. While the breadth of this epistemic turn in revolutionary discourse involves documents and archives as much as repertoires, I turn now to a history tour that took place in 2010 to bring people and places together, in part, through Bolívar in the twenty-first century.

Bolívar in Practice

Carmen Zulay Echenagucia and Jorman Valera, local historians and educators, pulled up two chairs in the middle of a small cultural center on the corner of the Plaza Bolívar in Ocumare de la Costa, west of Caracas. Carmen and Jorman had initiated a project called La Ruta Histórica (The Historic Route), one component of a comprehensive education project celebrating the bicentennial anniversary of the Revolution of Independence. Rain pounded down on the roof. Puddles of water pooled up around the steps that surrounded the wide front entrance of the room, open to the street through a wall-length garage door. A few stranded people dove under the doorway for refuge on their way to the library across the street. La Ruta, Carmen and Jorman told me, is a program in which local historians lead mainly students through seven historical sites in the area of the Ocumare coast. Jorman showed me photographs of about twenty young people standing in a circle around the Plaza Bolívar and at the beach of Playón approaching La Boca, the famous landing site of Bolívar in 1816 and of Francisco de Miranda ten years prior. Located between the major port cities of Puerto Cabello and La Guaira (nearest Caracas), Ocumare was at the center of the wars of independence and, in many ways, continues to play a central role in the current political moment. At the time, Carmen and Jorman were getting the word out about their history tours to other regions of the country and internationally, with some help from the Misión Cultura to pay for their brochure and publicity.

I first met Jorman Valera in the Misión Cultura meetings in 2007, sometime before the La Ruta project was started, so on this return trip to Ocumare in 2010, I was interested in finding out what Jorman and Carmen had been up to. So much had happened in a few short years. Their brochure was entitled "Afrodescendant Bicentennial Route: Bolívar and los Afros in the History of Emancipation from Key Coastal Towns on the Aragua Coast." As I paged through it, Carmen and Jorman told me the logistics of the program: students from the nearby towns of Maracay and Caracas were all invited to participate in the tours. They had also created a social media page to promote the project. The government aided them in this process, but decisions about the content of the tours were handled by residents and members of the local Misión Cultura. I held out some hope that students from the United States might be able to learn directly about what was happening in Venezuela until the United States imposed sanctions made it increasingly difficult to travel. The group's website in 2010 described the project:

> The Ruta Pedagógica 'Bolívar y las y los Afros' is a project that vindicates a civilized group that over years has been marginalized and excluded in the struggle for emancipation in the Americas. This revolutionary process allows us today to include Afropolitics in the law and constitution of the Republic … On this path, you will not encounter the history that you would normally find in books or the Internet. This is a social construct, a product of collective efforts of the Cumbe Afroaragueño. In the old educational model, it was not possible to approach these issues in our institutions but now, in these first years we have been working to bring these histories to our communities.[22]

Cultural producers insist on tours that are locally rooted and led by Afro-descendant historians as part of a more comprehensive education program that spans from early childhood to adulthood, to involve oral history projects and mentorship. They were open to school groups nationwide and worldwide and include site visits to places like the cacao cooperative, the landing site of Bolívar in La Boca, and the town of Cumboto. As the project has now evolved into other education initiatives since Covid-19 and the intensified sanctions by the U.S. government against Venezuela, cooperatives in Ocumare have moved to health care and food production as their primary work alongside annual cultural events.[23]

What is important about this form of popular state diplomacy is that the initiative of the Ruta Histórica challenged conventional historic accounts of the Revolution of Independence as a battle fought solely between Spain and the primarily white criollo oligarchy and instead asserts the Afro-Venezuelan political and cultural story that had been previously silenced. As we sit in the open front room at the Misión,

Jorman relates the importance of Bolívar's expedition in terms of the support received from Haití. "Haití," he says, "has been erased from our history, yet it was one of the most important countries to the foundation of independence in Venezuela. In 1816, when Bolívar landed in Ocumare, he came with the support of Alexandre Pétion under the condition that Bolívar support the emancipation of slavery."[24] Jorman goes on to explain that the dates are extremely important; 1806 and 1816 mark the history of a struggle for independence in the region. These dates for the region of Ocumare bookend the official date of the bicentennial of 1810. "We are still in this struggle of independence," Jorman says to me as he points my attention back to the brochure.[25] In it, I see an essay by Jorge Guerrero Veloz, who at the time represented Venezuela as a cultural ambassador in New Orleans, in which he spells out the connections between Miranda, Bolívar, and Haití as the principal motive for creating the tours.

According to Guerrero Veloz, the 200-year celebration of independence must take as its point of reference Haití and the emancipation of slavery. He argues that Haití played a much more important role in the history of Venezuela than what has conventionally been accepted by historians. He also suggests that this support from Haití must be considered central in the account because on two separate occasions the Haitian leaders Jean Jacques Dessalines and Alexandre Pétion made it possible for Miranda and Bolívar to carry out their expeditions to Venezuelan soil: "[It is] an historical debt that we maintain still today with this generous country." Quoting Toussaint Louverture, he continues, "What we want is not a liberty of circumstances conceded to ourselves alone, rather the absolute adoption in which all people who are born red, black or white cannot be the property of another."[26] To vindicate this claim for historical independence based on the Haitian model means to correct previous distortions of history and to reaffirm an ethics of rights for all as opposed to only the few. It also upholds a genealogy of independence within the Black abolitionist and Black independence revolutionary traditions, suggesting an altogether different alignment of power that supports activists and cultural producers on the Aragua coast—like those developing the bicentennial history tours—who have taken up these issues both within Venezuela and internationally.

To illustrate the political significance of Afro-descendant rights in the Chávez era, Eubel López, a spokesperson for the Afro-descendant movement, unequivocally backed Chávez's successor President Nicolás Maduro, saying, "We are fully with the Bolivarian Revolution, because through it we have been made visible, with great achievements such as the Organic Law against Racial Discrimination." The same year I visited Jorman and Carmen, the second annual Afrodescendiente festival brought together upward of ten thousand people, with thirty-four cultural-performance groups convening on issues of history, creation of knowledge, and building community networks. Activists strengthened existing networks and created new ones within the country and internationally through events and economic exchanges.[27]

A stronger demand exists today to bring forward these stories, to build on this praxis, and to continue to define new directions for the revolution through radical solidarity among Afro-diasporic networks.[28] Rather than extracting activism as a resource for the state to exploit, the local approach to historical reactivation that the history tours exemplified is about endogenous production. Ruette-Orihuela and Hortensia Caballero-Arias of the Instituto Venezolano de Investigaciones Científicas (IVIC) note this phase of state formation is part of what activists are calling "cimarronaje institucional," which they describe as a framework of collective action that brings together historical resistance against racial and social exclusion into new forms of participatory engagement with the institutional apparatus of the Bolivarian state.[29]

The bicentennial history project created a liberated space, like the *cumbes* themselves, within which participants defined their own political aspirations of the Bolivarian Revolution. These projects emphasize the value of endogenous production networks through the customs and spaces of everyday life. As performance in face-to-face encounters, the history project integrates fiestas and other cultural productions of the town as centrally important aspects of their work.

Together, these events connect people with places, strung together to make a path, where each place on that path opens more possibilities to map a historical and contemporary redress of power, of who tells history, and of how that story is told.

The various performances of Bolívar suggest that multiple forms of statecraft (bottom up, top down, horizontal, and communal) overlap and interact. In Graham-Jones's words, "present in iconic performances and their reception is a shared ambivalent mythopoesis, in which our 'historical' need to make the myth flesh runs up against our 'critical' desire to demystify the flesh through mediation and appropriation."[30] As a practice, statecraft 'from below,' mediates and appropriates the prefigurative celebrity of Bolívar in an active endeavor to historicize and broaden its reach for legitimacy. The twenty-first-century Bolívar has become a form of diplomacy among peoples of different countries of Latin America to unify against the aggressively imperialist policy of the United States in the region. Moreover, the staying power of this figure relies on its attachment to indigenous and Afro-descendant social movements as major proponents of the revolutionary state. To illustrate this further, I take up a last example, this time in the city of Caracas where murals have activated the presence of Bolívar in the city streets (Figure 8.1).

For decades, visual artists have contributed to defining the revolution through Bolívar in ways that build international solidarity in regional festivals, mural, poster and print making, and other aesthetic practices. Artists working in the urban scape of Venezuela's capital city actively integrate the figure of Bolívar in mural art including this painting by Ecuadorian artist Pavel Égüez. In the mural, entitled *La Patria Naciendo de la Ternura/The Nation Being Born of Tenderness* (2006), Bolívar is positioned with his accomplice and revolutionary companion Manuela Sáenz among several groups of indigenous and Afro-descendant peoples. They ride together on the horse at a gallop, turned to the left, closely placed as if they all fit in the saddle at the same time. The hooves of the horse are lifted out of the multitude against a cobalt-blue sky, arms, hands, and feet outstretched with Bolívar

Figure 8.1 Pavel Égüez, *La Patria naciendo de la ternura* (Patriotism Is Born from Tenderness). Mural on the Avenida Baralt in downtown Caracas, 2010. Courtesy of Angela Marino.

holding a dove in his hand. People are various shades of brown, some with small houses fleshing out their bodies, others with painted faces accented by a mosaic of eyes and leaves. Two faces are turned upward at the top, with mouths open, recalling the Lucumí-inspired paintings of the Cuban artist Wifredo Lam. Others are holding masks or shown in profile. No longer is Bolívar the sole commander in the saddle of governance.

When Chávez was asked to respond to the Spanish king Juan Carlos's rebuff at the Latin American Summit in Chile, he famously replied, "I'm not going to shut up, and they won't shut me up because I'm not speaking for myself, I am speaking for millions, the millions who are the children of Bolívar, the millions who are children of Guaicaipuro and Manuela [Sáenz], José Leonardo Chirinos, and all of those who the Spanish murdered, ambushed, and slaughtered here."[31] In the mural, the image of Bolívar suggests a similar kind of transitional solidarity with Black and indigenous peoples against colonial invasion, violence, and slavery.

Since Égüez's mural, street art in Venezuela has exploded. Stencils, murals, and graffiti art leverage Bolívar's memorial power as a popular icon to reach across national lines, to affirm indigenous and Afro-descendant struggles for rights and vindication in the hemisphere. Some groups are supported by the state and others work independently as artist collectives and print poster crews, taking their work to the streets in both urban and rural areas. Rather than unwittingly compelled to repaint Bolívar for state funds, many activists and artists express that they see Bolívar as potentially useful for popular education, regional expansion, and anti-imperialism. Moreover, this diplomacy asserts a broader platform of regional unification within the African diaspora and among indigenous communities of the hemisphere with its networks and ongoing debates and connections in the past and present.

Remaking Bolívar as mestizo, or mixed race, has been long recorded. Yolanda Salas de Lecuna wrote prolifically on these popular remakings of Bolívar in what is known as the "Cult of Bolívar." Her book *Bolívar y la historia en la conciencia popular* (1987) records dozens of interviews with people on the northern coast of Venezuela, in which they relate stories they heard about Bolívar. Among them is a story that Bolívar was the child of a Black woman enslaved in the town of Capaya in the western state of Barlovento.[32] Others believe he was a descendant from the lineage of Guaicaipuro, who was one of the first indigenous leaders to fight against the Spanish in the early colonial period.[33] Still others claim he was born in the state of Aragua, in San Mateo, La Victoria, or El Consejo.[34] Asked during an interview what Simón Bolívar meant to him, Chávez described him as an embodiment of those he sought to empower: "[I see Bolívar] in the face of the Yukpa and Yanomami Indians, trampled by the dominant sectors of our country; in the working class of Caracas; in university students and in schools."[35] The biographer Bart Jones writes, "Chávez's Bolívar was an expansive figure, sufficiently vast and heterogeneous to encompass a broad new coalition."[36] For Chávez, and more recently carried over by President Nicolás Maduro, Bolívar's legacy extends to the contemporary struggle by those seeking equality through state power.

Rather than statecraft in this sense operating like a sorcerer that covers up and obscures history (creating an illusion of stability), popular power through the revolutionary state pushes this memory to the European invasion. Referencing five-hundred-year histories enables an even wider vision of futurity to exist through and beyond Bolívar. This is not to say that Bolívar is an ideal or even necessary aspect of this negotiation. It is indeed not only possible, but perhaps necessary, that Bolívar's primacy is diminished in the process. A new horizontalism and pluralism is formed. What is interesting is that the process does not seek closure to the debate; it opens the power of the past and present as a transitional phase in which various forces are on the way out, or changing, and others are contending for state office to make way for future directions and guiding stories.

Witnessing the proliferation of Bolívar in Venezuela by dozens of arts collectives for the past twenty years, it seems the nineteenth-century figure of the independence wars is as much a product of a historical moment, as he is a very contemporary figure alive in the imagination of twenty-first-century socialism. Performance in this case offers a way to consider the various "forces" that enter a symbol of state beyond "magic" or crafting from above. Performing Bolívar becomes a vehicle for state transformation in which new meanings are being made toward cultural and racial justice as a basis for regional unification. Whether this very alive figure speaks today, or is but a shell of the past, the issue becomes more about how symbols remain useful (or not) to the revolutionary movement as the state itself transforms.

Notes

1 Portions of this chapter were previously published in Angela Marino, *Populism and Performance in the Bolivarian Revolution of Venezuela* (Evanston: Northwestern University Press, 2018).
2 This chapter selects only a few of these enactments and in no way pretends to be comprehensive in its review of them.

3 Juan Vidal, "Censorship, Street Art, Oil and the Future of Venezuela," *Hyperallergic*, July 12, 2012,https://hyperallergic.com/54105/censorship-street-art-oil-and-the-future-of-venezuela/ (accessed May 3, 2022).
4 Mayby Soraya Ugueto-Ponce, *Performance and Populism: Mobilization, Popular Power, and Embodiment on the Left*, University of Warwick and UC Berkeley, November 3–5, 2022, https://tdps.berkeley.edu/performance-and-populism (accessed May 3, 2022).
5 Trenzas Insurgentes, "Poder Popular, Género y Etnia: el Caso de Trenzas Insurgentes, Colectivo de Mujeres Negras, Afrovenezolanas y Afrodescendientes," in Revista Venezolana de Economía y Ciencias Sociales 20, no. 1 (2014): 157–78.
6 On September 1, 2021, Monasterio approved the formal agreement of the August 31 as an International Day of Afro-descendant Peoples (Proyecto de Acuerdo, Día Internacional de las Personas Afrodescendientes).
7 Casimira Monasterio is a Black woman, a teacher, and elected member of the national assembly. See Meyby Soraya Ugueto-Ponce, "La acción colectiva encarnada en mujeres Afrovenezolanas. Mobilización entre el poder popular y el poder constituido," (Keynote Roundtable: "Commune: Mobilizing Popular Power in Geo-Political Souths," Performance and Populism Conference, The University of Warwick and The University of California-Berkeley, November 5, 2021).
8 Bart Jones, *¡Hugo!: The Hugo Chávez Story from Mud Hut to Perpetual Revolution* (Hanover, NH: Steerforth, 2007), 81.
9 Partha Chatterjee, *The Politics of the Governed: Reflections on Popular Politics in Most of the World* (New York: Columbia Press, 2004).
10 See the now-classic edited volume by David Smilde and Daniel Hellinger, *Venezuela's Bolivarian Democracy: Participation, Politics, and Culture under Chávez* (Durham: Duke University Press, 2011) as one source among many that focus on the transformations of Venezuelan civil society in the first decade of the twenty-first century.
11 The Ministry of Popular Power for Education issued a series of publications that also critiqued the roles of Miranda, Bolívar, and others in avoiding, and in some cases being complicit with, the perpetuation of slavery in the independence wars. These publications were widely distributed and accessible, thus generating public debate.

12 Yolanda Salas de Lecuna, *Bolívar y la historia en la conciencia popular* (Colombia: Ediciones de la Universidad de Simón Bolívar, 1987), 89.
13 Jean Graham-Jones, *Evita, Inevitably: Performing Argentina's Female Icons before and after Eva Perón* (Ann Arbor: University of Michigan Press, 2014), 5.
14 Graham-Jones, *Evita, Inevitably*, 7.
15 See Anna Battista, "Subvert Your Visual (And Architectural) Codes: El Arte Urbano. Una Estética de la Subversión, The Venezuela Pavilion at the 55th International Venice Art Biennale," in *Irenebrination: Notes on Architecture, Art, Fashion, Fashion Law & Technology*, June 29, 2013, https://irenebrination.typepad.com/irenebrination_notes_on_a/2013/06/el-arte-urbano-venezuela-pavilion.html (accessed May 3, 2022).
16 Jesús "Chucho" García, "Demystifying Africa's Absence in Venezuelan History and Culture," *African Roots/American Cultures: Africa in the Creation of the Americas*, ed. Sheila S. Walker (New York: Rowman & Littlefield, 2001), 286.
17 García, "Demystifying Africa's Absence," 286.
18 García, "Demystifying Africa's Absence," 286.
19 See Meyby Soraya Ugueto-Ponce, "¿Negros? ¿Afros? Más allá de una respuesta maniquea y excluyente. Reflexiones en torno al caso venezolano," En: Identidades políticas en tiempos de la afrodescendencia: Auto-identificación, eds. Ancestralidad, Visibilidad y Derechos. Silvia Valero y Alejandro Campos García (Buenos Aires: Corregidor, 2015), 247–87.
20 See George Ciccariello-Maher, *We Created Chávez: A People's History of the Venezuelan Revolution* (Durham: Duke University Press, 2013), 146–8.
21 Ugueto-Ponce, Personal communication with author, February 3, 2021.
22 See website by the Nucleo Central de Redes Socioculturales del Eje Afrodescendiente de Aragua, 2010, http://redesculturalesafroaragua.blogspot.com/p/ruta-bicentenaria-afrodescendiente.html (accessed May 3, 2022).
23 Ugueto-Ponce, Personal communication with author, February 3, 2021.
24 Jorman Valera, personal interview, 2010.
25 Jorman Valera, personal interview, 2010.
26 Jorge Guerrero Veloz, *Comunidades afroaragüeñas* (Caracas: Ministerio de Educación, Cultura y Deportes; Viceministerio de Cultura;

CONAC: Dirección General de Desarrollo Regional, Plan de Sobremarcha, Proyecto de Redes Socioculturales, 2001).

27 Several members of the *La Red de Organizaciones Afrovenezolanas*, a prominent Afro-descendant transnational organization, including its founder Jesús 'Chucho' García, worked abroad in diplomacy as ambassadors. In 2012, García and prominent activist William Camacaro shared experience with cooperative movements in the United States in an event called "From Venezuela to Mississippi: African Culture and Unity."

28 See also Meyby Soraya Ugueto-Ponce, "¿Negros? ¿Afros? Más allá de una respuesta maniquea y excluyente. Reflexiones en torno al caso venezolano," in Identidades políticas en tiempos de la afrodescendencia: Auto-identificación, Ancestralidad, Visibilidad y Derechos, eds. Silvia Valero y Alejandro Campos García (Buenos Aires: Corregidor, 2015), 247–87.

29 Krisna Ruette-Orihuela and Hortensia Caballero-Arias, "'Cimarronaje Institucional:' Ethno-racial Legal Status and the Subversive Institutionalization of Afrodescendant Organizations in Bolivarian Venezuela," *Journal of Latin American and Caribbean Anthropology* 22, no. 2 (2017): 320–38, https://doi.org/10.1111/jlca.12259.

30 Graham-Jones, *Evita, Inevitably*, 7.

31 Quoted in Chris Carlson, "Venezuelan President Clashes with the King of Spain at Latin American Summit," *Venezuelanalysis*, November 12, 2007, https://venezuelanalysis.com/news/2827 (accessed April 22, 2022).

32 Salas de Lecuna, *Bolívar*, 25.

33 Salas de Lecuna, *Bolívar*, 41.

34 Salas de Lecuna, *Bolívar*, 41, 47.

35 Quoted in Alexander Philip Bercovich, *The Bolívar Archive* (Cambridge, MA: Harvard University Press, 2014), 62.

36 Bart Jones, *¡Hugo!: The Hugo Chávez Story from Mud Hut to Perpetual Revolution* (Hanover, NH: Steerforth, 2007), 24.

Afterword

The Future of Dissensus: Performance Postdiplomatic Postdemocracy

Tony Perucci

In the introduction to this volume, James Ball offers the concept of the "postdiplomatic theatre" as both an emergent practice and critical lens of contemporary international relations. Like its namesake, postdramatic theatre, the postdiplomatic is not an "ephochal" shift away from the stagecraft of what US President Dwight D. Eisenhower called diplomatic theatre's "statecraft."[1] If diplomatic theatre depended upon the willing suspension of disbelief in "good faith actors" available to negotiation and compromise, postdiplomatic theatre emerges from an incredulity toward diplomatic theatre's aesthetics of stability, consensus, and collective agreement in shared goals.

It is worth lingering for a moment with Eisenhower, as his presidency heralded the High Modernist period of diplomatic theatre. That is, during the early decades of the Cold War, the stagecraft of statecraft took on a new focus: audiences beyond the political leaders and financiers of the over-industrialized West. The Cold War was, in part, waged through spectacles that were staged primarily for the consumption of leaders of non-aligned countries, particularly of nations formed through anti-colonial revolutions in Asia, Africa, and Latin America. For instance, taking its cues from Madison Avenue advertising firms, the United States recast diplomacy as a marketing event to be managed by public relations experts. Indeed, the US State Department perceived anti-Black violence in the South as a diplomatic crisis precisely because it damaged the US's brand: *democracy*.[2]

The US's diplomatic "front" of democracy exemplified the arts of "impression management," which sociologist Erving Goffman described in his landmark Eisenhower-era book, *The Presentation of Everyday Life* (1959). As such, the US performance of Cold War diplomatic theatre cannot be simply marked as "real" or "fake," but in constant motion on the slippery continuum of cynicism and sincerity—amidst targeted assassinations and Jim Crow on the one hand, and a genuine belief in post-Second World War capitalism as an engine of democracy on the other. While Goffman attempted to trouble the distinctions between artifice and "real reality," he still accepted the premise of modern drama, the solidity of what Hans-Thies Lehmann terms the "closed fictive cosmos."[3] In the final pages *The Presentation of Everyday Life*, Goffman declares that an "action staged in a theater is a relatively contrived illusion and an admitted one. ... A character in a theater is not in some ways real, nor does it have the same kind of real consequences as does the thoroughly contrived character performed by a confidence man."[4] In the context of Donald Trump, for instance, the very idea that one could make Goffman's distinction between "theatrical character" from "con man" is now hard to fathom.

However, as Baudrillard and many others have argued, such a distinction of the "contrived illusion" and the "real" is not just inadequate, but to make that distinction is symptomatic of late capitalism. The political leader on the world stage in the neoliberal era is less an actor, and more a "brand ambassador." As neoliberal political leaders have spoken the language of the corporate HR department, Trump's appeal is in no small part due to his refusal to "do" PR speak. Trump highlighted the contrived qualities of this illusion as a means of realizing the template of the "populist" leader—a performer who claims to bypass representation (and representational democratic governance)—by means of a "direct relationship" to "the people."[5] How Trump did this—now, itself, a global template—was to undermine the foundations of diplomatic theatre, in favor of a postdiplomatic theatre that displaces "theatre" from Goffman's dramaturgical analogy.

Trumpian political performance posits that "action staged in [politics] is a relatively contrived illusion," but that *it* is "an admitted one," and thus more (than) real. This is either the realization of postdramatic theatre-as-politics or pure humbuggery—or both.

Postdiplomatic theatre preceded Trump, as diplomatic theatre had long failed to conceal its dependence upon neoliberal capitalism's performed front of "democracy." As James Harding has written, the confluence of totalitarianism and privatization has ushered forth "a period of postdemocracy from which there is no return, a period in which the institutional semblances of democracy remain intact despite all of its mechanisms having been thoroughly compromised by corruption and cooptation."[6] Such a conjuncture, Harding argues, need not bring about resignation. Rather, "performance postdemocracy" requires more than critique, instead demanding confrontation with anti-democratic agents and institutions by working from a diversity of tactics that includes works that amplify the postdramatic "carefully calculated aura of ambiguity" in support of "an effective radical antagonism for the twenty-first century."[7]

In this way, the postdiplomatic theatre is an intervention into the postdemocratic condition. It challenges any kind of "return to normal," to diplomatic theatre as usual. Instead, it offers the performance of social action, as detailed in this book, as a constructive alternative that does not turn a blind eye to the willing suspension of disbelief in the illusion that global techno-capitalism is a mechanism of democracy. Rather, it promotes democracy as a necessary antagonism to capital. Instead of the detached irony of the "savvy skeptic" who basks in the triumph of the spectacle while disavowing it, postdiplomatic theatre employs what I have called the "irritational aesthetics" of "reality frictions," that demand the responsibility of the decision to *act* in the moment of indecidability.[8] Postdiplomatic theatre does not offer a solution to the crises of postdemocracy. Rather it poses performance postdemocracy as *the problem* that a diplomacy of equals, rather than one of diplomats and financiers, must take up.

Notes

1 Tony Perucci, *Paul Robeson and the Cold War Performance Complex: Race, Madness, Activism* (Ann Arbor: University of Michigan Press, 2012), 34.
2 Penny M. Von Eschen, *Satchmo Blows Up the World: Jazz Ambassadors Play the Cold War* (Cambridge, MA: Harvard University Press, 2004) and Perucci, *Paul Robeson*.
3 Erving Goffman, *The Presentation of Self in Everyday Life* (Garden City, NY: Doubleday, 1959), 17; Hans-Thies Lehmann, *Postdramatic Theatre*, trans. Karen Jürs-Munby (New York: Routledge, 2006), 99. See also, Erving Goffman, *Frame Analysis: An Essay on the Organization of Experience* (Boston: Northeastern University Press, 1974).
4 Erving Goffman, *The Presentation of Self*, 254.
5 Benjamin Moffitt, *The Global Rise of Populism: Performance, Political Style, and Representation* (Stanford: Stanford University Press, 2016), 96. See also Tony Perucci, "The Trump Is Present," *Performance Research* 22, no. 3 (2017): 127–35. https://doi.org/10.1080/13528165.2017.1348607.
6 James M. Harding, *Performance, Transparency, and the Cultures of Surveillance* (Ann Arbor: University of Michigan Press, 2018), 224.
7 Harding, *Performance, Transparency, and the Cultures*, 230, 258.
8 Mark Andrejevic, *Reality TV: The Work of Being Watched* (Lanham, MD: Rowman & Littlefield Publishers, 2004), 212. See also Tony Perucci, "Irritational Aesthetics: Reality Friction and Indecidable Theatre," *Theatre Journal* 70, no. 4 (2019): 479.

Selected Bibliography

Abd Rahim, Baidruel Hairiel, Nurazzura Mohamad Diah, and Mohd Salleh Aman. "From Immigrants to Sports Figures: The Case Study of the IOC Refugee Team in Rio Olympics 2016." *Al-Shajarah: Journal of the International Institute of Islamic Thought & Civilization.* Special Issue: Migration and Refugee Studies (2018): 137–54.

Acquaah, Samuel, Emmanuel R. K. Amissah, and Patrique de Graft Yankson. "Dress Aesthetics of Smock in Northern Ghana: Form, Function, and Context." *Journal of Textile Engineering & Fashion Technology* 1, no. 2 (2017): 68–77.

Akou, Heather Marie. *The Politics of Dress in Somali Culture.* Bloomington: Indiana University Press, 2011.

Allman, Jean, ed. *Fashioning Africa: Power and the Politics of Dress.* Bloomington and Indianapolis: Indiana University Press, 2004.

Allman, Jean, and John Parker. *Tongnaab: The History of a West African God.* Bloomington and Indianapolis: Indiana University Press, 2005.

Anderson, Benedict. *Imagined Communities: Reflections on the Origin and Spread of Nationalism.* Revised Edition. London: Verso Books, [1983] 2006.

Anderson, Patrick, and Jisha Menon. *Violence Performed: Local Roots and Global Routes of Conflict.* London: Palgrave Macmillan, 2009.

Andrejevic, Mark. *Reality TV: The Work of Being Watched. Critical Media Studies.* Lanham, MD: Rowman & Littlefield Publishers, 2004.

Askew, Kelly. *Performing the Nation: Swahili Music and Cultural Politics in Tanzania.* Chicago: University of Chicago Press, 2002.

Assensoh, A. B., and Yvette M. Alex-Assensoh. *Kwame Nkrumah's Political Kingdom and Pan Africanism Reinterpreted, 1909–1972.* Lanham, MD: Lexington Books, 2022.

Austin, J. L. *How to Do Things with Words.* ed. J. O. Urmson and Marina Sbisà. Cambridge, MA: Harvard University Press, 1955.

Bairner, Alan. *Sport, Nationalism, and Globalization: European and North American Perspectives.* Albany: State University of New York Press, 2001.

Ball III, James R. *Theater of State: A Dramaturgy of the United Nations.* Evanston: Northwestern University Press, 2020.

Bell, Colleen. "Hybrid Warfare and Its Metaphors." *Humanity: An International Journal of Human Rights, Humanitarianism, and Development* 3, no. 2 (Summer 2012): 225–47.

Bell, Colleen. "War and the Allegory of Medical Intervention: Why Metaphors Matter." *International Political Sociology* 6, no. 3 (September 2012): 325–8.

ben-Abdallah, Mohammed. *Verdict of the Cobra*. Alexander Street Press, Black Drama Database, 1987. https://search.alexanderstreet.com/view/work/bibliographic_entity%7Cbibliographic_details%7C3607961 (accessed March 9, 2022).

Bercovich, Alexander Philip. *The Bolívar Archive*. Cambridge, MA: Harvard University Press, 2014.

Berlova, Maria. "Playing King." *Nordic Theatre Studies* 26, no. 1 (2014): 80–90.

Biney, Ama. *The Political and Social Thought of Kwame Nkrumah*. New York: Palgrave Macmillan, 2011.

Bjola, Corneliu, and Marcus Holmes. *Digital Diplomacy: Theory and Practice*. London: Routledge, 2015.

Botwe-Asamoah, Kwame. *Kwame Nkrumah's Politico-Cultural Thought and Politics*. New York: Routledge, 2005.

Bowdich, T. Edward. *Mission from Cape Coast Castle to Ashantee, with a Statistical Account of That Kingdom, and Geographical Notices of Other Parts of the Interior of Africa*. London: John Murray, Albemarle-Street, 1819.

Bradshaw, Samantha, and Philip N. Howard. *The Global Disinformation Order: 2019 Global Inventory of Organised Social Media Manipulation*. Oxford: Project on Computational Propaganda, 2019.

Breslin, Shaun. "Beyond Diplomacy? UK Relations with China Since 1997." *The British Journal of Politics and International Relations* 6 (2004): 409–25.

Brindley, Erica Fox. *Music, Cosmology, and the Politics of Harmony in Early China*. Albany: State University of New York Press, 2012.

Butler, Judith. *Excitable Speech: A Politics of the Performative*. New York: Routledge, 1997.

Carlyle, Thomas. *Sartor Resartus: The Life and Opinions of Herr Teufelsdrockh*. Urbana, Illinois: Project Gutenberg, [1831] 2012. https://gutenberg.org/files/1051/1051-h/1051-h.htm (accessed March 9, 2022).

Casey, Marion R. "1916: The Easter Rising." *Irish America*. February/March 2016.

Char, James. "Contesting for Supremacy in the Asia-Pacific in the Time of COVID-19: How the Pandemic May Have Already Unravelled China's

Long-Term Strategy in Southeast Asia." *Prospect and Exploration* 18, no. 9 (September 2020): 132–43.

Chatterjee, Partha. *The Politics of the Governed: Reflections on Popular Politics in Most of the World*. New York: Columbia Press, 2004.

Cheah, Pheng. *Spectral Nationality: Passages of Freedom from Kant to Postcolonial Literatures of Liberation*. New York: Columbia University Press, 2003.

Ciccariello-Maher, George. *We Created Chávez: A People's History of the Venezuelan Revolution*. Durham: Duke University Press, 2013.

Clarke, Peter. *West Africa and Islam*. London: Edward Arnold, 1982.

Cohen, Raymond. *Theatre of Power: The Art of Diplomatic Signaling*. London: Longman, 1987.

Colbert, Soyica Diggs. *Theory for Theatre Studies: Bodies*. New York: Methuen Drama, 2022.

Cole, David, ed. *The Torture Memos: Rationalizing the Unthinkable*. New York: New Press, 2009.

Colum, Padraic, Maurice Joy, James Reidy, Sidney Gifford, Rev. T. Gavan Duffy, Mary M. Colum, Mary J. Ryan, and Seumas O'Brien. *The Irish Rebellion of 1916 and Its Martyrs: Erin's Tragic Easter*. ed. Maurice Joy. New York: The Devin-Adair Company, 1916.

Conradi, Peter. *Hot Dogs and Cocktails*. London: Alma Books, 2014.

Constantinou, Costas. *On the Way to Diplomacy*. Minneapolis: University of Minnesota Press, 1996.

Coogan, Tim Pat. *1916: The Easter Rising*. London: Orion Publishing Group, 2016.

Cook, Scott. "'Yue Ji' 樂記—Record of Music: Introduction, Translation, Notes, and Commentary." *Asian Music* 26, no. 2 (April 1, 1995): 1–96.

Copeland, Daryl. "Guerrilla Diplomacy: Delivering International Diplomacy in a Digital World." *Canadian Foreign Policy* 11, no. 2 (Winter 2004): 165–75.

Copeland, Daryl. *Guerrilla Diplomacy: Rethinking International Relations*. Boulder, CO: Lynne Rienner, 2009.

Coulthard, Glen Sean. *Red Skins White Masks: Rejecting the Colonial Politics of Recognition*. Minneapolis: University of Minnesota Press, 2014.

Cowhig, Frances Ya-Chu. *Lidless*. New Haven: Yale University Press, 2010.

Deloria, Joseph Philip. *Playing Indian*. Yale Historical Publications. New Haven: Yale University Press, 1998.

Dershowitz, Alan, *Preemption: A Knife That Cuts Both Ways*. New York: W. W. Norton, 2006.

Donkor, David A. *Spiders of the Market: Trickster Performance in a Web of Neoliberalsm*. Bloomington: Indiana University Press, 2016.

Doty, Roxanne Lynn. *Imperial Encounters: The Politics of Representation in North–South Relations*. Minneapolis: University of Minnesota Press, 1996.

Edmondson, Laura. *Performance and Politics in Tanzania: The Nation on Stage*. Bloomington: Indiana University Press, 2007.

Esposito, Roberto. *Immunitas: The Protection and Negations of Life*. Cambridge: Polity Press, 2011.

Essel, Osuanyi Quaicoo. "Dress Fashion Politics of Ghanaian Presidential Inaguration Ceremonies from 1960 to 2017." *Fashion and Textiles Review* 1, no. 3 (2019): 35–55.

Essel, Osuanyi Quaicoo, and Emmanual R. K. Amissah. "Smock Fashion Culture in Ghana's Dress Identity-Making." *Historical Research Letter* 18 (2015): 32–8.

Esslin, Martin. *An Anatomy of Drama*. New York: Hill and Wang, 1976.

Fisher, Te Ata. *As I Remember It*. Te Ata Fisher Collection. WHC M1298. Western History Collections. Norman: University of Oklahoma Libraries.

Ford, Robert. "Powell and After: Immigration, Race and Politics in Britain." In *Lives and Afterlives of Enoch Powell: The Undying Political Animal*. Ed. Olivier Esteves, and Stephane Porion. Milton Park, Abingdon: Routledge, 2019.

Fosler-Lussier, Danielle. *Music in America's Cold War Diplomacy*. Oakland: University of California Press, 2015.

Franklin, M. I., ed. *Resounding International Relations: On Music, Culture, and Politics*. New York: Palgrave Macmillan, 2005.

Fu, Daobin. "Village People, Village Music and the Theoretical Significance of the Concept That Poetry Can Harmonize People." *Frontiers of Literary Studies in China* 2, no. 3 (2008): 321–48.

Fusheini, Mumuni Zakaria. "The Dagomba Smock (Bim'Mangli) of Northern Ghana in the Light of Contextualism and Instrumentalism Theories of Aesthetics." *Africa Development and Resources Research Institute* 29, no. 1 (2020): 58–72.

Fusheini, Mumuni Zakaria, Joe Adu-Agyem, and Eric Asante Appau. "Indigenous Aesthetic Qualities Inherent in the Dagomba Bim'Mangli

(Smock) in Northern Region of Ghana." *International Journal of Research and Innovation in Social Science* 3, no. 4 (2019): 237–48.

García, Jesús. "Chucho." "Demystifying Africa's Absence in Venezuelan History and Culture." *African Roots/American Cultures: Africa in the Creation of the Americas*. Ed. Sheila S. Walker. 281–90. New York: Rowman & Littlefield Publishers, 2001.

Garrison, James. "The Social Value of Ritual and Music in Classical Chinese Thought." *Teorema* 31, no. 3 (2012): 209–22.

Geertz, Clifford. *Negara: The Theatre State in Nineteenth-Century Bali*. Princeton: Princeton University Press, 1980.

Gentleman, Amelia. *The Windrush Betrayal: Exposing the Hostile Environment*. London: Guardian Faber, 2019.

Gerrits, André W. M. "Disinformation in International Relations: How Important Is It?" *Security and Human Rights* 29 (2018): 3–23.

Gibbs, Levi S. "Improvised Songs of Praise and Group Sociality in Contemporary Chinese Banquet Culture." *International Communication of Chinese Culture* 7, no. 2 (June 1, 2020): 133–46.

Gildea, Robert. *Empires of the Mind: The Colonial Past and the Politics of the Present*. Cambridge: Cambridge University Press, 2019.

Goeman, Mishuana. "From Place to Territories and Back Again: Centering Storied Land in the Discussion of Indigenous Nation-Building." *International Journal of Critical Indigenous Studies* 1, no. 1 (2008): 23–34.

Goffman, Erving. *The Presentation of Self in Everyday Life*. New York: Doubleday, 1959.

Goffman, Erving. *Frame Analysis: An Essay on the Organization of Experience*. Boston: Northeastern University Press, 1974.

Goody, Esther, and Jack Goody. "The Naked and the Clothed." In *The Cloth of Many Colored Silks*. Ed. John Hunwick, and Nancy Lawler. 67–89. Evanston: Northwestern University Press, 1996.

Graham-Jones, Jean. *Evita, Inevitably: Performing Argentina's Female Icons before and after Eva Perón*. Ann Arbor: University of Michigan Press, 2014.

Green, Richard. *Te Ata: Chickasaw Storyteller, American Treasure*. Norman: University of Oklahoma Press, 2006.

Grix, Jonathan. *Sports Politics: An Introduction*. London: Palgrave Macmillan, 2016.

Guerrero Veloz, Jorge. *Comunidades afroaragüeñas*. Caracas: Ministerio de Educación, Cultura y Deportes; Viceministerio de Cultura;

CONAC: Dirección General de Desarrollo Regional, Plan de Sobremarcha, Proyecto de Redes Socioculturales, 2001.

Harding, James M. *Performance, Transparency, and the Cultures of Surveillance*. Ann Arbor: University of Michigan Press, 2018.

Hall, Stuart. "Encoding/Decoding." In *Media and Cultural Studies: Keyworks*. Ed. Meenakshi Gigi Durham, and Douglas Kellner. 128–38. Malden, MA: Blackwell Publishers, 2001.

Hansen, Karen, and D. Soyini Madison. *African Dress: Fashion, Agency, Performance*. New York: Bloomsbury, 2013.

Haraway, Donna. "The Biopolitics of Postmodern Bodies: Constitutions of Self in Immune System Discourse." In *Simians, Cyborgs, and Women: The Reinvention of Nature*, 225–52. New York: Routledge, 1990.

Harris, Britney. "Diplomacy 2.0: The Future of Social Media in Nation Branding." *Journal of Public Diplomacy* 4, no. 1 (2013): 17–31.

Harris, Elizabeth. *Ghana: A Travel Guide*. Aburi: Aburi Press, 1976.

Hartigan, Karelisa. *Performance and Cure: Drama and Healing in Ancient Greece and Contemporary America*. Classical Inter/Faces Series. London: Duckworth, 2009.

Hayton, Bill. *The South China Sea: The Struggle for Power in Asia*. New Haven: Yale University Press, 2014.

Hayward, Fred M., and Ahmed R. Dumbuya. "Political Legitimacy, Political Symbols, and National Leadership in West Africa." *Journal of Modern African Studies* 21, no. 4 (December 1983): 645–71.

Hendrickson, Hildi. *Clothing and Difference: Embodied Identities in Colonial and Post-Colonial Africa*. Durham: Duke University Press, 1996.

Hewitt, Guy. "The Windrush Scandal: An Insider's Reflection." *Caribbean Quarterly* 66, no. 1 (2020): 108–28.

Hewitt, Guy, and Kevin M. Isaac. "Windrush: The Perfect Storm." *Social and Economic Studies* 67, nos. 2, 3 (2018): 293–302.

Hirsch, Shirin. *In the Shadow of Enoch Powell: Race, Locality and Resistance*. Manchester: Manchester University Press, 2018.

Hodder, B. W. "Indigenous Cloth Trade and Marketing in Africa." *Textile History* 11, no. 1 (1980): 203–10.

Irak, Dağhan. "Football in Turkey During the Erdoğan Regime." *Soccer & Society* 21, no. 6 (2020): 680–91.

Irak, Dağhan. "'Shoot Some Pepper Gas At Me!' Football Fans vs. Erdoğan: Organized Politicization or Reactive Politics?" *Soccer & Society* 19, no. 3 (2018): 400–17.

Irak, Dağhan. "Turkish Football, Match-Fixing, and the Fan's Media: A Case Study of Fenerbahçe Fans." In *Sports Events, Society and Culture*. Ed. Katherine Dashper, Thomas Fletcher, and Nicola McCullough. 115–28. Abingdon: Routledge, 2015.

Jacobi, Daniel, and Annette Freyberg-Inan. "Introduction: Human being(s) in International Relations." *Human Beings in International Relations*. Ed. Daniel Jacobi and Annette Freyberg-Inan. 1–33. Cambridge: Cambridge University Press, 2015.

Jeffrey, Alex. *The Improvised State: Sovereignty, Performance and Agency in Dayton Bosnia*. Chichester: John Wiley & Sons, 2013.

Jones, Bart. ¡*Hugo!: The Hugo Chávez Story from Mud Hut to Perpetual Revolution*. Hanover, NH: Steerforth, 2007.

Jones, Clement. *Race and the Media: Thirty Years' Misunderstanding*. London: Commission for Racial Equality, 1982.

Jones, Nicholas. "Enoch Powell: A Personal Insight." *The Political Quarterly* 89, no. 3 (2018): 358–61.

Kielman, Adam. "Sites and Sounds of National Memory: Performing the Nation in China's Decennial National Day Celebrations." *International Communication of Chinese Culture* 7, no. 2 (2020): 147–68.

Kowalski, Bartosz. "China's Mask Diplomacy in Europe: Seeking Foreign Gratitude and Domestic Stability." *Journal of Current Chinese Affairs* 50, no. 2 (2021): 209–26.

Lee, Hyunjung. *Performing the Nation in Global Korea: Transnational Theatre*. Basingstoke: Palgrave Macmillan, 2015.

Lehmann, Hans-Thies. *Postdramatic Theatre*. Trans. Karen Jürs-Munby. New York: Routledge, 2006.

Lepore, Jill. *The Name of War: King Philip's War and the Origins of American Identity*. New York: Vintage Books, 1999.

Levitas, Ben. *The Theatre of Nation: Irish Drama and Cultural Nationalism: 1890–1916*. Oxford: Clarendon Press, 2002.

Levtzion, Nehemia. *Ancient Ghana and Mali*. New York: Methuen and Company, 1973.

Levtzion, Nehemia. "Islam in the Bilad-al-Sudan to 1800." In *History of Islam in Africa*. Ed. Nehemia Levtzion and Randall L. Pouwels. 63–92. Athens: Ohio University Press, 2000.

Li, Han. "From Red to 'Pink': Propaganda Rap, New Media, and China's Soft Power Pursuit." *American Journal of Chinese Studies* 25, no. 2 (2018): 89–105.

Lopes, Dawisson Belém. "De-westernization, Democratization, Disconnection: The Emergence of Brazil's Post-Diplomatic Foreign Policy." *Global Affairs* 6, no. 2 (2020): 167–84.

MacAnna, Thomas. "Nationalism from the Abbey Stage." In *Theatre and Nationalism in Twentieth-Century Ireland*. Ed. Robert O'Driscoll. Toronto, Canada: University of Toronto Press, 1971.

Maguire, Joseph. "The Sports-Industrial Complex: Sports Sciences, Social Developments, and Images of Humankind." In *Power and Global Sport: Zones of Prestige, Emulation, and Resistance*. Ed. Joseph Maguire. 159–76. Abingdon: Routledge, 2005.

Mahiet, Damien. "The Diplomat's Music Test: Branding New and Old Diplomacy at the Beginning of the Nineteenth and Twenty-First Centuries." In *International Relations, Music and Diplomacy: Sounds and Voices on the International Stage*. Ed. Frédéric Ramel and Cécile Prévost-Thomas. 115–39. Cham: Springer, 2018.

McCaskie, T. C. "Innovational Eclecticism: The Asante Empire and Europe in the 19th Century." *Comparative Studies in Society and History* 14, no. 1 (1972): 30–45.

McCaskie, T. C. "Telling the Tale of Osei Bonsu: An Essay on the Making of Asante Oral History." *Africa* 84, no. 3 (2014): 353–70.

McConnell, Fiona. *Rehearsing the State: The Political Practices of the Tibetan Government-in-Exile*. Chichester: John Wiley & Sons, 2016.

McConnell, Fiona. "Performing Diplomatic Decorum: Repertoires of 'Appropriate' Behavior in the Margins of International Diplomacy." *International Political Sociology* 12 (2018): 362–81.

McGarry, Fearghal. *The Abbey Rebels of 1916: A Lost Revolution*. Dublin: Gill and Macmillan, 2015.

McGregor, JoAnn, Heather Akou, and Nicola Stylianou. *Creating African Fashion Histories: Politics, Museums and Sartorial Practices*. Bloomington: Indiana University Press, 2022.

McRobbie, Angela. *British Fashion Design: Rag Trade or Image Industry*. London: Routledge, 1998.

Menakem, Resmaa. *My Grandmother's Hands: Racialized Trauma and the Pathway to Mending Our Hearts and Bodies*. Las Vegas, NV: Central Recovery Press, 2017.

Mieszkowski, Jan. *Watching War*. Stanford: Stanford University Press, 2012.

Mirzoeff, Nicholas. *Watching Babylon: The War in Iraq and Global Visual Culture*. London: Routledge, 2005.

Mirzoeff, Nicholas. *How to See the World: An Introduction to Images, from Self-Portraits to Selfies, Maps to Movies, and More*. New York: Basic Books, 2016.

Mitchell, W. J. T. *Cloning Terror: The War of Images, 9/11 to the Present*. Chicago: University of Chicago Press, 2011.

Moffitt, Benjamin. *The Global Rise of Populism: Performance, Political Style, and Representation*. Stanford: Stanford University Press, 2016.

Monfils, Barbara S. "A Multifaceted Image: Kwame Nkrumah's Extrinsic Rhetorical Strategies." *Journal of Black Studies* 7, no. 3 (1977): 313–30.

Moran, James. *Staging the Easter Rising: 1916 as Theatre*. Cork: Cork University Press, 2005.

Nic Dhiarmada, Bríona. *The 1916 Irish Rebellion*. Forward by Mary McAleese. Notre Dame, Indiana: University of Notre Dame Press, 2016.

Nixon, Rob. *Slow Violence and the Environmentalism of the Poor*. Paperback Edition. Cambridge, MA: Harvard University Press, 2013.

Nwafor, Okechukwu. *Aso Ebi: Dress, Fashion, Visual Culture, and Urban Cosmopolitanism in West Africa*. Ann Arbor: University of Michigan Press, 2021.

Nyaaba, Ali Yakubu, and George M. Bob-Milliar. "The Economic Potentials of Northern Ghana: The Ambivalence of the Colonial and Postcolonial States to Develop the North." *African Economic History* 47, no. 2 (2019): 45–67.

Obiri-Addo, Ebenezer. *Kwame Nkrumah: A Case Study of Religion and Politics in Ghana*. Lanham, MD: University Press of America, 1999.

Osseo-Asare, Abena Dove. "Kwame Nkrumah's Suits: Sartorial Politics in Ghana at Independence." *Fashion Theory* 25, no. 5 (2021): 362–597.

Owusu-Ansah, David. *Islamic Talismanic Traditions in Nineteenth-Century Asante*. Lewiston: Edwin Mellen Press, 1991.

Owusu-Ansah, David. "The Asante Kramo Imammate: Conflicting Traditions." In *The Cloth of Many Colored Silks*. Ed. John Hunwick and Lawler Nancy. 355–65. Evanston: Northwestern University Press, 1996.

Ozouf, Mona. *Festivals and the French Revolution*. Trans. Alan Sheridan. Cambridge, MA: Harvard University Press, 1988.

Passoth, Jan-Hendrik, and Nicholas J. Rowland. "Who Is Acting in International Relations?" In: *Human Beings in International Relations*. Ed. Daniel Jacobi, and Annette Freyberg-Inan. 286–304. Cambridge: Cambridge University Press, 2015.

Perani, Judith, and Norma H. Wolff. *Cloth, Dress and Art Patronage in Africa.* New York: Berg Publishers, 1999.

Perucci, Tony. *Paul Robeson and the Cold War Performance Complex: Race, Madness, Activism.* Ann Arbor: University of Michigan Press, 2012.

Perucci, Tony. "The Trump Is Present." *Performance Research* 22, no. 3 (2017): 127–35. https://doi.org/10.1080/13528165.2017.1348607.

Perucci, Tony. "Irritational Aesthetics: Reality Friction and Indecidable Theatre." *Theatre Journal* 70, no. 4 (2019): 473–98. https://muse.jhu.edu/article/715917.

Phillips, Mike, and Trevor Phillips. *Windrush: The Irresistible Rise of Multi-Racial Britain.* London: HarperCollins, 1998.

Plange, Nii-K. "Underdevelopment in Northern Ghana: Natural Causes or Colonial Capitalism?" *Review of African Political Economy* 15/16 (May–December 1979): 4–14.

Powell, Enoch. "Enoch Powell's 'Rivers of Blood' Speech." April 20, 1968. https://anth1001.files.wordpress.com/2014/04/enoch-powell_speech.pdf (accessed April 21, 2022).

The Provisional Government of the Republic of Ireland. "Proclamation of the Irish Republic." *Proclamation of the Irish Republic, 24 April 1916.* CAIN, n.d. Web. http://cain.ulst.ac.uk/issues/politics/docs/pir24416.htm (accessed November 1, 2016).

Rabine, Leslie. "Photography, Poetry and the Dressed Body of Leopold Sedar Senghor." In *African Dress: Fashion, Agency, Performance.* Ed. Karen Hansen and D. Soyini Madison. 171–85. New York: Bloomsbury, 2013.

Rahman, A. *The Regime Change of Kwame Nkrumah: Epic Heroism in Africa and the Diaspora.* New York: Palgrave MacMillan, 2007.

Ramel, Frédéric, and Cécile Prévost-Thomas, eds. *International Relations, Music and Diplomacy: Sounds and Voices on the International Stage.* Cham: Springer, 2018.

Rancière, Jacques. "The Fools and The Wise." Trans. David Fernbach. January 22, 2021. https://www.versobooks.com/blogs/4980-the-fools-and-the-wise (accessed March 31, 2021).

Reeck, Darrell. "The Castle and the Umbrella: Some Religious Dimensions of Kwame Nkrumah's Leadership Role in Ghana." *Africa Today* 23, no. 4 (October–December 1976): 7–27.

Regev, Motti. *Pop-Rock Music: Aesthetic Cosmopolitanism in Late Modernity.* Cambridge: Polity, 2013.

Reid, Fiona. *Medicine in First World War Europe: Soldiers, Medics, Pacifists.* London: Bloomsbury Academic, 2017.
Richards, Christopher. *Cosmopolitanism and Women's Fashion in Ghana: History, Artistry and Nationalist Inspirations.* New York: Routledge, 2022.
Roach, Joseph. *Cities of the Dead: Circum-Atlantic Performance.* New York: Columbia University Press, 1996.
Roach, Joseph. *It.* Ann Arbor: University of Michigan Press, 2007.
Rossol, Nadine. *Performing the Nation in Interwar Germany: Sport, Spectacle and Political Symbolism, 1926–36.* New York: Palgrave Macmillan, 2010.
Rovine, Victoria. *African Fashion, Global Style: Histories, Innovations, and Ideas You Can Wear.* Bloomington: Indiana University Press, 2015.
Ruette-Orihuela, Krisna, and Hortensia Caballero-Arias. "'Cimarronaje Institucional': Ethno-racial Legal Status and the Subversive Institutionalization of Afrodescendant Organizations in Bolivarian Venezuela." *Journal of Latin American and Caribbean Anthropology* 22, no. 2 (2017): 320–338.
Salas de Lecuna, Yolanda. *Bolívar y la historia en la conciencia popular.* Colombia: Ediciones de la Universidad de Simón Bolívar, 1987.
Salois, Kendra. "The Ethics and Politics of Empathy in US Hip-Hop Diplomacy: The Case of the Next Level Program." In *Popular Music and Public Diplomacy.* Ed. Mario Dunkel, and Sina Nitzsche. 233–53. Bielefeld: Transcript Verlag, 2018.
Schechner, Richard. *Performance Theory.* Revised and Expanded Edition. London: Routledge Classics, 2003.
Schildkrout, Enid. "The Ideology of Regionalism in Ghana." In *Strangers in African Societies.* Ed. William A. Shack and Elliott P. Skinner. 183–207. Berkeley: University of California Press, 1979.
Seib, Philip. *Real-Time Diplomacy: Politics and Power in the Social Media Era.* London: Palgrave Macmillan, 2012.
Sekyi, Kobina. *Blinkards, a Comedy.* Oxford: Heinemann, 1977.
Servitje, Lorenzo. *Medicine Is War: The Martial Metaphor in Victorian Literature and Culture.* Albany: State University of New York Press, 2021.
Shewell, Christina. "Poetry, Voice, Brain, and Body." *Voice and Speech Review* 14, no. 2 (May 3, 2020): 143–66. https://doi.org/10.1080/23268263.2020.1743502.

Shimakawa, Karen. *National Abjection: The Asian American Body on Stage.* Durham: Duke University Press, 2003.

Siegel, Daniel J. *Pocket Guide to Interpersonal Neurobiology: An Integrative Handbook of the Mind.* New York: W. W. Norton & Company, 2012.

Smilde, David and Daniel Hellinger, eds. *Venezuela's Bolivarian Democracy: Participation, Politics, and Culture under Chávez.* Durham: Duke University Press, 2011.

Spencer, Ian R. G. *British Immigration Policy Since 1939: The Making of Multiracial Britain.* London: Routledge, 1997.

Spohr, Arne. "Concealed Music in Early Modern Diplomatic Ceremonial." In *Music and Diplomacy from the Early Modern Era to the Present.* Ed. Rebekah Ahrendt, Mark Ferraguto, and Damien Mahiet. 19–44. New York: Palgrave Macmillan, 2014.

Stephens, James. *The Insurrection in Dublin: An Eyewitness Account of the Easter Rising, 1916.* New York: Barnes and Noble, 1999.

Strauss, Julia C. *State Formation in China and Taiwan: Bureaucracy, Campaign, and Performance.* Cambridge: Cambridge University Press, 2020.

Strauss, Julia C., and Donal B. Cruise O'Brien, eds. *Staging Politics: Power and Performance in Asia and Africa.* London: I.B. Tauris, 2007.

Straw, Will. "Systems of Articulation, Logics of Change: Communities and Scenes in Popular Music." *Cultural Studies* 5, no. 3 (1991): 368–88.

Tallbear, Kimberly. *Native American DNA: Tribal Belonging and the False Promise of Genetic Science.* Minneapolis: University of Minnesota Press, 2013.

Tarlo, Emma. *Clothing Matters.* Chicago: University of Chicago Press, 1996.

Taussig, Michael. *The Magic of the State.* New York and London: Routledge, 1997.

Taylor, Diana. *Disappearing Acts: Spectacles of Gender and Nationalism in Argentina's "Dirty War."* Durham: Duke University Press, 1997.

Taylor, Diana. *Performance.* Durham: Duke University Press, 2016.

Taylor, Lou. *Studying Dress History.* Manchester: Manchester University Press, 2002.

Thomas, Roger G. "Forced Labor in British West Africa: The Case of the Northern Territories of the Gold Coast 1906–1927," *Journal of African History* 14, no. 1 (1973): 79–103.

Trenzas Insurgentes. "Poder Popular, Género y Etnia: el Caso de Trenzas Insurgentes, Colectivo de Mujeres Negras, Afrovenezolanas y

Afrodescendientes." *Revista Venezolana de Economía y Ciencias Sociales* 20, no. 1 (2014): 157–78.

Tuch, Hans N. *Communicating with the World: U. S. Public Diplomacy Overseas*. New York: Palgrave Macmillan, 1990.

Turner, Victor. *Dramas, Fields, and Metaphors: Symbolic Action in Human Society*. Ithaca: Cornell University Press, 1974.

Ugueto-Ponce, Meyby Soraya. "¿Negros? ¿Afros? Más allá de una respuesta maniquea y excluyente. Reflexiones en torno al caso venezolano." *Identidades políticas en tiempos de la afrodescendencia: Auto-identificación, Ancestralidad, Visibilidad y Derechos*. Ed. Silvia Valero, and Alejandro Campos García. 247–87. Buenos Aires: Corregidor, 2015.

Ugueto-Ponce, Meyby Soraya. "La acción colectiva encarnada en mujeres Afrovenezolanas. Mobilización entre el poder popular y el poder constituido." Presented in Performance and Populism conference Keynote Roundtable, "Commune: Mobilizing Popular Power in Geo-Political Souths." The University of Warwick and The University of California-Berkeley. November 5, 2021.

United States. *Department of the Army. The U.S. Army/Marine Corps Counterinsurgency Field Manual: U.S. Army Field Manual No. 3–24. Marine Corps Warfighting Publication No. 3–33.5*. Chicago: University of Chicago Press, 2007.

Van der Kolk, Bessel A. *The Body Keeps the Score: Brain, Mind, and Body in the Healing of Trauma*. New York: Viking, 2014.

Vernon, Patrick. "Many Rivers to Cross: The Legacy of Enoch Powell in Wolverhampton." In *Windrush (1968) and "Rivers of Blood" (1968): Legacy and Assessment*. Ed. Trevor Harris. Milton Park. Abingdon: Routledge, 2019.

Viestad, Vibeke Maria. *Dress as Social Relations: An Interpretation of Bushman Dress*. New York: New York University Press, 2018.

Von Eschen, Penny M. *Satchmo Blows Up the World: Jazz Ambassadors Play the Cold War*. Cambridge, MA: Harvard University Press, 2004.

von Falkenhausen, Lothar. *Suspended Music: Chime-Bells in the Culture of Bronze Age China*. Berkeley: University of California Press, 1993.

Warner, Michael. *Publics and Counterpublics*. Cambridge, MA: MIT Press, 2002.

Watterson, John Sayle. *The Games Presidents Play*. Baltimore: Johns Hopkins University Press, 2006.

Wilcox, Laura. *Bodies of Violence: Theorizing Embodied Subjects in International Relations*. New York: Oxford University Press, 2015.

Williams, Wendy. *Windrush Lessons Learned Review*. HC-932020-21. Crown Copyright. March 19, 2020. https://assets.publishing.service.gov.uk/government/uploads/system/uploads/attachment_data/file/876336/6.5577_HO_Windrush_Lessons_Learned_Review_LoResFinal.pdf (accessed December 26, 2021).

Yankah, Kwesi. *Beyond the Political Spider: Critical Issues in African Humanities*. Makhanda, RSA: African Books Collective, 2021.

Yung, Bell, Evelyn Sakakida Rawski, and Rubie S. Watson. *Harmony and Counterpoint: Ritual Music in Chinese Context*. Stanford: Stanford University Press, 1996.

Contributors

James R. Ball III is an Associate Professor at Texas A&M University in the Department of Performance Studies. His research focuses on spectatorship, immersive aesthetics, politics, and diplomacy. His book *Theater of State: A Dramaturgy of the United Nations* (2020) offers an innovative theory of global political spectatorship. Related work has been published in *TDR: The Drama Review*, *The Journal of Dramatic Theory and Criticism*, *e-Misférica*, and elsewhere.

Sean Bartley is Assistant Professor of Theatre History at Northwestern State University of Louisiana. His research interests include contemporary site-based and immersive performance, sporting events and arenas, systems of new play development, and experiential pedagogy. He has published in *Sporting Performances: Politics in Play* (2020), *Theatre History Studies* (2019), *TDR: The Drama Review* (2018), and *Theatre Journal* (2017). His dramaturgy work includes productions with American Repertory Theatre *(Julius Caesar, Romance)*, New Repertory Theatre *(BOOM)*, and Company One *(Learn to be Latina)*.

Mary Karen Dahl is a Professor of Theatre at Florida State University where she codirects the Theatre and Performance Research graduate program. Her longstanding interest in the relationship between performance, politics, and violence has resulted in such publications as *Political Violence in Drama: Classical Models, Contemporary Variations* (Choice Outstanding Academic Book, 1987); "Postcolonial British Theatre: Black Voices at the Center" in *Imperialism and Drama* (1995); and "Sacrificial Practices: Creating the Legacy of Stephen Lawrence" in *Violence Performed: Local Roots and Global Routes of Conflict* (2008).

David Afriyie Donkor is an Associate Professor at Texas A&M University in the Department of Performance Studies and the Africana Studies Program. Donkor's publications include the book, *Spiders of the Market: Ghanaian Trickster Performance in a Web of Neoliberalism*

(2016); journal articles in *Theatre Survey*, *The Drama Review (TDR)*, *Cultural Studies*, and *Ghana Studies*; chapters/entries in the volumes *Legacy of Efua Sutherland: Pan-African Cultural Activism* by Ann Adams and Esi-Sutherland Addy, and *Cambridge Encyclopedia of Stage Actors and Acting* by Simon Williams; and a book review in the *Journal of West African History*.

Christiana Molldrem Harkulich is a theatre historian, director, and dramaturg. She has presented work at ASTR, ATHE, and MATC. She has previously published in *Theatre Annual* and *Theatre History Studies*. Her research focuses on decoloniality, Indigenous performance, and politics. She received her PhD in Theater and Performance Studies at the University of Pittsburgh, and her BA from Wellesley College. She currently teaches at Eastern Illinois University.

Adam Kielman is Assistant Professor of Music in the field of ethnomusicology at The Chinese University of Hong Kong, and is the author of *Sonic Mobilities: Producing Worlds in Southern China* (2022). His research examines evolving forms of musical creativity and modes of circulation in southern China as they relate to shifts in conceptualizations about self, publics, state, and space. His broader research interests include popular musics of East Asia, music and mobility, music and language, music and technology, jazz and improvised music, and sound studies.

Warren Kluber is a Lecturer in Discipline in English and Comparative Literature at Columbia University. His research on war, medicine, and modern theater has been published in *Modern Drama*, *Theatre Journal*, *The Journal of Dramatic Theory and Criticism*, and *PAJ: A Journal of Performance and Art*.

Angela Marino is an Associate Professor at the University of California, Berkeley in the Department of Theater, Dance, and Performance Studies. Her research focuses on Latinx and Latin American political cultures and performance studies.

Tony Perucci is Associate Professor of Performance Studies at the University of North Carolina at Chapel Hill. Recent articles have appeared in the journals *TDR: The Drama Review, Performance Research, Theatre Journal,* and *Theatre Topics,* as well as in the books *Culture Jamming: Activism and the Art of Cultural Resistance, Affective Movements, Methods and Pedagogies* and *Performing Arousal: Precarious Bodies and Frames of Representation.* His is the author of *Paul Robeson and the Cold War Performance Complex: Race, Madness, Activism* (2012) and *On the Horizontal: Mary Overlie and the Viewpoints* (forthcoming).

Jared Strange is a PhD candidate in Theatre and Performance Studies at the University of Maryland. His dissertation research focuses on the performativity of soccer as realized on the pitch and on the stage. His research and reviews can be found in *Theatre Research International, Journal of Dramatic Theory and Criticism, Comparative Drama, Theatre Journal,* and *TDR: The Drama Review.* He is also a playwright, dramaturg, and theatre artist based in the Washington, DC area, where he has worked with such companies as The National Theatre, Rorschach Theatre Company, and Young Playwrights' Theater.

Áine Josephine Tyrrell is an interdisciplinary scholar with a PhD from the Department of Theatre and Performance Studies at Stanford University currently working as a Foreign and Defense policy researcher in Washington, DC. She also holds a BA in English Literature and Drama Studies from Trinity College Dublin. Her PhD thesis, "Countering Counter-Terror: The Impact of Security Policy on American, British and French Publics Post 9/11," reframes counter-terrorism law as performance. Áine has published peer-reviewed articles in *Cultural Dynamics* and *TDR: The Drama Review.*

Index

Abdallah, Mohammed ben- 77
Adonis, Andrew 98
Akufo-Addo, Nana 21, 63–5, 79–82
Allman, Jean 64
Anderson, Benedict 9
Anderson, Marian 49, 61 n.15
Anderson, Patrick, and Jisha Menon 35
Austin, J. L. 10, 33
Ayisoba, King 79

Bakri, al- 84 nn.11–12
Ball, James R. III 24 n.3, 108, 144
Bangayan, Jhonvid 145–8
batakari 21, 64, 65–7, 69–71, 73–83
Baudrillard, Jean 208
Bell, Colleen 122–3
Berdymukhamedov, Gurbanguly 166
Berlova, Maria 10
Biden, Joseph 13, 185 n.27
Biney, Ama 73
Blige, Mary J. 4
blood-quantum policy 51, 55
Bolívar, Simón 23, 189–202
Bradshaw, Samantha, and Philip N. Howard 157
British Nationality Act 94–5, 100, 101, 110
Bryan, Anthony 104, 109
Bush, George H. W. 18
Bush, George W. 1–6, 181–2
Bush, Laura 4
Butler, Judith 93, 101

Caesar, Glenda 109
Carlyle, Thomas 63
Castiglione, Baldassare 142, 144
Ceannt, Éamonn 32
celebrities. *See* "It Effect"
Chatterjee, Partha 191

Chávez, Hugo 190–4, 200–1
Cheah, Pheng 31, 39
China
  "mask diplomacy" 22, 139, 146–56
  music and statecraft 140, 143–4, 158–9
  social media 157–8
Chirinos, José Leonardo 193–4, 200
Clarke, Tom 32, 43 n.15
Clinton, Bill 76, 78, 165, 182, 185 n.27
clothes and politics 64–5, 73–6
Cohen, Raymond 12–13, 14
Colbert, Soyica Diggs 133
Cold War diplomatic theatre 141, 207–8
Collins, Michael 33–4
Collor de Mello, Fernando 4
Colum, Pádraic 40
Coming to America (film) 78
Connolly, James 29, 30, 31–3, 43 n.13
Constantinou, Costas 12
Cook, Scott 143
Cooke, Pat 37
Copeland, Daryl 93, 105, 108
Coulthard, Glen Sean 49
Covid-19 pandemic 22, 139, 147–50, 152, 174, 196
Cowhig, Frances Ya-Chu 22, 121–2, 126–34

diplomatic performance 5–12, 13, 48, 52–3, 159
discrimination, 47–55, 59–60, 91–111, 190–1
Donkor, David 18
Doty, Roxanne 10
Durel, Joey 3
Duterte, Rodrigo 149, 151, 154

Easter Rising 20, 29–41
Echenagucia, Carmen Zulay 195–6, 198
Ede, James Chuter 94–5
Edmondson, Laura 25
Éguez, Pavel 199–201
Eisenhower, Dwight D. 181, 207
Erdoğan, Recep Tayyip 22, 165–7, 168, 172–5, 176–83
Esposito, Roberto 131–2
Esslin, Martin 43 n.17
Estefan, Gloria 4

Ferguson, George Ekem 72
Fisher, Clyde 51, 55
Fisher, "Te Ata." *See* Te Ata
Flores, Wilson Lee 156
Ford, Gerald 181
Ford, Robert 96, 98
Fosler-Lussier, Danielle 141
Franklin, M. I. 142

Galvez, Carlito, Jr. 149
García, Jesús "Chucho" 190, 193–4, 205 n.27
Garrison, James 143–4
Geertz, Clifford 8–9, 11
General Post Office (Dublin) 30, 33–5, 36, 38, 41 n.4
Gentleman, Amelia 94, 95, 104, 108
George VI and Elizabeth (Queen Mother) 47–8, 52, 57, 58–9
Ghana 21, 63–4, 67, 73–80
Gildea, Robert 100
Goeman, Mishuana 52
Goffman, Erving 142, 172, 208
Goldman, Benjamin 2, 3
Graham-Jones, Jean 193, 199
Green, Richard 55
Gregory, Augusta 30, 31
Griffith, Arthur 32
Guerrero Veloz, Jorge 197
"guerrilla diplomacy" 93, 105–10
Gustav III 10

Haaland, Deb 60
Hall, Stuart 99, 109, 141
Haraway, Donna 131
Harding, James 209
Harris, Elizabeth 73
Hartigan, Karelisa V. 133
Hayton, Bill 152
Havel, Václav 4
Heath, Edward 97
Hewitt, Guy 92–1, 95, 105–8
Hirsch, Shirin 100
Hollande, François 4
Holloway, Joseph 30
Holmes, Jack 166
Hot Dog Summit 20–1, 47–59
Huang Xilian 139, 145
Hui Yuanqiong 145
Hyde, Douglas 30, 31–2

Ibn Battuta 65–6
"Iisang Dagat" (music video) 22, 139–40, 142, 144–56, 158–9
Immigration Act 101–2, 104
Indian Citizenship Act 54
"Indigenous" term 52
Iraq War 119–21, 134 n.4
Ireland. *See* Easter Rising
Isaac, Kevin M. 107
Ish-Ti-Opi 55
"It Effect" 179–81

Jazz Ambassadors program 141
Jeffery, Alex 11
Jessop, David 106–7
Jones, Bart 201
Jones, Clement 97–8, 107

Kanter, Enes 179
Karasz, Palko 175
Kasparov, Gary 172
Kelly, Megyn 171
Kielman, Adam 10
Kilmainham Gaol 30, 36–7, 44 n.28
Kim Jong-Il 166

Kimmel, Michael 135 n.10
Kowalski, Bartosz 150–1
Kwaku Duah 68

Lafayette, Marquis de 1–7
Lam, Wifredo 200
Lammy, David 110
Latour, Bruno 8
Law Against Racial Discrimination (Venezuela) 190–1, 198
Lawrence, Doreen 109–10
Lawrence, Stephen 93, 109, 111 n.7
Lehmann, Hans-Thies 15–16, 208
Li, Han 158
Locsin, Teodoro, Jr. 149, 150, 155
López, Eubel 198
Louverture, Toussaint 197

MacDonagh, Thomas 30, 31–3
MacNeill, Eoin 42 n.10
Maduro, Nicolás 198, 201
Mahama, John 79
Mahiet, Damien 141
Malissa, Dean 2, 3
Mao Zedong 166
"mask diplomacy." *See under* China
Maulding, Reginald 102
Maxwell, John Grenfell 35–6, 44 n.26, 45 n.29
May, Theresa 92, 103, 107
McConnell, Fiona 13
McCoy, Alfred 123
McDermott, Séan 32, 39
McFaul, Michael 172
McRobbie, Angela 64
Menakem, Resmaa 122, 132–3
Milbank, Dana 3
Miranda, Francisco de 195, 197
Mirzoeff, Nicholas 125–6
Monasterio, Casimira 190–1, 203 n.7
Morgan, Piers 109
Mount Vernon 1, 5
musical diplomacy 22, 140–4, 156–9
Musulmani, al- 84 nn.11–12

nationalism 158
  African 74
  ethnonationalism 21, 97
  Irish 31, 37, 39–40, 44 n.28
  sartorial 74, 87 n.37 (*see also* clothes and politics)
  transnationalism 190
New Deal policies 53, 58, 62 n.27
Nixon, Richard 182
Nkrumah, Kwame 21, 73–6, 79, 87 n.41

Obama, Barack 167, 185 n.27
Olusoga, David Adetayo 96
Osei Bonsu 68, 70
Osei Tutu Kwame 69, 70
Ousley, Heman 106

Papin, Imelda 145, 147
Passoth, Jan-Hendryk, and Nicholas J. Rowland 8
Pearse, Pádraig 29, 30, 31–4, 38
"performance postdemocracy" 209
Phillips, Mike and Trevor 92, 100, 102, 107
Plunkett, Joseph 30, 32, 33
Pocahontas 51, 59
"popular power" (in Venezuela) 190–1, 196, 202
postdiplomatic theatre 14–17, 141, 207–9
postdiplomacy 28 n.44, 207
postdramatic theatre 15–16, 205, 209
Powell, Enoch 21, 91–3, 96–110
"publics" concept. *See* Warner, Michael
Putin, Vladimir 22, 165–76, 179–83, 184 nn.11–12, 186 n.37

racism. *See* discrimination
Rajan, Amol 98
Ramel, Frédéric, and Cécile Prévost-Thomas 142

Rancière, Jacques 14
Rawlings, Jerry 76-9
recognition and misrecognition 20, 49-50, 59-60, 102-3, 172
Reed, Lou 4
Reynolds, Emma 110
Roach, Joseph 40, 180
Roosevelt, Eleanor 47-9, 53, 61 n.15
Roosevelt, Franklin Delano 20, 47-9, 52-3, 59
Rothkopf, Arthur J. 3
Ruette-Orihuela, Krisna, and Hortensia Caballero-Arias 198
Russia. *See* Putin, Vladimir

Saddam Hussein 22, 119-21, 125, 131
Sáenz, Manuela 199-200
Salas de Lecuna, Yolanda 192, 201
Samonte, Mauro Gia 153
Sarkozy, Nicolas 1-7, 140
scenarios 167-8
Schechner, Richard 5
Seib, Philip 157
Servitje, Lorenzo 122
Shimakawa, Karen 9
Social Drama 5, 25 n.13
social media 13, 80, 139-40, 151-2, 157
Sommerfield, William 3
South China Sea/West Philippine Sea controversy 22, 139, 152-6
sovereignty claims
 China 152
 Indigenous nations 49, 51, 52, 54
 Venezuela 190, 192
"spectatorial anesthesia" 126
Spencer, Ian R. G. 102
sports-as-politics 22-3, 165-83
state dinners 1, 3-4, 18, 140
state-sanctioned violence 22, 35
state visits 1-7

Strauss, Julia C. 10-11
Straw, William 142
Stuever, Hank 4
Sweeney, Joe 38-9
Sweney, Mark 97

Tallbear, Kim 51
Tarlo, Emma 64
Taussig, Michael 9
Taylor, Diana 10, 124, 167-8
Te Ata 20-1, 48, 50-9
theatre-as-medicine metaphor 133
Thompson, William Irwin 43 n.17
torture 120-5, 127, 130, 136 nn.20, 33
Trump, Donald (and Trumpism) 4, 13, 14-15, 167, 185 n.27, 208-9
Turkey. *See* Erdoğan, Recep Tayyip
Turner, Victor 3
24 (TV series) 125

Ugueto-Ponce, Meyby Soraya 190-1, 194
United Kingdom 122, 178. *See also* Easter Rising; George VI and Elizabeth; Windrush scandal

Valera, Jorman 195-7, 198
Venezuela. *See* Bolívar, Simón
Vernon, Patrick 92, 96, 98
Vučić, Aleksandar 151

Wale, Shatta 80-1
war-as-medicine metaphor 22, 119-26, 135 n.6
Warner, Michael 42 n.5, 44 n.20, 180-1
Washington, George 1, 3, 5-6
Williams, Sonia 109
Williams, Wendy 101, 103, 107
Wilson, Paulette 91-2, 93-4, 98, 101-4, 108-11
Windrush scandal 21, 91-111

Wittes, Benjamin 171–2
Wolf, Armin 170

Xia Wenxin 146, 147–8
Xi Jinping 149, 151

Yeats, William Butler 30, 31, 40
Yu Bin 145, 147, 148, 153
Yue Ji 22, 143–4, 158, 160 n.14

www.ingramcontent.com/pod-product-compliance
Lightning Source LLC
Chambersburg PA
CBHW062144300426
44115CB00012BA/2036